AF552458

HOTEL MANAGEMENT AND CATERING

HOTEL MANAGEMENT AND CATERING

M. C. METTI

ANMOL PUBLICATIONS PVT. LTD.
NEW DELHI - 110 002 (INDIA)

ANMOL PUBLICATIONS PVT. LTD.

H.O.: 4374/4B, Ansari Road, Darya Ganj,
New Delhi-110 002 (India)
Ph.: 23278000, 23261597

B.O.: No. 1015, Ist Main Road, BSK IIIrd Stage
IIIrd Phase, IIIrd Block
Bangalore - 560 085 (India)
Visit us at: www.anmolpublications.com

Hotel Management and Catering

ISBN 978-81-261-3237-9

PRINTED IN INDIA

Printed at Mehra Offset Press, Delhi.

Contents

Preface *vii*

1. Off-Premise Catering 1
2. Catering and Customer 37
3. Organizational Forms in the International Hotels 65
4. Hotel Load 98
5. Globalization in the Hotel and Catering Sector 130
6. Rethinking Catering Business 149
7. Importance and Usage of Dress Codes 173
8. Sociability and Models of Catering 205
9. Catering and Social Occasions 235

Index 267

Preface

Catering is the business of providing food (and often, service) for events. Social caterers are one of the fastest-growing segments of the hotel industry. This book is a comprehensive guide to successful catering business management. In addition to creating and executing a great menu, successful catering also takes know-how for marketing your business, keeping costs in line, and ensuring the entire operation runs smoothly.

"Hotel Management and Catering" offers professionals and aspiring caterers detailed advice on all the crucial business aspects of the subject for on- and off-premise catering. Updated to meet the needs of this fast-growing industry, the book features material on non-hotel catering operations—such as small business management and running your own catering operation.

It presents fresh information on menu design and pricing, complete with illustrative menu examples and tips for using software tools to create enticing menus. Hope the book is very beneficial to all the readers especially to Hotel Management Students.

Author

Chapter 1

Off-Premise Catering

OFF-PREMISE CATERING MANAGEMENT

Off-Premise Catering Management fills you in on all crucial legal and financial aspects of the subject, including catering contracts, legal requirements, finding and working with a lawyer, preparing income statements, cost control, and much more. Off-premise catering is serving food at a location away from the caterer's food production facility. One example of a food production facility is a freestanding commissary, which is a kitchen facility used exclusively for the preparation of foods to be served at other locations.

Other examples of production facilities include, but are not limited to, hotel, restaurant, and club kitchens. In most cases there is no existing kitchen facility at the location where the food is served. Caterers provide single-event foodservice, but not all caterers are created equal.

They generally fall into one of three categories:

- Party food caterers supply only the food for an event. They drop off cold foods and leave any last-minute preparation, plus service and cleanup, to others.
- Hot buffet caterers provide hot foods that are delivered from their commissaries in insulated containers. They sometimes provide serving personnel at an additional charge.

- Full-service caterers not only provide food, but frequently cook it to order on-site. They also provide service personnel at the event, plus all the necessary food-related equipment—china, glassware, flatware, tables and chairs, tents, and so forth. They can arrange for other services, like decor and music, as well. In short, a full-service caterer can plan an entire event, not just the food for it.

Off-premise catering can mean serving thousands of box lunches to a group of conventioneers; barbecuing chicken and ribs for fans before a big college game, serving an elegant dinner for two aboard a luxury yacht, or providing food, staff, and equipment for an upscale fundraiser with hundreds of guests. On a "degree of difficulty" scale from one to ten—one meaning "easy" and ten meaning "most challenging"—on-premise catering is a two, and off-premise would rank a ten!

Off-premise caterers meet the needs of all market segments, from the low-budget customer who looks for the greatest quantity and quality for the least amount of money, to the upscale client with an unlimited budget who wants the highest level of service, the ultimate in food quality, and the finest in appointments—crystal stemware, silver-plated flatware, and luxurious linens. Between these two extremes is the mid scale market segment, which requires more quality than the low-budget sector, but less than the upscale.

Off-premise catering is an art and a science. The art is creating foods and moods, as the caterer and client together turn a vision into reality. The science is the business of measuring money, manpower, and material. Successful off-premise caterers recognize the importance of both aspects—art and science—and are able to work at both the creative and the financial levels. In off-premise catering, there is only one chance to get it right.

Many events, such as wedding receptions, occur only once in a lifetime. Other events are scheduled annually, quarterly, or on a regular basis, and the caterer who fails to execute all details of such an event to the satisfaction of the client will seldom have another chance. Unfortunately for some, off-premise catering can be like living on the brink of disaster unless they are experienced.

Uninitiated amateurs may not recognize a volatile situation until it becomes a problem, later realizing they should have recognized it earlier. Catering off-premise is very similar to a sports team playing all of its games away from home, in unfamiliar surroundings, with none of the comforts of home to ease the way. There is no home field advantage, but there is a minefield disadvantage!

As caterers plod their way toward the completion of a catered event, there are thousands of potential "land mines" that can ruin an otherwise successful affair.

Some examples follow:

- Already running late for a catering delivery, the catering van driver discovers that all vehicle traffic around the party site is in gridlock. The traffic has been at a standstill for more than an hour, the police say it will be hours before the congestion can be eliminated, and the clients and their guests are anxiously awaiting dinner.
- The only freight elevator in a high-rise office building has been commandeered for the evening by moving and cleaning people, thus preventing access to the floor where a caterer is to stage an event scheduled to start in two hours.
- The wrong hot food truck is dispatched to a wedding reception. The error is not discovered until the truck has reached the reception and the bride and groom are ready for their guests to be served. It will take more than an hour to send the correct truck with the food that was ordered.
- A cook wheels a container filled with cooked prime ribs down a pier toward a yacht where the meat will be served to a group of 80 conventioneers in half an

hour. Suddenly, the cook is distracted, and the prime rib container tumbles over the edge of the pier into 40 feet of water.

- The table numbers have vanished, and the guests are ready to be seated for dinner.
- The fire marshal arrives at a party site 20 minutes before a catered event and refuses to allow guests access to the party site because the space had not been authorized for party use.
- The catering crew arrives at the party site with a van full of food, cooked to order—exactly one week early.
- A new customer places an order and asks that the caterer deliver to a home where family members and guests will have gathered prior to a funeral service. The caterer sends the food and, upon arrival, is told that the person with the checkbook is at the funeral home and is asked to please stop back in an hour for the money. The delivery person leaves without obtaining a signature. Upon returning, there is no one home and no one from whom to collect payment.
- While using a garbage disposal in a client's home, the caterer suddenly hears a terrible noise and watches in horror as water and garbage spew from the disposal all over the floor. The irate customer refuses to pay the caterer and threatens to sue for the cost of replacing the garbage disposal that was ruined because of (in the customer's words) the caterer's "negligence."
- After catering a flawless party at a client's home and loading the catering truck to capacity, the caterer is shocked to learn from the client that all 15 bags of trash must be removed from the client's property because of the neighbourhood's zoning ordinances.
- The caterer's rental company representative calls the caterer the morning after an event and advises the caterer that the $600 rented chafing dish is missing.

It was there the night before, when the caterer left the client's home. Get the picture? We could tell horror stories all day! Seasoned off-premise caterers agree, these are only a few of the thousands of obstacles that stand in the way of completing a catered event. This book addresses the various ways to professionally and successfully deal with difficult situations. With all of these very real potential problems, why are there more than 50,000 off-premise caterers in the United States? Why are more young people studying catering at two-year and four-year colleges and universities? Why are thousands of people starting their own catering companies, risking their savings on their dreams of future success? The reasons are numerous.

They may love the adventure of working in new and exciting places. They look forward to the peaks and valleys of the business cycle. They love the intense feeling of satisfaction that comes after successfully catering a spectacular party. They love the myriad challenges of this very difficult profession. Many are their own bosses, with no one to answer to but the client. Many pick and choose the parties they wish to cater. Many make six-figure incomes each year, and others cater occasionally, just for the fun of it.

What are the differences between off-premise catering and on-premise catering? Let's examine these differences, from both the client's and the caterer's viewpoints. Most clients fail to consider the cost of the rental equipment such as tables, chairs, linens, china, glassware, and flatware when they consider engaging an off-premise caterer. They think it will be less expensive to entertain in their homes, or at unique off-premise sites, than in hotels.

In fact, it can be more expensive, considering not only the cost of the rental equipment, but also other costs such as transportation of food and supplies to the site, the costs of special labour and décor, the need for tenting, air-conditioning and/or heating, and other expenses. Clients may save some money by buying their own liquor, but this can be insignificant as compared with the added costs.

For many clients, the additional costs are far outweighed by the benefits of entertaining in the privacy of their own homes or the uniqueness of a special off-premise location such as a museum, state-of-the-art aquarium, antique car dealership, or historical site. From the Caterer's Viewpoint Off-premise caterers must plan menus that can be prepared successfully at the client's location. For example, foods to be fried should not be cooked in unventilated spaces, like small kitchens in high-rise office buildings. On-premise caterers are not as limited in this regard, and they are generally supported by built-in equipment that can support a wider variety of menus.

On-premise party personnel are more familiar with the party facilities than those who work at a variety of unfamiliar locations. Off-premise catering generally has greater seasonal and day-to-day swings in personnel needs, which can create a greater challenge for the off-premise caterer, who is constantly recruiting and training staff; turnover is usually high because such work is on an "as-needed basis."

There is definitely a greater potential for oversights in off-premise catering. Backup supplies, food, and equipment can be miles away or even inaccessible when catering, for instance, aboard a yacht miles from shore. In spite of the uncertainties, off-premise catering offers the opportunity to work in a greater variety of interesting locations. The work is more likely to be different each day, resulting in less boredom and more excitement. For those looking for unlimited challenges and rewards, off-premise catering may be the answer.

Advantages and Disadvantages of Off-Premise Catering

Advance deposits Limited start-up investment Limited inventories Controllable costs G Additional revenues Business by contract Direct payment Advance forecasting Free word-of-mouth advertising Selectivity Let's discuss a few of these items in more detail. First, most off-premise caterers require some form of advance deposit prior to an event.

This deposit provides the caterer with some security if the event is canceled and also can be used to purchase some or all of the food and supplies for the party. There is no need for large amounts of capital to get started, since most off premise catering operations begin by using the existing kitchen facilities of a restaurant, club, hotel, church, or other licensed foodservice business. (It is common knowledge that many start their catering businesses in their home kitchens, but it is imperative to state that this is in direct violation of most local zoning ordinances.)

In addition, all of the necessary catering foodservice equipment such as china, glassware, flatware, tables, chairs, and linens can usually be rented, thus avoiding having to invest in expensive equipment inventories. Food and supply inventories, as well as operating costs, are much more easily controlled, because clients must advise the caterer in advance as to the number of guests that are expected.

Off-premise caterers need buy only the amounts necessary to serve the event, unlike a restaurant where there is a large variation from day to day regarding the number of patrons and their menu selections. Off-premise catering generates additional revenues for existing operations like hotels, clubs, and restaurants. They can generate even more profit by providing other services—rental equipment, flowers, décor, music, entertainment, and other accessory services.

Both the client and the caterer have expectations regarding the outcome of the party. These expectations should be clearly spelled out in a written contract. Payment for an event is normally made directly to a manager or owner, eliminating a middleman, whether it's a wedding planner, on-site food and beverage director, or one of the caterer's own staff members. This form of direct payment provides for better cash control and fewer folks to share the profit. Advance forecasting is more accurate for off-premise caterers, because parties are generally booked weeks, months, or years in advance.

Moreover, each part of the country has seasonal swings, which make revenue forecasting somewhat easier. For example, in the South the summer months are generally less busy, but in the North these are the busy months. Off-premise events generate tremendous amounts of free word-of-mouth advertising, which can produce future business without the necessity of advertising. Many off-premise caterers feel that satisfied guests at one party will either directly or indirectly book another party by speaking favourably to friends and co-workers about the event and the caterer. In other words, one party can create future parties.

Caterers also have the advantage of being somewhat selective about their clients. There are no laws that require you to accept every request to cater. If the job doesn't Advantages and Disadvantages of Off-Premise Catering meet your standards, politely decline. In sticky situations where you've already begun to work with a client but find that your communication styles just don't mesh— or, as sometimes happens with weddings, the client is not heeding your advice and you can't even decide who's really in charge—you can walk away, as long as you do so within the terms of your written agreement.

Off-premise catering does have some disadvantages too: Catering managers, owners, and staff undergo periods of high stress during very busy periods. Deadlines must be met. There are no excuses for missing a catering deadline: Stress is compounded because the workload is not evenly spread throughout the year. For most off-premise caterers, 80 per cent of the events are scheduled in 20 per cent of the time. For most, weekends are generally busier than weekdays.

Certain seasons, including Christmas, are normally busier than others. Of course, caterers must maintain general business hours too! Many have left the catering field, burned out by the constant stress and high energy demands. The seasonality of the business makes it difficult to find staff at certain times. Revenues are inconsistent, making cash management very difficult, particularly during the slower periods when expenses continue yet revenues do not. For those caterers who operate hotels, restaurants, clubs, and other businesses, the time away from the main business—spent on the off-premise business—can hurt. It is difficult for even the well-organized person to be in two places at the same time. Many hoteliers and restaurateurs find the rigors of off-premise catering too great. Some quit after realizing the difficulty of catering away from their operations. They feel that the financial benefits are insufficient compared with the effort required to cater off-premise events.

Elements of Successful Off-Premise Catering

What does it take to become a successful off-premise caterer? What experience is necessary, and what personality traits are desirable? Work Experience. Prior experience in the catering profession or the foodservice industry is important. Experience in food preparation and foodservice (both back of-the-house and front-of-the-house) helps caterers understand the procedures and problems in both areas and how the two areas interface. Those with a strong kitchen background, for example, would be wise to gain some front-of-house experience, and front-of-house personnel should learn the kitchen routine. Many successful off-premise caterers began by working as accommodators.

Accommodators are private chefs who are hired to prepare food for parties. Many assist the client with planning the menu, purchasing the food, and even arranging for kitchen and service staff. The food is prepared and served in the client's home or facility, eliminating the need for a catering commissary. Accommodators receive a fee for their services. The party staff is paid directly by the client.

Passion

Successful professionals are passionate about their work, and caterers are no exception. They love what they do! Clients and staff members will quickly detect a lack of passion, and it will cost you business and good workers. If you don't love what you do, move on and try something else. The desire to be an entrepreneur is a trait that is highly desirable for off-premise caterers. An entrepreneur must be willing to spend extraordinary amounts of time and energy to make the off-premise catering business successful, possess an inherent sense of what is right for the business, have the ability to view all aspects of the business at once rather than focusing only on one or two parts, and demonstrate a strong, incessant desire to be his or her own boss and become financially independent.

Accounting and bookkeeping skills are necessary to understand the financial aspects of operating a catering business.

The ability to prepare and interpret financial statements is essential:

- Learn as much about computers as you can. You'll be amazed at how much you can accomplish by using e-mail, having a website, and using specialized programmes for everything from budgeting to menu planning.
- It's also important to understand the legal aspects of catering. Laws that affect caterers include regulation of licensing, contracts, liability, labour, and alcoholic beverage service. _ A caterer, like any other businessperson, must have some human resource skills. Knowing how to recruit, train, motivate, and manage personnel is critical.
- Off-premise caterers should be knowledgeable about how to develop and implement a marketing plan. Ability to Plan, Organize, Execute, and Control. These are the four basic functions of management. To plan, a caterer must visualize in advance all of the aspects of a catered event and document the plans so they are readily understood by the client and easily executed by the staff.

Organizing is simply breaking down the party plans into groups of functions that can be executed in an efficient manner. Execution is the implementation of the organized plans by the party staff. Controlling is the supervisory aspect of the event.

All well-organized and well-executed plans require control and supervision. The adage is, "It is not what you expect, but what you inspect." The premier off-premise catering firms in the United States insist on excellent supervision at each event. Ability to Communicate with Clients and Staff. Listening is the key to good communication with clients and prospective clients. Off-premise caterers must listen carefully and attentively to determine what the client needs.

A client who calls and asks, "Are you able to cater a party next Friday?" should be dealt with differently from one who calls and asks, "How much will it cost for a wedding reception?" The first caller is ready to buy your services, whereas the second caller is shopping. Astute caterers must be able to respond to client requests in such a manner that the client will immediately gain confidence in the caterer.

Communicating with staff is a complex issue. In simple terms, it can be reduced to the ability to tell staff what is expected so that they understand, and the ability to receive their feedback regarding problems, both actual and potential. The result of effective communication is an off-premise catering staff that professionally executes a well-planned party that meets or exceeds the client's expectations.

Off-premise catering is a very risky business. It is not for the fainthearted who are afraid of the unknown. For example, it is more risky catering a corporate fund-raiser at the local zoo under a tent than serving the same group in a hotel ballroom. Off-premise caterers must know when the risk outweighs the gain. In this particular example, catering the event at the zoo without adequate cover in case of rain would probably be too risky. The event could be ruined. The tent makes the risk of rain a calculated one.

Off-premise catering requires working long hours without rest or sleep, lifting and moving heavy objects, intense pressure as deadlines near, and even long periods of little or no business, which can cause concern. Successful caterers should be in good physical shape, have a high energy level, and be able to mentally deal with seasonal business cycles that range from nonstop activity to slow periods with little or no business. Off-premise caterers must be self-confident, but at the same time realize that they must always find ways to improve the quality of their food and services. In this profession a fondness for people and feeling comfortable in crowds is important. A "cool head" when under pressure will keep both staff and client calm while potential problems are resolved professionally and efficiently.

This is the benchmark of all outstanding caterers. Creative caterers are able to turn a client's vision into reality by creating the appropriate look, feel, menu, service, and ambiance. Those who are not very creative can learn to be, or they can employ those who are creative.

Dependability is a major cornerstone of success in off-premise catering. When a caterer fails to deliver what was promised, the negative word of mouth travels fast among clients and potential clients. Even in those situations where circumstances change, making it more difficult to perform as promised, the outstanding caterer will find a way to deliver rather than use the changed circumstances as an excuse not to deliver.

Open-Mindedness

Open-minded caterers read up on catering trends and try new recipes and menus. They are willing to prepare unfamiliar dishes requested by clients, after thoroughly testing and understanding the recipes. They discover and try new dishes. They are always learning better ways to run their businesses. The needs of the client must always come first. Success in this business comes from identifying these needs and satisfying them. Unsuccessful off-premise caterers are those who get lost in trying to satisfy their own needs for money, equipment, and greater self-esteem. They forget that the primary goal is to serve the needs of the client. When a client's needs are met, the caterer's needs for revenues, profits, and positive feedback will automatically be met.

Prospective clients hire caterers based on their perceived image of the caterer and what the caterer will provide. In some sense, then, caterers are selling themselves more than their food. Off-premise caterers must be able to project a favourable image to the client, one that is in accord with the client's expectations. For example, a caterer whose image is sophisticated and upscale will be hard-pressed to sell a Little League banquet with a low budget. Successful caterers understand their projected images and target their marketing efforts at those clients who desire that image.

In this pressure-packed, deadline-oriented, and stressful business, it is easy to get carried away with the magnitude of the undertakings and become so tense and uptight that work ceases to be fun. Laughter at the right time can relieve that tension and stress, putting a renewed sense of fun into the work at hand. How do caterers serve shrimps? They bend down! Managing an Off-Premise Catering Operation Even those who possess the qualities that indicate off-premise catering success must know how to put these talents to use effectively.

Off-premise caterers should be hands-on managers who are constantly customer focused. They must be able to lead staff and clients alike, while conducting business in a professional manner. They must be able to make timely, ethical decisions, while understanding what makes for a successful event. They must also avoid those situations that cause a business to fail.

Developing a Strategic Plan Yogi Berra, the zany former New York Yankee catcher, is famous for his many witticisms, such as, "Nobody goes there anymore—it's too crowded." But his best quote may be this one: "If you don't know where you're going, you will wind up somewhere else." That's the reason you need a strategic plan—a roadmap to help you determine the direction in which you wish to go, and the specific goals you'll need to accomplish to get there. A strategic plan starts with a statement of core values, which may include things like client satisfaction; ethical business practices; staff satisfaction, training, and motivation; community service; and operating an environmentally conscious business. G

From these core values, a caterer can develop a Mission Statement—a succinct sentence that sums up the company's mission. Here's an example: "To meet the catering needs of the corporate community, providing high levels of service and food quality that result in repeat business and vital growth." After the Mission Statement comes the Vision Statement—a concise summary of where you want to be in the future. Again, an example: "Within five years, our company will be the top-ranked catering firm in our area, with continuing sales and profit growth, while giving back to our community." It's not enough to brainstorm about these statements. Writing them down is the first step to making a commitment—to make them a reality.

Only after they are put in writing can you develop more specific objectives to increase sales and profits, measure customer satisfaction, size up your competitors, and plan the ways in which you will give back to the community. Your Mission and Vision Statements lead naturally to the next step—to establish goals for the operation. You may have heard time management experts use the term "SMART" when describing goals.

The acronym stands for:

- *Specific:* The goals to be accomplished must be easily understood, concise, and unambiguous.
- *Measurable:* There should be no question about whether one attains, or falls short of, a goal. It may be measured in terms of quality, cost, quantity, or time.
- *Attainable:* The goals may be just out of reach, but they're not out of sight! The best goal challenges and motivates you and your team. If it's practically impossible, it may be too frustrating.
- *Relevant:* The goals must fit well with your long-term mission and vision, your objectives, and the results you expect.

- *Time-bound:* There must be a specific deadline for completion of each goal. An example of a SMART goal might be to increase sales and profits by 20 per cent each year for the next five years. Once a caterer has set goals, there must be certain trade-offs.

To increase sales, for instance, may require raising prices, hiring more staff to be able to cater more events, or spending money on advertising. The major goals can be broken into smaller, intermediate steps, with a time line to keep the company on track. And remember, goals are not just for the owner of a company. The staff and other professionals employed by the company—tax preparer, banker, attorney—should also be well aware of the goals. You'll need their help to achieve them, and you want them on your side, committed to your goals.

Too often, caterers believe they can do everything themselves. They fail to ask for or accept advice from outside consultants and colleagues. It is far more intelligent to ask for assistance when you need it. Someone familiar with your plans and your passion for them is far more likely to be helpful. Finally, as soon as a goal is set, take some action on it. The last part of a strategic management process is to reevaluate your mission, vision, and goals periodically. Times change, trends change, and you become aware of new information. Let's say a caterer's sales year showed a 50 per cent increase, when he or she had set a 20 per cent annual goal. In this case, the next year's goal might be more realistically revised to a 30 per cent increase.

Hands-on Attention to Detail Management

The devil is in the details. Have you ever heard that old saying? Another way to put it: We've all been bitten by a mosquito or stung by a bee, but how many of us have been bitten by an elephant? It's always the little things that get us! In catering, the details are virtually endless, a stream of tiny elements that might go wrong and result in a catastrophe. One thing forgotten, misheard, or misplaced can ruin an event. So it's important to check and recheck and to be prepared for last-minute emergencies. It is simply not possible to run this kind of business from behind a desk, reading computer printouts and delegating all tasks.

Off-premise catering companies must be managed from the centre of the action, whether that is with the guests or preparing foods in the kitchen. It comes from checking and rechecking every detail to ensure that it meets the highest of standards. It comes from inspecting for the best and expecting the best. Some call this management style "management by walking around." In one sense that is true, but there is more to it than walking around.

Astute offpremise caterers must:

- Obtain feedback from clients and guests regarding the food and service.
- Oversee the catering staff to ensure they are performing as directed and as expected.
- Help out when a table needs to be cleared or when the bar suddenly becomes very busy.

Help in the kitchen during critical times such as hot food dish-up, and even help scrape, stack, and wash dirty dishes if that's what is necessary. It's a roll-up-your-sleeves kind of profession, and you should never be totally satisfied with the way things are. Always look for new ways to present food and make it more flavorful, and for better and more efficient ways to do things. Customer-Focused Management An off-premise caterer's full-time mission must be to satisfy the needs of clients. Mike DeLuca, editor of Restaurant Hospitality, puts it this way: Companies that are 100% customer focused make the customer's satisfaction their only goal. They do not have as goals, increasing sales by a certain percentage, raising a profit margin, or reducing debt. They believe... that if you strive to sell only the highest quality product and strive to please every customer, sales, profit and success will follow.

This is a difficult concept for many of us to grasp. It means letting go of a financial accounting structure passed down from generation to generation of Harvard MBAs who've instilled in us that the only way to build your bottom line is to raise your top line and squeeze the middle.... That can work... but wouldn't you rather make the quality of your food, the dining experience and your customer's satisfaction your primary concern? The moral is simple: If you satisfy your customers while charging a fair price and controlling costs, profits will follow.

Managerial Decision Making Off-premise catering managers must make decisions that keep their operations running smoothly. They realize that some decisions will be better than others, that there is no perfect solution to every problem, and that the best decision-making goal is to find the best possible solution with the least number of drawbacks. Connie Sitterly, a management consultant and author, states that to be a good decision maker you should "plan ahead so when problems crop up, you're prepared to act, not react.

Control circumstances, instead of allowing them to control you. Take the initiative by anticipating and solving business problems." Although hundreds of books have been written about decision making, the following tips from Ms. Sitterly should be helpful. They're paraphrased from an article she wrote back in 1990 in The Meeting Manager, but they are still up-to-the-minute when it comes to making tough decisions successfully.

- Remember that there's seldom only one acceptable solution to the problem. Choose the best alternative.
- Make decisions that help achieve the company objectives.
- You need to consider feelings whenever people are involved. Even if you must make an unpopular decision, you can minimize repercussions... if workers know you have taken their feelings into account.
- Allow quality time for planning and decision making... pick a time when you are energetic and your mind is fresh.

- Realize that you'll never please everyone. Few decisions meet with unanimous approval... the appointed authority, not the majority, rules.
- Make time for making decisions... in business, delaying a decision can cost thousands of dollars.
- Put decision making in perspective. Every executive feels overwhelmed at times by either the enormity or the number of decisions made during a business day.... For peace of mind accept that you are doing the best job you can with the time, talent, and resources you have.
- Don't 'vait for a popular vote. Rallying your colleagues around your decision before you take action or waiting for their vote of confidence before deciding anything may cost too much in time. There are times when you just have to do something.

Leadership

There are major differences between those who lead and those who manage. Catering companies need both types of executives, and some who can do both. If a catering company is earning seven- and eight-figure annual revenues, it is most definitely being led by people with leadership skills. Leaders are able to get people to do things they don't necessarily like to do, but they do them and even enjoy them. You might say: Maintains Develops Administers Innovates Relies on systems Relies on people Counts on controls Counts on trust Does things right Does the right things Works within the system Works on the system Manages things Leads people A leader is more like a thermostat than a thermometre. A thermostat sets the standard temperature for the space it's in.

A thermometre simply records the temperature; it can't change anything. And one more important trait: Leaders take a little more than their share of the blame and a little less than their share of the credit. Professionalism and Common Business Courtesy Off-premise caterers who are not professional in their business practices will never reach the pinnacle of success in the field.

Before we address the technical aspects of catering in the succeeding chapters, it is of utmost importance that we define professionalism.

The following guidelines are adapted from an article by Carol McKibben in Special Events magazine:

- Become known for doing what you say you are going to do.
- Give price quotes and commitments only when you know everything about the event.
- Treat clients and staff members with respect.
- Build relationships with clients. Do not look at them as accounts or projects.
- Be on time, or a bit early, for appointments. Be prepared for an appointment.
- Be honest; don't play games.
- Stand behind your work. If it is wrong, make it right.
- In the face of abuse from others, don't respond by becoming abusive. Try to detach yourself from it emotionally and handle it logically. Of course, do not use your position of power to abuse others.
- Dress professionally.
- Enjoy your work as an off-premise caterer. When work ceases to be enjoyable, it is time to quit and find a new career.

Ethics in Management

The Roman philosopher Publilius Syrus said, "A good reputation is more valuable than money." This is as true today as it was in ancient times. And yet, lack of ethics is perhaps the most widely discussed topic in today's business world. We read and hear of illegalities, scandals, and other forms of questionable behaviour bringing down some of the nation's largest corporations. Off-premise caterers are in no way exempt from ethical concerns.

Even the smallest caterers deal in issues of fairness, legal requirements, and honesty on a daily basis. Examples include truth in menu, misleading advertising, unexpected and unjustified last-minute add-ons to the party price, and even underbidding a competitor when the client has disclosed your competitor's price. The truly ethical caterer will assume responsibility for the host to ensure that the host plans an event in the best interest of the guests. A host who wishes to serve alcohol to underage guests or barbecued ribs to a group of elderly people (tough to eat with dentures) is out of line and needs to be advised that this will not work. In fact, an ethical caterer will refuse to cater an event that is clearly not being planned in the best interest of the host or guests.

There are times when a caterer is given a free hand in planning a menu. Perhaps a grieving client calls for food after the funeral of a loved one, saying, "Please send over food for 50 guests tomorrow night. You know what we like!" The ethical caterer will not take advantage of this situation by either providing too much food or overcharging the client. Another temptation arises when the caterer is pressed to cater more events on a certain day or evening than he or she can reasonably accommodate. The extra money looks good.

Unethical caterers will rationalize that they can handle all the events, even if an inexperienced supervisor or staff must oversee these events, or even if the kitchen staff will not be able to prepare the caterer's usual high-quality food because of lack of time and personnel. Caterers who take on more work than they can reasonably accommodate are greedy and are considered by many observers to be unethical.

In the foregoing situation the caterer should decline the work and perhaps recommend another caterer. Some caterers refuse to recommend another catering firm because they feel that if the client is not pleased with the other firm, the caterer who turned down the business will be blamed for the recommendation. Other caterers freely recommend one or more companies when unable to cater events. There are times when it is very hard not to bad-mouth a competitor, but this is considered unethical as well as rude.

Those who are ethical would rather point out their own strengths than downgrade the competition. It can be very tempting for self-employed caterers to underreport income or overstate expenses. They rationalize that no one will know if they accept cash for a party, then fail to report it as income and pay the associated tax, or that no one will know if they happen to charge personal expenses now and then to the business. Some caterers who are licensed to sell liquor by the drink or by the bottle are tempted to bill clients for beverages that were not consumed.

These practices are not only unethical—they are illegal. Other ethical violations occur when caterers receive under-the-table cash "kickbacks" from suppliers, misrepresent their services to potential clients, or bid on party plans or ideas stolen from other caterers. Caterers also soon learn that some clients are unethical. A few are masterful at finding fault with a wedding or other important event, then demanding a "discount" based on whatever flaw they feel they have uncovered. Some will refuse to pay for linens that were damaged by candles they lit on them! You'll find people who, mid- party, will ask you to stay "a couple hours of overtime, just to wrap things up"— then not show up to pay you for the extra time the next day, as agreed.

Others will haggle over the tiniest details on an invoice or try to engage more than one caterer in a bidding war to lower prices. Caterers who deal with "middleman" organizations, like destination management firms or production companies, may find that a client of one of these companies will come back later to try to deal directly with you, thus cutting out the middleman who recommended you! As a catering professional, you need to expect a certain amount of this behaviour and must protect yourself if you suspect an ethical question may arise.

Insisting on security deposits, having a valid and authorized credit card number on file for unforeseen charges, refusing to look at other caterers' written bids, and standing firm on your own invoice prices are just a few ways ethical problems can be avoided. And rather than cut out a legitimate middleman-type of vendor, you can either refuse to deal directly with a client who tries such a maneuver or suggest a commission be paid to the middleman. You will also be put in some sticky situations as—during tough times, and even good times—certain clients will make unrealistic requests.

They've often been good, regular clients too! But they'll promise you future business if you'll cater their party "at cost," or defer payment for them, or ask some other special favour "just this once." These requests are unfair, and you're right to be squeamish about them. Offpremise caterers should be extremely wary when approached in this fashion. As a general rule, clients who do not pay their bills in a professional manner, or who are not willing to pay a fair price for catering services, are not worth the headaches they cause.

The Jefferson Centre of Character Education has set forth a list of ten "universal values": honesty, integrity, promise keeping, fidelity, fairness, caring for others, respect for others, responsible citizenship, pursuit of excellence, and accountability. These values should provide some solid guidance for any businessperson who considers him- or herself a true professional. Separating yourself from the Competition Great caterers do more than imitate—they innovate. There are distinct advantages for those who offer a unique menu, a unique service, or perhaps a unique location.

They may build and improve on someone else's concept, but they strive to take the idea to the next level. Rather than mimicking another's success, they imprint their own signature on their menus. To illustrate, let's take a look at two simple, self-service mashed potato bars. Mashed potatoes Sweet potatoes Sour cream Crème fraiche Bacon bits Canadian bacon Chopped chives Chopped fresh basil Shredded cheddar cheese Crumbled Stilton The "Unique" bar may include all the traditional accompaniments too—but what a difference a little imagination makes! There might even be a bit of caviar to top the mashers at the Unique bar, and perhaps they'll be served in martini glasses.

Why not have fun with it? One of America's top chefs, Charlie Trotter, looks at food trends differently in his book Lessons in Excellence. Says Trotter, "It's important that you foster a company culture that spurs you and your employees to search for innovative opportunities. Innovations can satisfy needs that are unmet or offer solutions to time-worn problems, or they can be new ways of saving time, space and money." Trotter says he and his staff use input from their travels, readings, television, radio, and even hobbies to hit upon trends. They keep up on the latest changes in public opinion and demographics to search for interesting, potentially high-growth markets.

Currently, they've identified ethnic cuisines such as Pan-Asian and Nuevo Latino as hot areas for menu innovation. The bottom line is that they create their own trends. Similarly, as with any career, catering professionals need to reexamine their business strategies from time to time. Some caterers do what they do best, are well known for it, and never vary their formulas. Their clients love them and get exactly what they expect. Other caterers blindly copy everybody else. They ricochet from one recipe to the other, never bothering to see if it meets their clients' needs.

If they read about it in Food Arts magazine, they feel they have to serve it! But most caterers lie somewhere between these two extremes, blending the successful ideas of the past with new twists. Great caterers also separate themselves from competitors by using the resources around them to build their businesses. In South Florida, for example, one caterer specializes in event planning for doctors, through his hospital foodservice management job.

Another has an exclusive off-premise contract for a sports facility; a third was the on-premise caterer for a city club, which resulted in off-premise jobs for the club members. Capitalize on the audience you have—they're (almost) already yours! Personal Management Off-premise caterers must learn how to deal with principles of stress management, time management, and personal organization if they are to manage at peak efficiency. Time is our most precious commodity, and to waste it because of being overstressed or disorganized will inevitably result in less-than-desirable results. Stress Management Stress comes from interaction with others, and from having to meet deadlines.

A certain amount of stress and tension is necessary to achieve the best results—those who are too laid back generally do not maximize their potential—but too much stress causes chronic fatigue, irritability, cynicism, hostility, inflexibility, and difficulty in thinking clearly. Catering managers who are overstressed are unable to perform at maximum capability.

Stress can often be controlled through:

- Daily exercise such as brisk walking, running, or other aerobic pursuits that increase the pulse rate. Some folks purposefully take their minds off work when they exercise; for others, the daily walk or run is a time to get their day mentally organized.
- Relaxation techniques, including meditation and yoga.
- Writing down the issues that cause stress. Identify those issues in your life that can be controlled, and simply decide to make the best of those that cannot. List ways to deal with the controllable stress factors.
- Reading articles and books on stress reduction. It is important to remember that some stress in catering is good. An arrow would not be propelled from a bow if the bow was not stressed.

However, too much stress can break the bow, as well as ruin catered events. Time Management There are only 168 hours in each week, and the greatest rewards come to those who accomplish the most meaningful things during this fixed amount of time. Offpremise caterers realize that if they can accomplish more meaningful production in less time, they will have more time for things other than work. They also realize that working smarter, not harder, through the effective use of time will produce greater results.

The key to effective time management is to set goals for a lifetime, for five years, and for each year, month, week, and day. (Use some of the tips for putting SMART goals in writing—not just for "big picture" goals, but as part of your daily business.) Without written goals, off-premise caterers cannot effectively manage their time. Because time management involves choosing how to spend time, it is impossible to make proper choices without knowing your desired goals.

The captain of a ship without a destination cannot choose the proper course. He will cruise aimlessly at sea, never reaching his port of call. It is equally important to schedule "downtime" for yourself—for family, friends, hobbies, and interests other than work. You are guarding against burnout when you insist on some personal time. Off-premise caterers can choose from an array of time-saving techniques and technical advances to help them in the quest to efficiently manage time:

- Make those daily, detailed lists of goals and objectives.
- Use technical advances to speed up paper handling, such as fax machines and computers with word processing, accounting, and menu-planning software.
- For heaven's sake, if you don't have a computer, get one! You can purchase one nowadays for a monthly payment of less than $40. You can take classes to learn how to use it or hire someone to teach you individually.
- Use cellular phones to stay in touch while away from the office. These are lifesavers at off-premise catering locations when emergency and other calls are necessary, and if you have downtime, a cellular phone can make it easy for you to use this time to return phone calls.

- Handle incoming papers only once. Here's the rule: Do it, delegate it, discard it, or file it. (Better yet, hire someone else to file it!)
- Do your most important work at times when you happen to be most alert. Most of us know whether we are "morning people" or "night owls." Take advantage of your peak energy periods to handle your most challenging tasks.
- Sign up for a seminar or course in time management to learn more tips.

One of the biggest time wasters for a caterer is also the source of much business— the prospective client who calls to ask questions—so it's an interruption that cannot be ignored, but can be controlled.

Whoever answers the phone at your business should always qualify the incoming call by asking:

- The date of the event
- The location of the event
- The number of guests
- The budget for the event Why?

First of all, time can be wasted talking about an event before you ask the date and discover you're not able to do it in the first place because of a scheduling conflict. Perhaps the number of guests is too small or too large for your particular company, the budget is insufficient, or the proposed location is already booked for another event. Always focus on results by asking yourself, "Will this activity help me achieve any of my goals?" Prioritize tasks in order of their importance and know when to delegate them to others.

Most people waste countless hours, days, weeks, and years chitchatting on the phone, shuffling papers, running errands, and doing other things that are easy enough but offer little or no payoff. Learn to delegate these types of tasks whenever possible. Pay other people to do them, and don't tell yourself you can't afford it—you can always make more money, but you have only so much time.

The true achievers—in catering and in other fields—minimize their time on low priority, low-payoff tasks and turn their attention to those things that will bring the greatest rewards. These tasks are often difficult to accomplish, take a great deal of time, and involve at least some risk. For example, a caterer could spend the entire day showing prospective clients numerous suitable locations for a major event. The caterer would then spend the next three days preparing a written proposal for an event at each of the locations, with no guarantee that the event will even take place. However, if the caterer is hired, there's a five-figure profit to be made. Worth the risk? Certainly! Another high-payoff task might be to write a new catering menu.

Both this and the aforementioned task require large chunks of time and involve some risk, but more than likely will produce major rewards in increased revenues and profits. In summary, off-premise caterers who best manage their time in the long run will be the most successful. They become the leading caterers in their communities, in their states, and in the country. Getting Organized When projects, tasks, catering kitchens, and offices are organized, things run much more smoothly and efficiently. The time spent looking for things and jumping from job to job is wasted time that could be put to much better use.

Many off-premise caterers have found various methods that work for them:

- Establish a filing system using hanging folders and manila folders. Categories can include upcoming events, projects to do, and projects pending. Files should be stored vertically, rather than stacked atop one another, for greater accessibility.
- Take a tip from event planners who start a separate notebook for each event they are working on. Into this three-ring binder go all notes, contracts, sketches, colour samples—anything for that particular job.

- Consider hiring a professional organizer to come to your office and set up a filing and record-keeping system that works for your business.
- Keep those items that are used frequently close by.
- Focus on one project at a time, rather than jumping from one thing to another. This can be easily accomplished by blocking out some time during the day to work on major projects and arranging for no interruptions.
- Whenever possible, try to schedule time to return phone calls and/or e-mail messages. That way, you can handle them all at once, instead of scattering them (and your thoughts) in five-minute intervals throughout the day.
- Either at the end of each day or first thing in the morning, prepare a list of things to do for the day.

Those off-premise caterers who can effectively deal with stress, who properly manage their time, who learn to delegate and keep things organized will lead their peers into the future. They will set the standards for others to follow. They will accomplish more and will be in a position to receive the greatest rewards as a result.

Looking Ahead—Catering in the Future

What does the future hold for caterers in this new century? First of all, we know that catering is neither rocket science nor brain surgery. Change is inevitable in this business, but not at the same rate as, say, in molecular theory or medical technology. In fact, in catering, rediscovering foods of the previous century is trendy! Many caterers still feature the signature dishes—honey coconut shrimp, beef tenderloin, Caesar salad—that they've served for decades. Why? The customers demand, and enjoy, them.

This certainly doesn't mean things stay stagnant in our industry. Innovative buffet and food station décor will continue to evolve. Most catering companies will continue to build their reputations on elegant, "over-the-top" food presentations, and the healthy competition shows no signs of abating. Other caterers prize research, developing cutting-edge menu items to set them apart from the pack.

More women are entering the off-premise catering field. Paula LeDuc in the San Francisco Bay area, Katherine Farrell in Ann Arbor, Abigail Kirsch in New York, Mary Micucci in Los Angeles, and Joy Wallace in Miami are but a handful of enterprising women who have grown their companies into catering's elite. Staffing woes will continue to be monumental, as hiring, training, and retraining get tougher. Foodservice has always been a somewhat transient industry.

Astute caterers will use pre-employment aptitude and personality testing, master online staff scheduling systems, and develop their own training programmes. They will also realize, if they haven't already, that they must treat their employees at least as well as they treat their clients. Along the same lines, in a top-tier catering operation, the employees treat each other as well as they treat their clients. Caterers of the future will come to realize that bigger is not necessarily better.

Having a large volume of business is admirable—but only when the quality of your work rises to the same level. A company can grow to the point where quality slips, gross profit margins lag, more equipment is needed, overhead costs expand, and the bottom line shrinks proportionately. The intelligent caterer will downsize, watch margins and profits grow—and overall stress levels diminish—as they become more selective about the clientele they service. Caterers are realizing that "high tech" will never replace personalized service, or "high touch"—but without high tech, they'll limit their potential for high touch.

In an industry where, amazingly, some caterers still don't accept credit cards, the savvy businessperson is learning to embrace new technology, launching interactive websites and e-mail marketing campaigns. They're creating improved computer generated proposals, rental orders, packing lists, staffing schedules, and instant financial statements. And they're realizing that computer-savvy business owners have more time to do what they love—which is run their business! Competition will continue to increase.

Sales will grow, but not without some dips, because economic woes, terrorist attacks, and the resulting fears cannot help but impact the catering profession. More caterers were hurt financially by the recession at the beginning of this century than by the September 11 terrorist attacks, but both left their marks on the industry. An increased use of security cameras at high profile events (and in some cases, to thwart theft) is one result of the heightened awareness. Mega-event catering is acknowledged as an excellent way to grow business—at golf and tennis tournaments, NASCAR races, air shows, boat shows, and more.

In addition to being profitable events, they expose the caterer to a wider range of potential clients. Then again, a caterer from Augusta, Georgia, generates enough revenue from serving sandwiches and beverages at the Masters' Golf Tournament that he need not cater at all the rest of the year! The pressure experienced in servicing huge, multiday events is as big as the events themselves, but the rewards can be significant. At the end of the 1900s, B. Joseph Pine II wrote The Experience Economy, a primer about the "new rules of engagement" for businesses.

Pine asserts that a new economic model is taking shape as we move from a service-based economy into an experience-based economy, where successful vendors literally create an "experience" for clients by using props and services to engage them in an "inherently personal way." Pine claims that Walt Disney was the founding father of the "Experience Economy," and in today's restaurant industry there are plenty of examples—Rainforest Cafe, Planet Hollywood, Hard Rock Cafes, and other themed eateries that combine food, service, and atmosphere to create a more "complete" dining experience. This kind of trend is adaptable for off-premise caterers too, with elaborate themes, staff members who double as costumed performers, team-building events, and imaginative menu items presented in wild new ways to delight and entertain the crowd as well as feed them!

For those who love to have fun, and who are as adventurous as they are practical, it's a great time to be an off-premise caterer. The Seven Habits of Highly Successful Caterers Let's examine some additional techniques, philosophies, and real-life ways to be successful in the challenging field of off-premise catering. Habits are things we do automatically, like brushing our teeth, combing our hair, or straightening a tablecloth that's uneven. We hardly think about them, we just do them. Stephen R. Covey wrote The Seven Habits of Highly Effective People, which has been a bestseller for years—you should read it if you haven't already. But what are some habits that mark successful caterers? What separates star performers from the rest of the crowd? With a nod to Mr. Covey, here are seven key traits.

One of our favourite sayings is, "A turtle goes nowhere until it sticks its neck out." In order to succeed, we must be continually growing and improving, and the only way to do this is to leave our comfort zones—and stick our necks out! If you're right-handed, you feel quite comfortable writing with your right hand. Try writing with your left hand. You're definitely out of your comfort zone. But after a while, you'll find you can actually write with either hand.

Successful caterers make things happen by taking calculated risks, whether it is trying new menu items, new buffet display concepts, or accepting a job in a new and challenging off-premise location. Caterers who refuse to take risks fail to grow and learn are left behind. Sincere Concern for Others Nobody cares how much you know until they know how much you care. Empathy and genuine concern for your clients and staff are paramount to long-term success. What are their needs, wishes, and desires? What are their concerns and their "hot buttons"? By putting ourselves in their positions, we can begin to show concern for others and understand them.

When we do this, we develop meaningful relationships and, not coincidentally, loyalty. We give them what they want, and we get what we want. Keeping Up with Current Trends It's not just a matter of food and presentation and theme trends. Caterers who are not wired to do business online through the Internet and e-mail are missing out on huge opportunities. The online catering referral service, Leading Caterers of America (founded by the book's co-author Bill Hansen), receives 5 to 20 inquiries per day from clients looking for catering services coast to coast, in Alaska, Hawaii, and occasionally overseas. People do shop for catering online, and the companies that lead the way have high quality websites and diligently reply to e-mailed requests in a timely manner.

Caterers need to get in the habit of responding to e-mail correspondence as soon as possible, as well as providing e-mailed proposals to those clients who prefer to do business via their computers. Event planners who book caterers for their clients love receiving e-mailed proposals, because they are easy to copy-and-paste into their own proposals. If you're not in the habit of working online, you're behind the times. Excellent Priorities and Time Management You get 20 per cent of your sales and profits from 80 per cent of your clients, and 80 per cent of your sales and profits from 20 per cent of your clients. None of us ever go home at night thinking that all the work is done—it never is. It's simply a question of what's most important, as well as what's most urgent. Urgent things are never really an issue.

There's no question that if you have a catered event today, it will get done. But what's most urgent is not necessarily what's most important. You must understand the difference. For example, you could spend a day catering three small parties for 25 guests each, but fall behind on preparing a proposal for another job, in three months, for 500 guests—and lose it to a competitor whose proposal was simply submitted on time. Successful caterers spend their time in those areas that generate the biggest paybacks in terms of money, quality, and other rewards. They make a habit of planning their days, leaving time for the most important, as well as the most urgent.

At the start of each day they prepare an agenda that details both short-term objectives and long-term goals. If you're a student, you should already be using this technique to accomplish as much as you can in school. Quality before Quantity Bigger is not necessarily better. Still, many of us get caught up in that way of thinking. If our sales are $1 million, let's go for $2 million. If they're $2 million, what's wrong with $4 million? And if $4 million is good... There's nothing wrong with building sales if quality does not suffer. However, when the quality of our products and services suffers so does the quality of our lifestyle. More business means more hours at work. And doctors will tell you they've never met a man or woman who, on a deathbed, expressed a wish that he or she had spent more time at work.

If we can grow our businesses with no adverse effects on the quality of our lives or our products, then we should go for it! But if we find profits slipping and clients complaining, and we need a letter of introduction when we stumble home at 3:00 A.M., then something's very wrong. We need to make of habit of continually asking ourselves whether we might be better off with less business and more time for ourselves and for our families. We need to continually examine the quality of our work to ensure that it's not slipping because we've allowed ourselves to take on too much. Being Detail Oriented A baseball player who bats.250 gets three hits for every 12 times at bat. One who bats. 333 gets four hits for every 12 times at bat. The difference—one more hit for every 12 times at bat—means the difference between an average major league ball player and a Hall of Fame inductee. Do you make it a habit to continually look for the little things?

A good caterer isn't nitpicky, but is forever finding something that needs to be tweaked, adjusted, redone, or improved—little things that most customers won't notice, but that greatly impact the overall professionalism of an event.

Being aware of the details in flavors, looks, aromas, and tidiness separates the average caterers from the superstars. And, by all means, check the spelling, grammar, and punctuation in all your written materials, from brochures to contracts—or hire someone to do it. Again, the goal is to present a professional image. Remember? The devil is in the details. Setting High Standards If you refuse to accept anything but the very best, you very often get the best. Successful caterers set their standards high and expect excellence from themselves and their staff members. They're never happy with the status quo, always striving to make each party, wedding, or event better than the last.

They debrief after an event, asking staff for input and improvements. They know that if they fail to improve, they're leaving the door open for their competitors to capture a good customer or a larger share of the market. Successful caterers also make a habit of lifelong learning. They're forever reading, attending trade shows, and exploring areas that will help them improve their own businesses with new ideas. They challenge and reward their staff members for having the same attitude.

Vince Lombardi, the late NFL coach, who during his career coached the first team to ever win the Super Bowl, put it this way: "The quality of a person's life is in direct proportion to their commitment to excellence, regardless of their chosen field of endeavor." How Does an Off-Premise Caterer Gauge Success? There are a number of signs to look for when evaluating an existing off-premise catering business. Healthy companies rate highly in all of these areas.

Those that are unhealthy, or even on the brink of failure, will not rate nearly as well.

- Management thoroughly plans, organizes, executes, and controls each catered event.
- Proper controls are in place for costs, accounts receivable and payable, and liquid assets such as cash and inventories. Theft prevention is also a priority.
- Food and service quality is well-controlled and meets or exceeds clients' approval.

- Pricing for food and services is fair and competitive with other firms in the marketplace. There is a spirit of healthy competition.
- The catering firm enjoys good working relationships with both clients and suppliers.
- Time and attention are given to food safety in storage, preparation, and display. Employees know the local health codes and follow them.
- There is sufficient working capital to operate the business. The firm can make loan payments as they become due. Excessive credit is not extended to clients.
- Budgets are prepared and followed. Business records, insurance coverage, and licenses are kept up to date. The information derived from these records is used to provide data to help manage the business.
- Sales growth is controlled. There are sufficient financial and personnel resources to operate as business steadily grows.
- Market trends are anticipated.
- Management and staff have a good working knowledge of the off-premise catering field.
- There are solid, trusting relationships between management and staff. Staff members are well trained and feel truly appreciated—because they are.
- Management works closely with a qualified accountant to plan for payment of taxes.
- And, finally, management is willing to seek qualified professional assistance if problems arise.

The Off-Premise Catering Model is the factors that enter into the off-premise catering arena. It shows how managerial philosophies and techniques, as well as laws regarding personnel, business, alcoholic beverage service, and sanitation and safety, must all be interrelated to guide the company. It then depicts how marketing efforts produce clients, which in turn creates needs for site inspections and logistical plans, including planning in these specific areas: menus, beverages, equipment, personnel, and any other related services.

Once the planning is complete, it is possible to provide clients with written proposals, which include all the aforementioned plans along with pricing. Normally, proposals are modified somewhat. Once modification is complete and all provisions meet with the approval of both caterer and client, a contract is prepared that contains all the conditions outlined in the proposal. As the party date approaches, certain operational elements are addressed, such as:

- Hiring and scheduling staff
- Purchasing and pre-preparation of menu items
- Ordering equipment as needed from party rental companies
- Obtaining licenses and permits, as needed, for use of the site, serving alcohol, etc.
- Preparing a "pull sheet" that details all items supplied by the commissary to produce the party.
- Coordinating all beverage and accessory services with the client and the vendors.

All the preplanning elements culminate on the day or night of "The Show." That's when staff, equipment, food, and other services arrive at the party site, and the event is executed. After the event, there are certain outcomes, which include: Positive and/or negative word of mouth about the event Revenues, expenses, profits, and cash Accounting records

Chapter 2

Catering and Customer

CATERING TO DIVERGENT

It sounds rather crass, but when they die, in the next 10-15 years, all of their money—some $10 trillion dollars—is going to another group of people, most of whom don't like banks. They would rather go to Fidelity, play the market, not having lived through a downturn. One of the challenges as we go forward is how the banking industry is going to transform itself, move from the current group who provides the bulk of our earnings, to a second group who will assume society's wealth, and who does not realty like us.

Who likes banks? Those 55 years and older plus those who have lower incomes and less education, according to a 1997 ABA survey—valued customers,.but not a group we can solely survive on. Also, as the chart below indicates, customer satisfaction is slipping somewhat for banks.

You need to know when you should allocate resources from the group giving you the bulk of your earnings now, to the group that does not like you. You will also get a boost from the federal government's change to electronic benefits transfer (EBT) on January 1, 1999. Most states will have an EBT environment by the end of 1998. The people who now get a Social Security check will have to become accustomed to an electronic transaction, and that's in your favour. A lot of the back-office work, you can change through electronic transactions.

EBT will provide a large infusion of the infrastructure required for electronic commerce, by increasing the number of point-of-sale terminals. The ABA asked the Federal Reserve and the Treasury to review the regulations surrounding transaction accounts, because the existing regulations are all in the realm of paper-based accounts. We would really like to get rid of the periodic statement under Regulation E because a purely electronic account will not have any outstanding items so you don't realty need a statement. Banks will have to do some new things, though—electronic benefits transactions on automated teller machines, and maybe statements on demand.

What can you do today on the Internet? You can do consumer education; you can have interactive advertising; you can distribute forms and applications; you can provide account information. You can do some internal transactions (transferring between a checking and a savings account), some bill payment (for payees like the power and the gas company), and, perhaps, some electronic commerce for the more daring. Electronic commerce, a broader term than electronic banking, better describes what ultimately we might want to do. What customers want today is not necessarily what they are going to want next year. You have to continually reassess.

RELIABILITY ON TOMORROW'S SYSTEMS

Today, most of you keep your real stuff on a mainframe, a rather secure system. On the Internet, how are you going to let people like me hack around in your computer? You are going to be doing the same kinds of things on the Internet that you do today to render service and security to your customers. You will have a lot of the same, concerns. You could have a saboteur on the inside. You could have a huge virus or software that fails.

The new one is the hackers, but then you've got people who forge checks, too; they just attack in a different way. Whatever system you have must be reliable, sound, and secure. What kinds of things will give you these qualities? Well, you have technical standards (ABA is secretariat for the x.9

financial services committee of the American National Standards Institute); you have best practices, and the regulators providing guidance to the industry. You are going to a much more efficient system and you should have greater margins as you implement it, but meanwhile, many larger institutions have proprietary systems that work very well. Probably nobody here has had a customer question, in the past 50 years, whether her check is going to clear. You are coming off of that kind of reliability.

Bankers have systems that, perhaps, can be expanded to an Internet environment. Determining who has the best products to help you is part of creating a plan. You want, perhaps, to start small, with, say, electronic bill payment, see how secure it is, how your customers accept it, and then go forward. You may lose money, but you are going to do it because your customers want it.

There are threats to banks' dominance of the payments system, one of the biggest of which is the post office. You may say that will never happen because it is not an insured depository, but I would submit, for example, that the largest financial institution in Japan is the post office. Financial modernization, after 30 years, seems finally to be coming. Companies with unlimited capital, such as, say, General Electric Corp., will be able to compete very effectively, not for the little old ladies' $50,000 CDs but for their kids' money. That's why ABA is very concerned.

With direct deposit, a customer need never walk into a branch. A customer in Alaska can directly deposit funds into a bank in Alabama and write checks or use his debit card all day long in Alaska. All across the country, community bankers are saying to themselves "Aha! Maybe I have an opportunity here." This stuff is coming. How are you going to respond? You are concerned about how your customers perceive you. Are you stodgy—as one of ABA's new industry ads shows — or are you out there on roller-blades? Now, you have to be concerned about customer perception beyond the community where you do business.

The Growth of Service Activities

Service sector economics now constitutes a major branch of economic studies although it is a field which no more than a decade ago was variously referred to as the 'poor relation' and the 'Cinderella of academics and politicians alike'. The explanation of the interest recently evinced in the economics of the service sector is to be found in the extent to which service industries have expanded relative to other economic activities. Whilst the tendency for the tertiary sector to grow in comparison to primary and secondary activities has been identified and commented on for many decades special factors, such as the potential for services to generate new jobs, have helped thrust the sector to the forefront of economic analysis in the last few years.

The relative growth of services in the British economy since 1971, quantified on the basis of official statistics, could well stand as on outline of events in most developed economies during this period. Between 1971 and 1986 the output of the service sector (defined as distribution, catering, transport, banking and finance, and other services) increased by 2.5 per cent a year, or more than twice the rate, 1.1 per cent, achieved by other economic activities (agriculture, energy, manufacturing and construction).

Within the sector commercial services—distribution, catering, financial, business, recreational and personal services—expanded faster than other services, 3.1 per cent compared with 1.7 per cent a year, whilst specific commercial services grew very rapidly indeed—banking and business services by as much as 5.1 per cent per annum. As a result, by 1985, service activities in Britain accounted for three-fifths of GDP and commercial services themselves were responsible for a third of total output.

The importance of service activities is no less when judged by labour force size. On the basis of both numbers of employees, and by numbers of employees plus the self-employed, by 1985 services accounted for 66 per cent of

Britain's labour force compared with 53 per cent in 1971. Commercial services alone provided jobs for 37 per cent of all employees in 1985.

The Need for New Measures

At a time when the bases, compilation, accuracy and usefulness of a range of official economic statistics have come under close scrutiny, the measurement of service outputs has not escaped attention. Recently there has been some shift away from a simple acknowledgement that service output measures may be subject to a degree of unreliability towards an apprehension that any errors they contain might lead to a downward bias in the measure of service output, and therefore, GDP growth rates. It has in fact been suggested that output increases in services may have been underestimated in recent years by as much as 2-1/2 per cent a year implying that annual growth of GDP itself should have been substantially higher.

For both conceptual and practical reasons the outputs of many service activities are notoriously difficult to quantify both absolutely and in terms of change over time. Yet because of their size and growth it is especially important that a reasonable degree of accuracy must attach to service output measures which should reflect current best practice given the data and resources available. If this is not the case then, because of the weight of service activities in the total economy, the accuracy of the registred change in GDP and national productivity, the relative contribution to growth of service and non-service activities, the pattern of structural change within the service sector and the policies to which these various phenomena have given rise, must all be called in question.

This assembles some of the principal results which have emerged from a study of alternative output measures for British service industries. The study reviews the methods currently used by the CSO to measure real output changes in specified services and seeks to devise, develop and implement new measures for these activities. For this purpose an empirical approach has been adopted. Whilst basic conceptual considerations are taken fully into account in that the alternative measures which are compiled can be integrated into the national accounting framework, it is felt that the theoretical complexities associated with service output measurement have received due attention elsewhere whilst very little has been done at the practical level.

When compiling new service output measures the two principal uses for which they are employed must be borne in mind. The original raison d'etre for measuring service sector output is for use, in conjunction with output indicators for industrial activities, to yield a measure of real growth in total GDP. This is the primary role for which the CSO devises and compiles output measures for service sector activities. Increasingly, however, as the weight of services in the economy has grown service output indicators are now used extensively, in conjunction with labour force and other relevant economic series, for the analysis of long-term developments in individual service industries.

Their employment in the latter context accentuates the requirement that they fulfill minimum reliability criteria: it is possible that offsetting errors in individual service industry output measures may modulate their impact on the reliability of overall GDP measurement but this does not apply when attention is focused on the analysis of developments in a specific service industry.

The results obtained in the present exercise suggest that official measures of GDP growth may well have been marginally understated as a result of the methods used to track service output changes. Even more significantly, perhaps, the alternative measures which have been compiled portray patterns of development for some individual commercial service industries which are very different from those yielded by official output measures.

When considering alternative output measures attention has been directed first at the strengths and weaknesses of official practice as a prelude to an attempt to improve the rationale and reliability of the resulting output indicators. However in some cases it is necessary to regard the new measure simply as an alternative to the official index: an alternative with a different, rather than superior, base and/or derived from quite separate data sources. Another feature of the search for alternative indicators is that it has been conducted with an eye to the improved reliability of service output measurement in the future. To some extent this means that data series which are available only for recent years have been drawn upon.

Nevertheless a major objective of the study has been to assess the extent to which the official picture of past service sector developments is changed if alternative output measures are used. The alternative measures have therefore been carried backwards in some cases to 1971, in others to 1973 and for a large number to 1978, using 1985 as the base year. There are three reasons for the latter choice. First data limitations mean that all series cannot be uniformly taken back to a common early date so that a recent year must be adopted as the base.

Secondly at the time when the research was initiated 1985 was the latest year for which data—whether values, 'quantities' or 'weights'—were generally available. Thirdly, the CSO was then in the process of re-basing its output indicators using 1985 GDP weights.

The new output measures draw much more extensively on unofficial data sources than do those compiled by the CSO. Broadly such sources can be divided into two types: those which yield data series covering an industry-wide set of activities; and those which contain data relating to individual service industry organisations and firms. Typically the assistance of the latter was enlisted to provide weights with which industry-wide quantity series for different kinds of output can be combined to produce a single output measure for the service sector in question.

It is to the credit of the CSO that there has been a continuous attempt to modify service output measures in the light of methodological developments and the emergence of alternative data sources. Whilst this has had the desired result of improving the reliability of service output measurement inevitably it also introduces inconsistencies and breaks in the time series where – either on practical or other grounds – the new methods have not been carried back to earlier years. A feature of the new measures postulated below is that every effort has been made to ensure temporal consistency in the series which they yield.

It has not proved possible to devote to 'quality' aspects of service output the attention they properly merit. In part this reflects the fact that the incorporation of quality changes in output measures may be even more difficult in services than in goods-producing industries where frequently its assessment is equally neglected. This in turn is due to the consideration that the quality of a given service varies greatly (no two football matches are the same in this respect) and in many cases (as with say opera performances) is highly subjective.

Nevertheless the results do have implications for this aspect of service output measurement, especially in the case of the catering trades. Were quality aspects taken into account more fully, further consideration would need to be given to the relative merits of measures based on deflated value series and service output units.

Coverage of the Measures

The search for alternative output measures has been restricted to the commercial service industries, essentially distribution, catering, financial, business and personal services, for which suggests that output has risen especially rapidly. Within this group of commercial services the CSO distinguishes for output measurement purposes as many as 37 service industries, output changes in which are currently assessed by a total of 114 indicators. These services accounted for some 30 per cent of total GDP in 1985 and about a third of people employed in Great Britain.

Given the vast range of service activities which must be covered by official output measures it is natural that the CSO makes use of readily available, relevant, series to yield the required indicators, series which themselves are normally official in the sense that they are compiled by other government departments. Since the quest for new measures has entailed a search for and detailed examination of, alternative data, involving the identification, location and perusal of non-official sources and also the co-operation of individual firms and organisations it proved necessary to regard the full range of commercial service activities as no more than a frame from which individual service industries could be selected for intensive analysis.

When choosing industries from this list for which alternative measures of output change are identified and implemented, several criteria have been applied. A principal consideration has been to direct efforts to services where, on the face of it, current practice appears to be weak. At one end of the scale this principle tends to divert attention away from activities such as retailing, where the measures are generally regarded as being relatively sound, towards such services as advertising where the official output indicator is based on an employment series.

Secondly some priority was given to activities for which at first blush—sometimes deceptive—alternative measures appeared feasible. Thirdly an attempt has been made to cover the larger service industries such as banking and insurance, and ceteris paribus, attention was focused on service activities which, a priori, are thought to be rapidly expanding, a criterion which points to the inclusion of, especially, financial and business services.

Since a systematic attempt has been made to base alternative output measures on numbers of service units produced, such service industries as estate agents, stockbroking and legal services where official output measurement is already founded on numbers of service units—of property transfers, transactions, and court proceedings—have not been considered as candidates for alternative measures.

The service industries for which new measures were ultimately compiled fall neatly into three groups. First, there are ten selected financial and business services: banking, building societies, finance leasing, hire-purchase, insurance, accountants, architects, advertising, computer services and construction plant hire. Secondly eight recreational services have been covered: broadcasting, theatres, libraries, museums, professional sports, participatory sports, local authority leisure centres and betting and gaming. Thirdly, the five catering trades—restaurants, public houses, clubs, catering contractors and hotels—have also been included.

Alternative output Measures

Continuous CSO action to modify and improve service output measures means that they have developed from year to year in an essentially ad hoc manner with considerable diversity in their conceptual underpinning. Output measures for the commercial service sector rely heavily on deflated value and employment indicators and whilst output measurement for some service activities, noted above, is based on counting numbers of service units, such practice applies to only a fraction of the output of the commercial service sector.

In fact it has emerged that the use of this type of measure can be extended to a considerable number of commercial services and an attempt has therefore been made to generalise and implement this approach, especially in the case of the financial and recreational services.

This method can be summarised as the compilation of [sigma]poqo where q represents the industry's output quantities (in the present context, service output units) p the industry's output prices and 0 and 1 refer to the years compared. This is 'the traditional [measure] used for multi-product industries wherein an index of production is constructed from a weighted sum of various outputs produced by the industry'.

Such a deflated value approach to output measurement will yield the required result—as measured by the traditional direct method based on weighted quantities—only if the deflator, the price index, relates specifically to the products or services in question. This condition is not fulfilled in the case of many service output measures where for practical reasons some form of general price index is used. It is partly to remedy this weakness in service output measurement that, wherever possible, alternative measures have been based in this exercise on the traditional direct methodology using numbers of service output units.

A fundamental requirement for the use of this 'traditional' or 'direct' approach is that, for purposes of practical measurement, the outputs of the industry or service in question should be relatively homogeneous. No economic activity yields a single, identical, product or service so that in practice it is sufficient if the bulk of an industry's activity is represented by a limited range of output types. It is their supposed inability to fulfill this criterion which has discouraged the application of the traditional, direct, measurement methodology to service activities. Generally it has been assumed that there exists, virtually, an infinite variety and range of outputs in the case of most, especially financial, services: that no two life insurances, mortgages, bank accounts, and the output activities associated with them, are the same.

It is argued that this view is based largely on a misconception, associated with what, for want of a better term, we shall call the 'digit illusion', and that in fact many service industries—including betting and gaming—fulfil the basic criterion for the application of the traditional, direct measurement methodology in that the bulk of their output is accounted for by a limited range of essentially homogeneous activities.

For the impression of enormous diversity in the output of most financial services derives from the fact that the values associated with a specific activity—the sums assured by a life company, sizes of mortgages provided by a building society, the amounts loaned under hire-purchase agreements by a finance house, the values of cheques cleared by a commercial bank, the car insurance premiums charged by an insurer etc—do have an infinitely large range.

It has been assumed in the search for new output measures that such differences can be essentially ignored. In the case of mortgages, for example, the output associated with writing 500,000 pounds sterling in a deed is, with some relatively minor qualifications, little different from that associated with inscribing 50,000 pounds sterling or even 5,000 pounds sterling; differences in the numbers of digits required in this and other financial instruments—cheques, insurance policies, hire-purchase agreements, betting slips—have relatively little bearing on the amount of output involved.

In brief for a given type of financial activity it is normally legitimate, when measuring output, to ignore the 'digit illusion'. This has the effect of rendering homogeneous, by the above definition, a wide range of financial activities, making them amenable, in principle, to the traditional direct, measurement methodology. It means, by way of illustration, that output changes for the life insurance industry can be based on changes in numbers (not values of sums assured, expenses or premiums) of policies.

It must be stressed however that a distinction must be drawn, and numbers counted, for each major type of service/activity provided by the service industry in question where value added per service unit varies significantly between activity types. This means, for instance, in the case of the life insurance industry, that numbers of policies must be counted separately for ordinary life insurance, industrial life, annuities and personal pensions.

It also means that attention needs to be drawn to a feature of this approach which is peculiar to financial service industries: the distinction between stocks and flows. Clearly, the resources devoted to, and therefore the amount of output associated with, the annual 'maintenance' of pre-existing mortgage will be substantially less than required when initiating a new mortgage. In principle, and where practical, it is as important therefore to draw a distinction when measuring output between numbers of existing mortgages issued in a given year (the 'flow') and the numbers of existing mortgages (the 'stock') as it is to count separately the numbers of, say, different kinds of policy issued by life insurance companies. Indeed the same distinction needs to be drawn in the case of life insurance—between new policies and policies in force—and in principle at any rate in many other financial service industries: between new and existing contracts for hire-purchase and finance leases for instance.

The practicability of extending the traditional measurement methodology to commercial services thus hinges, in the case of each activity, on the availability of two kinds of data: industry-wide series of numbers of each type of principal (homogenous) product, the series q; and appropriate weights with which these various product series can be combined to yield an aggregate output measure for the service industry in question, the series p.

To a degree inadequacies in the measurement of service output changes simply reflect the relative lack of interest with which they were regarded in the past and a consequent failure to devote sufficient resources to the collection of basic output data. Also, it is to some extent, due to the 'insubstantiality' of most services, the fact that they 'pass away' in the moment of production, that a systematic effort has not been made to base their output measurement to a much larger extent on numbers of service units produced. In fact regardless of whether or not a service has any kind of physical embodiment, in the vast majority of cases there exists a physical record or token that a particular service has been performed.

The outputs of all kinds of commercial service industries are very well 'documented'—by the ticket required for entrance to Wimbledon, the bill for a meal, the contract which records the finance leasing of a fleet of aircraft—in a form which in principle allows the numbers of each type of service to be recorded. In this sense, and at this level, the output of service activities is registered at least as well as the products of industrial pursuits. The nig universal existence, at the 'grass roots' level, of this detailed record of service sector outputs, to an ever increasing extent in computerised form, augurs well for the future extension and development of the kind of direct output measurement advocated here.

This comprehensive data base has not yet been properly exploited to yield aggregate series of the numbers of each type of service produced on an industry-wide basis. However research and enquiry have revealed that representative bodies of various kinds at the industry level—especially trade associations—have come to regard the compilation of aggregate numbers of each kind of service produced, using these data bases, as one of their primary tasks, and such sources have been widely drawn upon.

That they may not be based on series for numbers of service units which are fully comprehensive for the industry in question should not be regarded as a major weakness of the alternative output measures which are presented in the following. Usually only the major 'products' are counted and in this respect the circumstances are no different from those which exist when the method is applied to industrial activities. For both industrial and service activities so measured the implicit assumption is the same: that real changes in the non-covered outputs parallel the aggregate change measured for the covered operations.

Unfortunately, with few exceptions, service industry organisations, do not collect, process or publish, the kind of data (relating to expenses for example), which are needed to obtain the 'weights' required for aggregating these various output series into a single measure for the industry in question. In these circumstances it has proved necessary to have recourse inter alia to the goodwill of individual (if major) firms in order to derive suitable weights which must be accepted as typical for the service industry in which they operate.

Wherever possible alternative measures have been derived from an application, along the above lines, of the traditional, direct methodology based on numbers of service output units. However even when allowance is made for the 'digit illusion' some service industries – such as architecture and accountancy – remain in that class where output units are, in essence, infinitely variable in nature. In these cases an attempt has nevertheless been made to upgrade the output measure, usually by identifying and compiling a more appropriate price deflator.

This presents the results of the search for new output measures for the selected commercial activities. Initially the new output series are presented separately for the three major service complexes – financial and business services, recreational services and the catering trades – which have been covered and compared with the official measures. In each case the nature of both the alternative and official series are stated only in brief: it is planned to describe the methods used in full detail elsewhere. The section concludes with a consideration of the implications of the results for future developments in the measurement of service output.

Financial and Business Services

In 1985 the ten financial and business services for which new output measures have been compiled contributed, in total, about 35 pound sterling billion to GDP and employed approximately a million people. In the case of banking, the largest of the services in this sector, it proved possible to base the new measure wholly on numbers of service units – numbers of accounts, clearings, cash and credit card transactions. This contrasts with official practice in which indicators derived from deflated series for deposits and loans, as well as employment, carry the bulk of the weight.

In life insurance, also, numbers of policies of various types, distinguishing between new policies and policies in force, replace the official series comprising deflated consumer expenditure. Similarly the new building society measure is founded wholly on numbers of service units – shareholders, existing borrowers and new loans – instead of, as is the case with the official measure, a combination of deflated liabilities, employment and numbers of advances. For general insurance, a measure reflecting broadly the stock of insurable assets has been substituted for the official indicator based on deflated premiums.

In the case of two services, architects and advertising, a deflated value series places officla measures based on employment. The primary feature of the new measures used for accountants, computer services and hire-purchase, is the use of deflators which have been specially constructed to reflect more closely than those officially employed developments in the activities in question. The official practice for both construction plant hire and finance leasing has been to base indicators on output developments in user industries.

Instead of this approach the new measures are derived from gross output in the case of construction plant hire and the value of assets newly leased and of the stock of leased assets in the case of finance leasing, each deflated by price indices specifically compiled for the activities in question. The new measures for the covered financial and business services are set alongside the official indicators.

The basic date series from which these were derived are such that not all of them cover the full span of years, 1971 to 1986, so that it is convenient to combine them into three groups: five industries – building societies, hire-purchase, insurance, advertising and construction plant hire – for which growth rates are available for the whole period 1971-86; six industries – the above five together with banking – where the information is shown for 1973-86; and all ten covered financial services – the above six plus accountants, architects, finance leasing and computer services – for which alternative and official growth rates can be compared for the period 1978-86.

In the case of the first group, for which measures extend over the full period 1971-86, whilst there are some very significant differences between alternative and official growth rates – for building societies the former is appreciably higher than the latter whilst the opposite is true for hire-purchase – the (unweighted) arithmetic average growth rate for all five services, at 4.1 per cent per annum, is identical for both alternative and official measures. The same generalisation applies to the group of six industries over the period 1973-86: for hire-purchase, advertising, construction plant hire and banking the two measures yield quite different results but these contrasts offset each other so that the (unweighted) average alternative growth rate is identical with the average official growth rate.

Results for the group of ten industries, relating to the period 1978-86, paint a very similar picture; of individual industry diversity but overall similarity. In this case only for building societies, insurance, advertising and accountants do alternative and official methods yield rates of output change that are at all akin. Yet, overall, the (unweighted) average alternative growth rate, 7.4 per cent per annum, is not much greater than the 7.0 per cent registered officially. The official measure for finance leasing is constructed to minimise distortion in GDP measurement whilst the alternative measure has been compiled in such a way as to enhance the reliability of the industry's growth indicator per se.

If this service industry is left out of account, the average alternative growth rate, at 6.6 per cent, is below the average official rate, 7.6 per cent. This set of results contains a further point of interest. Whilst, as pointed out, there are substantial differences in the case of most industries between the alternative and official measures, the inter-industry growth patterns are remarkably similar whether gauged by alternative or official indicators: again leaving out finance leasing the correlation coefficient for the remaining nine pairs of, alternative and official, growth rates is +0.95.

Although comparisons of unweighted average growth rates can be quite instructive more attention should be focused on differences between alternative and official measures revealed by weighted aggregate indices of the kind.

These output indices, derived from the alternative and official measures for individual industries and relating to the same groups of industries and periods specified have been obtained from an aggregation procedure which is based on 1985 contributions to GDP. The results contained are summarised in the form of average annual rates of growth that also contains growth rates obtained from weights derived from 1980 industry contributions to GDP and 1985 industry employment levels, to test the sensitivity of the results to alternative weighting systems.

In the case of the five industries for which there is full coverage over the period 1971 to 1986 the alternative growth rate is 4.4 per cent and the official one 4.8 per cent on the basis of 1985 GDP weights. A discrepancy of no more than a tenth between the two versions is also suggested by 1980 GDP weights. This group of five industries accounted for only 20 per cent of the contribution to GDP and an estimated 27 per cent of employment of all financial and business services in 1985. In contrast the group of six was responsible for 56 per cent of output and an estimated 42 per cent of employment and the group of ten for as much as 74 per cent of output and 56 per cent of employment.

Greater significance should therefore be attached to the results obtained for these latter two groups. All three weighting systems show that for the group of six industries, over the years 1973 to 1986, the official measure understated growth by about a fifth when compared with the aggregate alternative measure; much the same picture emerges for the group of ten industries during the period 1978 to 1986 where, on the basis of both 1985 and 1980 GDP weights, the official measure, compared with the alternative, underestimates growth by about a fifth.

When considering this disparity two industries merit special attention: banking which is by some way the largest of the ten industries; and finance leasing on account of the fundamental difference, referred to above, in the methods underlying the alternative and official measures. In fact if banking—with alternative and official growth rates of respectively 8.2 and 6.5 per cent per annum for the period 1978 to 1986—is left out of account the picture hardly changes at all: the alternative aggregate growth rate for the remaining nine industries over the period 1978 to 1986 (based on 1985 GDP weights) emerges as 8.0 per cent per annum compared with an official growth rate of 6.0 per cent. This is in sharp contrast to the effect of excluding finance leasing. In this case the alternative growth measure for the nine remaining industries falls to 7.5 per cent whilst the official measure rises to 7.2 per cent so that most of the differential disappears.

Recreational Services

In 1985, recreational services, SIC class 97, contributed almost 6 billion pounds sterling to GDP and provided employment for 430,000 people. Apart from cinemas, for which the official output indicator is based on numbers of attendances, the measures used by the CSO rely for the most part on deflated series of turnover or consumers' expenditure on the service in question. In the case of local authority libraries, however, employment-based indicators are used.

In the search for alternative measures it has proved possible, for these services, to base the new indicators largely on numbers of service units. Thus the output index for 'group' 974, broadcasting and theatres, reflects changes in numbers of radio and television hours transmitted (in the absence of adequate series for numbers of viewing/listening hours) and of attendances at theatres etc, whilst that for libraries and museums has been founded on numbers of books issued and numbers of visitors.

The new measures for sport, 'group' 979, an activity that accounts for almost half of the output of recreational services, has been derived from a variety of indicators which reflect, inter alia, changes in numbers of attendances at paying spectator sports, sports hours transmitted by television and radio, membership of participatory sports clubs and measures which trace changes in numbers of betting slips and football coupons. Only in the case of local authority leisure facilities was recourse made to conventional deflated value series.

The output series set out for cinemas and for authors and artists are those used officially: that for cinemas being already based on numbers of service units whilst no alternative measure could be readily identified for 'group' 976.

For comparison with the overall official measure for recreational services the five component output measures have been combined into a single output index using weights based on 1985 contributions to GDP.

The official measure suggests that the output of this service industry complex grew, between 1973 and 1988, at an average annual rate of 2.9 per cent; the alternative points to a significantly slower rate of increase of 2.0 per cent. One factor which may go some way towards explaining this discrepancy is that whilst in principle the alternative measure includes local authority libraries and leisure facilities throughout the period, the official indicator embraces these activities only since their transfer to class 97 of the 1980 SIC. Yet it can be seen that even in recent years the official measure has registered a significantly higher rate of growth for this industry than that shown by the alternative measure.

THE CATERING TRADES

In 1985 the catering trades' contribution to GDP totalled 7-1/2 pounds sterling billion and the industry employed more than a million people. Output measures for these trades are summarised, in terms of average annual growth rates. In the early years of the period covered the official indicator was based on turnover data supplied by a voluntary panel of catering organisations deflated by price indices specific to each of the catering trades.

From the beginning of the 1980s the official measure has been derived from changes in the margins of the individual catering trades as recorded in the DTI's annual catering trades' enquiry, again deflated by specific price indices. Although in principle it should be possible to measure output in the catering trades on the basis of numbers of service units—hotel bed occupancy, numbers of bar transactions etc—attempts to use this approach proved, for practical reasons, to be fruitless.

Therefore to test the sensitivity of the official measure alternative output series were constructed using the price indices officially compiled but applying them throughout to turnover data (as opposed to the gross margins used officially in recent years) yielded by the catering trades inquiries, interpolating results for early years where no such inquiries were conducted.

It is clear that these alternative measures alter the picture quite significantly for some trades. Whilst for restaurants, clubs and catering contractors changes in output are not greatly different whether measured on the official or alternative bases, sharply contrasting developments emerge for public houses and the hotel trade: the substantial growth recorded for public houses by the official measure virtually disappears with the alternative, whilst the opposite occurs in the case of hotels.

These quite significant modifications to the subsectoral picture, in effect, cancel out: on both official and alternative methods catering output increased over this period by about 1 per cent a year. The reliability of catering output changes cannot, however, be allowed to rest there. For when these changes are compared with labour force developments there would seem to have been substantial long-term declines in labour productivity: taking the official output measure in conjunction with changes in the number of employees in catering, labour productivity appears to have fallen by as much as 1.7 per cent a year between 1971 and 1986.

To help determine whether these results reflect real developments in this service industry or whether they arose from statistical series which are sufficiently unreliable as to produce a misleading picture of events, alternative, more sophisticated, full-time equivalent labour force series have been constructed. Since both part-time working and self-employment are important features of the catering trades' labour force, allowance for developments in both these aspects has been made in the FTE series shown.

Whilst the introduction of FTE labour force series improves the productivity picture there nevertheless remains an apparently substantial fall in catering productivity: an annual average decline of 1.7 per cent a year using numbers of employees is modified to a deterioration of 1.2 per cent on an FTE basis. Of the individual trades only catering contractors emerge with enhanced FTE productivity, displaying an improvement of 1.7 per cent a year.

The other four trades register deteriorations: restaurants by 2.1 per cent a year, public houses 0.1 per cent, clubs 3.6 per cent and hotels 1.2 per cent. It is theoretically feasible, on the basis of most formulations of the production function, that in certain circumstances output in any economic activity might increase over the long term at a rate below that registered for labour inputs. This could arise in particular if there were a fall in capital intensity but such a development does not appear to have been a feature of catering during this period.

A measure compiled for the industry suggests that between 1971 and 1986 the stock of equipment grew at an annual average rate of 3.6 per cent a year which, in conjunction with an annual rise of 2.3 per cent in the FTE labour force, points to a 1.4 per cent annual increase in capital intensity.

In these circumstances it is difficult to accept that either the official or alternative output measures presented adequately reflect output growth in the catering trades. A probable explanation of this deficiency is that the measures fail to take sufficient account of developments, in some general sense, in the quality of catering output, be it a reflection of changes in the range of services offered, the milieu in which they are provided, the nature of the food and drink supplied or the standards of customer service.

It is relevant that following comparatively little change in its size during the 1950s and 1960s the catering industry's labour force has grown substantially over the last two decades, especially during the early 1970s. These developments have generally been explained by contrasts in the nature of the labour market between, on the one hand, the earlier decades and on the other the 1970s and 1980s.

The earlier prevalence of full employment meant that because catering work was notoriously unattractive and ill-paid the industry was able to adjust its labour force towards its basic manning requirements. This kind of effect was reinforced by the impact of the selective employment tax which led to a significant fall in catering employment when it was implemented during the later years of the 1960s and a rapid increase in the early years of the 1970s after its abandonment.

This thesis is also supported by case studies of the impact on the industry of technological innovations (computers, microwave ovens etc). A recent survey of organisations operating in the catering trades revealed that rather than causing redundancies 'the time saved by new technology and improved productivity was being used wherever possible to enhance customer service'. A stagnant productivity performance in catering is equally difficult to reconcile with the rapid growth of both take-away food facilities and self-catering accommodation.

In the event it has been decided to use labour inputs, to be precise the FTE measure shown, as a surrogate output measure for this industry. It is felt that whilst far from ideal it provides a less unsatisfactory output measure, over the period in question, than either the official index or the alternative indicator compiled above. On this basis an annual average growth rate of 2.3 per cent emerges for catering output, hardly an unreasonable achievement for what is largely a leisure industry during a period when GDP increased, on average, by 1.7 per cent a year.

Furthermore when applied to the individual catering trades this labour force based method yields results, for changes in real output over these years, which are intuitively much more plausible than those derived from either the official or alternative methods. It suggests that between 1971 and 1986 output in all five trades increased substantially: in restaurants by 2.4 per cent a year, in public houses by 2.5 per cent, in clubs by 3.1 per cent, in catering contractors by 2.8 per cent and in hotels by 1.6 per cent.

Measure for all Covered Services

The alternative output measures compiled for financial services, recreational services and the catering trades are combined and compared with their official counterparts. Group 1, for which the series relate to the full period 1971-86, comprises five financial services (building societies, hire-purchase, insurance, advertising and construction plant hire) and the catering trades. Group 2 covering the period 1973-86 includes in addition banking and recreational services.

Whilst group 3, for which the output indicators are available for the period 1978-86, embraces all the service industries for which alternative measures have been compiled. These aggregate output indices, both official and alternative, are derived from those presented in the relevant tables using as weights the 1985 contribution of each activity to GDP. The results are summarised in the form of average annual rates of change. To check the sensitivity of these final results alternative and official measures of growth are also compared using as weights the services' 1985 employment levels and 1980 contributions to GDP.

The picture which emerges is one in which the alternative measure consistently points towards a higher growth rate than that indicated by its corresponding official index. Moreover the size of the differential varies comparatively little regardless of the group, period or weighting system to which attention is directed. If most attention is attached—in view of the size of their coverage—to the results for groups 2 and 3, it appears that compared with the alternative methods the official indicators have understated growth by between 13 and 18 per cent. Given that in most cases the alternative measurement methods differ radically from those officially employed it is perhaps remarkable that, overall, the discrepancy should be no greater than this.

To what extent, as it stands, would the official measure of GDP growth be changed if the alternative measure is substituted for the official indicator? The answer is: very little. Basing this adjustment on the alternative/official differential revealed for group 2 the annual average GDP growth rate for 1973-86 is unchanged at 1.3 per cent per annum, and using the group 3 results the annual growth rate for 1978-86 rises from 1.6 per cent to 1.7 per cent. If the disparity between official and alternative growth rates depicted held for the commercial services excluded from this exercise then the official GDP growth rate of 1.3 per cent registered for the period 1973-86 is boosted to 1.5 per cent per annum and the GDP growth rate of 1.6 per cent for the years 1978-86 is raised to 1.9 per cent a year.

There are good reasons for supposing that these upward revisions to the GDP growth rate will understate rather than overstate the actual shortfall. In the first place output measures which lean towards numbers of service units will to some extent be biased downwards compared with those derived from deflated sales or turnover values because the data sources in question tend to cover any new services in the latter but not the former. Secondly whilst official output measures which rely on employment series usually incorporate some productivity improvement, this has not been applied to the FTE based measure compiled above for catering so that it may well underestimate actual output growth in this activity.

Thirdly salary indices which have been used as surrogate price deflators in the case of accountancy and computer services will tend to overestimate actual output price increases—and therefore bias downwards the resulting output measure—since no allowance is made for the impact on unit labour costs of any productivity improvements in these services.

While the implications for GDP measurement of the substitution of alternative aggregate service output indicators may not be unduly significant it is clear that they are more substantial for the commercial service sector as a whole. They are even more significant for individual service complexes. Although the new measure for financial and business services differs relatively little from the official measure, especially if account is taken of the contrasting conceptual treatment of finance leasing in the respective approaches, the alternative obtained for recreational services points to a significantly lower growth rate and that compiled for catering is about twice the official growth rate. Contrasts between alternative and official measures are even more pronounced for individual service industries.

Service output Measurement

Substitution of the new output measures for those officially compiled would have made little difference to GDP growth rates in recent years. In effect discrepancies which emerged between alternative and official output measures for individual service industries have tended to offset each other. There is no guarantee that this condition would hold in the future and for this reason alone the search for alternative, improved, measures of service output change should be pursued.

In contrast significantly large differences between alternative and official output measures have emerged for particular services and these have very important implications for the analysis of economic developments in individual service industries. The validity of the economic analyses to which these activities are now widely subjected depends crucially on the accuracy of the output and productivity measures that are employed to map their development over time. For this reason, especially, new and improved service output measures are required.

A lesson of the research which lies behind the above results is that new service output measures can be further developed both extensively and intensively. Whilst the service industries examined were chosen as systematically as possible on the basis of specific criteria, only limitations imposed by time and resources prevented other service activities being subjected to a similar kind of scrutiny. Moreover in many of those service industries which have been surveyed scope for further measurement improvements remain. In this connection attention needs to be drawn to the results obtained for building societies and the catering trades.

In the case of the former serious doubts attach to the alternative measure which, although it yields a growth rate higher than the official one, nevertheless implies, as it stands, a long-term fall in labour productivity in this service industry. Also it is clear that the search for improved catering output measures needs to be continued: the labour force indicator adopted for the purpose of this exercise must be regarded as no more than a stop-gap stratagem though on the basis of existing statistical sources there is at present little immediate prospect of new measures being based on numbers of service output units.

None the less the data deficiencies are essentially practical, not conceptual, in nature and with appropriate statistical arrangements could no doubt be remedied eventually: already there is some experience of collecting data relating to hotel room utilisation which some time in the future might form the basis of a service unit-based measure. Generally there seems to exist a large reservoir of data relating to both output indicators and weights, collected by a variety of service industry organisations, which lies outside the purview of official sources.

It is difficult to avoid the impression that the current exercise has barely scratched the surface of this fund of material and that, in particular, much is available at the firm level which has yet to be systematically collated in a way that it can be used to measure developments for whole industries. Certainly it is clear that within the firms in question most service outputs are documented in detail, increasingly in computerised records, so that alternative measures based on numbers of output units should become progressively more practicable.

There appear to be two basic options for tapping into this kind of data base. One would comprise an official periodic survey of each of the main service industries in which, as in the case of some industrial censuses, questionnaires would seek information about numbers and values of those output units which are best measured for each service.

The inquiries into the distributive, catering and service trades periodically conducted by the Business Statistics Office might be developed in this direction. The alternative is to adopt the approach followed, in the main, in this exercise and base new output measures on the information which is collected by trade associations and other industry organisations. This option is less attractive than the systematic collection of the requisite data, on a comprehensive and consistent basis, by means of an official census.

Chapter 3

Organizational Forms in the International Hotels

CHOICE IN A WORLD OF ALLIANCES

In the new management landscape, interfirm collaborations are common, and control is only loosely correlated with ownership. Firms may collaborate with each other by forming equity joint ventures. However, a large number of interfirm collaborations are based on no equity investment at all, but are contractual or quasi-contractual in nature. The principals have concluded in these cases that the optimal level of ownership is zero. Given several choices, ranging from full ownership to a partial equity position to various contractual modes, such as management service and franchise agreements, the key question tackled by this paper is "What organizational mode is best?"

This study focuses on the global hotel business, which is especially suitable for an investigation of the organizational modal choice question, since non-equity modes are at least as widespread as equity ownership, if not more. Alliances with other firms used to be considered a minor component of overall strategy in many sectors. Today, competitive advantage can equally well be derived from interfirm cooperation in non-equity-based agreements such as management service contracts. This is especially true in service sectors such as hotels, where the capital-intensive elements (such as real estate) can be separated from the knowledge-based or managerial expertise elements of competitiveness.

In the hotels sector, management service contracts (between the owners of the physical capital or real estate and the global hotel company, which supplies the managerial expertise) appear to be the single most common governance mode. Franchising is also ubiquitous. Interfirm cooperation is therefore not peripheral, but central to global strategy. The global hotels business may be a precursor for other service sectors in terms of the prevalence of non-equity modes of doing business. By covering many foreign markets, our data enable us to examine the extent to which environmental (i.e., market or country-specific) variables, as opposed to firm-specific variables, affect the choice of organizational mode.

With the relaxation of investment controls and the general growth in alliance formation worldwide, managers today face a spectrum of available choices. The key question this paper tackles is: "For a particular foreign operation (a particular hotel in a foreign location), should a firm choose full ownership of the operation, an equity joint venture or contract-specified modes, such as franchising, or management service agreements?" This paper proposes that the choice is not determined by country characteristics or transaction-cost considerations alone. The characteristics of the firm and its global strategy comprise the other leg of the new syncretic theory.

Four literatures have a bearing on the modal choice question. These are:

i. The traditional market entry literature from International Business;
ii. Transaction cost theory exemplified by Anderson and Gatignon (1986);
iii. The strategic theory of organizational capability and knowledge in firms.

There is a considerable literature on corporate alliances, but less on when it is better for a firm to choose an alliance over its own fully owned operation, or vice versa, and very little indeed on which type of alliance is best, under which circumstances. The aims of this paper are to advance the theory and testing of the entire spectrum of modal choices, including relatively neglected modes, such as management service contracts and franchising. The latter are more prevalent in service sectors, especially in hotels.

This synthesizes several academic literatures with a bearing on the modal choice issue, and presents a unified framework. The results show that both host country environment and firm strategy influence the selection of organizational mode. They also show that contractual alliances can effectively substitute for equity ownership in several circumstances, and comprise an important part of global strategy.

This is organized as follows: A survey of various organizational forms in the international hotel business is followed by a review of the modal choice literature. This is followed by presentation of hypotheses, data, and statistical tests. The paper concludes by examining the implications of the empirical findings for management practice and further theory development.

THE GLOBAL HOTELS BUSINESS

One first needs to understand various organizational forms and their idiosyncrasies in the global hotel business before one can formulate hypotheses. Some of the hypotheses this paper will propose are peculiar to the hotel business although most are applicable to other service and manufacturing sectors. Hence we first present an overview of the hotel business.

Since the focus of this paper is the determinants of foreign strategy, we focus only on hotel properties outside the home nation of the firm. Hotel firms listed in the International Hotels Group Directory have more than half a million rooms outside their home nation. From the directory, we first identified firms that listed at least one property outside their home nation as part of their global group of hotels. The directory provides a comprehensive coverage of the business worldwide, but does not show the organizational mode (fully owned, joint venture, management contract, or franchise) for each property. This was obtained from questionnaires.

For the purpose of this paper, therefore, a global hotel firm is defined as one that either has an equity stake in a foreign property, or operates the hotel under a management service agreement, or is a franchisor to the foreign hotel property. Thus, a company could be a global firm without any ownership of a foreign property. However, as a matter of fact, virtually every hotel company in our sample had some equity ownership in at least one foreign property, thus providing a range of organizational choices in the sample.

A questionnaire was sent to all listed firms with foreign hotel operations. The questions covered data on the hotel firm as a whole (e.g., the firm's overall size, international experience, distribution and number of hotel properties worldwide). The questionnaire also asked what organizational mode was used for each hotel property abroad. The questionnaire response provided a sample that covers 1,131 hotels and comprises over 60 per cent of all "foreign" properties and rooms listed in the directory (355,169 out of some half million rooms). Despite reminders, a large firm response bias remains in the sample. Our data base therefore includes the organizational mode chosen for each hotel property, and other details on the global hotel company involved, as well as characteristics of the nation where the hotel property is located.

For the world as a whole, 37 per cent of foreign properties were under management service contract, making this the single most common organizational modality in the international hotel business. 34.6 per cent of foreign hotel properties were fully or partially owned, while the remaining 28.4 per cent were franchised. While the prevalence of management service contracts is high across all major regions where hotels are located, there appear to be variations in equity ownership and franchising by region. Equity ownership is lower, and franchising more frequent in North America.

In Asia, by comparison, franchising is less common, and equity ownership modes are most common. Non-equity modes, thus, account worldwide for 65.4 per cent of foreign operation properties, and arrangements involving two companies account for as much as 81.2 per cent of the total number of hotels worldwide. But this should not make us jump to the conclusion that managerial control or strategic direction are weak in the joint venture or non-equity organizational forms. In some service sectors, such as hotels, control has been de-linked from equity ownership - but control, and an overall global strategy exist.

What are the dimensions of management "control" in alliances? For both its short and long term strategy, the global firm today must deal with a multiplicity of partners and organizational forms, each having its own degrees of required control. In the international joint venture context, Schaan and Geringer and Hebert described different mechanisms whereby each firm may exercise control over the joint venture.

For alliances in general. the means of control can be classified as "participatory" control (by the act of actively participating in the management of an enterprise), control exercised by "withholding" or threatening to withhold some asset or capability desired by the other partner, and "proscriptive" control (by legal or de facto prohibitions). We break these down further between (a) daily operational and quality control in each hotel property; (b) control over the physical assets or over the real estate and its attendant risks; (c) control over tacit expertise embedded in the routines of the firm; and (d) control over the codified assets, such as a global reservation system and the firm's internationally recognized brand name.

Equity Investments

In fully owned operations, all four control criteria (a) through (d) are under the strong control of the hotel firm. In equity joint ventures, (a), (b), and (c) are shared, although typically control of the global brand name and reservations system remains with the global hotel company to retain its leverage over the local partner. Since organizational control has many attributes, especially in international business, where culture and national differences prevail, it is difficult to develop an overall measure for control in international joint ventures.

As depicted, the global hotel company may retain strong control over (d) (its reservations system and global brand), but have shared control over day-to-day management, quality, and physical assets. Tacit expertise (c) is inevitably shared with the local partner, to some extent, which may erode the global hotel company's knowledge advantage over time. Equity investment does provide stronger long-term strategic control compared with management service agreements, for the simple reason that the latter are time-bound and, on expiry of the agreement, subject to cancellation by the property owners. By comparison, an equity stake is not so easily dissolved.

Management Service Agreements

A management service contract is a long term agreement, of up to ten years or even longer, whereby the legal owners of the property and real estate enter into a contract with the hotel firm to run and operate the hotel on a day to day basis, usually under the latter's internationally recognized name. Quality control, daily management and senior staffing (a) principally rest with the international hotel firm and not the property owners. But the operation is run as if the property were part of the global chain. Customers cannot tell the difference.

The international hotel firm, as operator, earns management fees often expressed as a percentage of gross revenues (sometimes with annual minimums and lump-sum payments). In addition, the global hotel firm may earn extra profit margins on any supplies and material it sells to the particular property. In some cases, there may be bonuses linked, not to revenues, but to profits - as a profit-sharing formula.

Finally, in several cases, the property is charged a small fee for every reservation booked through the global reservation system of the global hotel firm. Such codified strategic assets (d) remain in the control of the global firm. Nevertheless, local partners may not always be content to merely remain as passive owners of the real estate. Since much of the middle management and staff are local personnel, they acquire tacit expertise on the job.

There have been a few cases, for example, as the Oberoi Hotels Group, which initially had an agreement with Intercontinental Hotels, but learned the business well enough to launch its own international hotel chain after terminating its partnership with Intercontinental Hotels. While it is possible that a few minority joint venture investments may provide the firm with lower control over global strategy than a management service agreement, in general we posit that a joint venture equity stake provides superior long-term strategic control, compared with contractual alternatives.

In effect, for the global hotel firm, management service agreements provide strong day-to-day (if not long term) control without ownership, as depicted in Tables 2a and b. Moreover, such contracts can amount to surer returns without real estate investment risk. Even ordinary commercial or economic risk is greatly reduced since the hotel operator's take is often a percentage of revenues (akin to a royalty), and not expressed as a percentage of profits, as would be the case in an equity joint venture. It is axiomatic that over a business cycle, revenues are far less volatile than profits. The latest indicator of this trend is Marriott Corp., which in 1993, split itself into two firms - one a profitable hotel management firm, and the other a debt-laden real estate owning company.

Franchises

In franchising, (a) daily management and quality control and (b) control over physical assets reside with the franchisee, and not with the global hotel firm. In this case, the international hotel firm does not run the hotel's management, but trains and guides it under a contractual relationship, sharing only some tacit expertise (c). But it would be a mistake to assume that the franchisor exercises no control. Typically, hotel standards are sought to be zealously enforced. Codified assets (d), such as brands and reservation systems reside with the global hotel company. The franchisor earns fees linked to revenues and profits, additional margins on material supplied to the franchise, booking fees for clients booked via the global reservations network, and training fees for personnel trained. Franchise relationships accounted for 28 per cent of properties.

For the international hotel firm, even without ownership or management involvement, we hypothesize that a network of franchisees enable it to capture at least some economies of global scale in logistics, supplies, architectural design, reservations, training, and brand recognition. Certainly, not all firms replicate hotel architectural designs "cookie cutter" style in every nation; nor do all franchisees purchase from the global hotel firm's central procurement channel. But we hypothesize that enough do so to provide significant economies in a worldwide operation.

Factors influencing the Modal Choice

The question addressed by this paper is:

> "For a firm intending an investment in a particular hotel property located in a particular nation, what determines whether the investment will be fully owned, or an equity joint venture, or whether it will be a non-equity arrangement involving either a management service contract, or a franchise?"

This is written from the perspective of a global hotel firm willing to consider different entry modes in various nations. It does not refer to the local owners of a hotel property as franchisees, or as the local partners in a management service agreement. In this we take a syncretic approach to the modal choice question, similar to Hill, Hwang and Kim, or Contractor. The approach is not merely the minimization of transaction costs, with a focus on one transaction or market entry at a time, nor does it treat only the conditions in the host nation (which was the focus of traditional market entry literature).

The firm seeks the maximization of profits based on long-term global strategy. This forces a look at the revenue side as well. Moreover, the maximization of long term global profits is not merely a matter of maximum rent extraction from a particular market, but building the capabilities and knowledge of the company as a whole. Zajac and Olsen (1993) describe the modal choice decision as determined by the need to create long-term "value" in the global firm. Increasingly, the use of corporate allies and partners to create a global network is being seen to be as valid a pathway to building value as an ownership-linked company. Since non-equity modes are more prevalent internationally in the hotel business, this process is well along on its way in this sector.

In alliances, the firm must deal with other agents, such as franchisees, local owners of the real estate, and joint venture partners, whose predilections, incentives, and motivations may differ from the strategic objectives of the global firm. Agency theory also provides some insights into such different objectives. A robust theory of modal choice must therefore incorporate country-specific and transaction-specific variables, as well as factors relating to the strategy of the global company and the agents with which it interacts.

Market Entry Literature

Interest in the modal choice question began in the marketing and international business fields, where the question was couched as the choice between exporting and foreign direct investment. Root and Goodnow and Hansz reflect the traditional marketing focus on conditions or the environment in the host country. This country focus remains as one of the legs of our empirical analysis later in the paper. Locational or country-specific advantages were one part of Dunning's OLI theory.

However, non-equity forms such as licensing were then considered of lesser interest, and joint ventures were not explicitly considered on the spectrum of governance choices until the mid-1980s. Buckley and Casson (1976) expanded the choice to include licensing as a means of reaching customers abroad. But in their perspective, the multinational firm would usually prefer to "internalize" transactions via direct equity investment rather than license its capability. The multinational firm's raison d'etre was its superior ability to extract rents from each nation it invested in - a rent that was supposed to be almost always far higher than potential returns via cooperative or contractual modes of entry, such as licensing or franchising. Recent work by Buckley and Casson (1996) considers cooperative modes of organization as far more likely.

Transaction-Cost Explanations

The core of the transaction-cost explanations deal with asset specificity, bounded rationality, the free-rider problem, and opportunism. The principal focus is on one transaction or negotiation - one market entry - at a time. The choice of organizational mode is that which minimizes transaction costs. The other strand of Dunning's (1988) OLI theory, namely Ownership, makes a related argument - that the multinational firm will prefer to "internalize" via equity ownership when the "market" for knowledge transfers "fails."

Transaction-cost explanations will comprise a significant input in the development of this paper's hypotheses. However, since they are sufficiently well known, it would be more useful to discuss how these arguments relate to global hotel operations when formally proposing hypotheses later in the paper.

A useful perspective on many alliances is that they involve the transfer of knowledge between partners over some duration of time, rather than as a transaction. Winter (1987) focused on the creation of knowledge and competence within the enterprise, and on how expertise is embedded in tacit organizational "routines." Ghoshal has a learning focus, but on cross-affiliate knowledge transfers within the multinational enterprise.

Teece distinguishes between tacit, unwritten or informal knowledge, and formally registered intellectual property which is far more easily transferable or shared with another firm. Contractor points out those intellectual properties, such as patents, trademarks or copyrights, are only of minor strategic importance - as an all-industry generalization.

However, in the hotel business, registered brand names, as well as unregistered, but proprietary reservations and logistics systems, are a potent source of control. In control over codified strategic assets occurs typically in all four modes. The potential threat of withdrawing permission to use the global company's brand, reservations and support systems, moderates the opportunistic behaviour of partners in each nation. In fact, this may be one factor which explains the high prevalence of equity and non-equity alliances in the hotel business.

It is nevertheless true that codified strategic assets are only the visible, formalized tip of a vast iceberg of tacit information embedded in trained personnel and technicians, and in implicit routines. Hence the cost of transferring such knowledge to another partner firm can be protracted, difficult, costly and incomplete. This also partially depends on the "absorptive capacity" of the partner firm learning the new routines. If the local partner is in a lesser-developed nation (here we connect the transaction-cost argument with a country variable), the transfer of complex tacit knowledge is more difficult, and we hypothesize later that non-equity forms, such as franchising, will be less prevalent in developing nations, ceteris paribus.

If knowledge is so extremely embedded, or tacit, as to prevent its accurate valuation by the negotiators, then in the worst case, "bounded rationality" may prevent the "transaction" or partnership itself from taking place. In the earlier literature such "market failure" left the firm with no choice but to opt for the hierarchical, full-ownership mode. Today, however, the ubiquity of cooperative modes, especially in the hotel business, suggests that such market failure is not common.

Learning across organizational boundaries in partnerships can also be unintended, lack reciprocity, or be unequal. Unequal cross-flows of knowledge can lead to perceptions of "free riding," and unintended leakage of knowledge can lead to opportunism in the form of partners terminating the relationship to become competitors. However, retaining legal or de facto control over strategic assets, such as brands or a global reservations system, can moderate such opportunism on the part of local partners. (Here again, this firm-level literature connects with the transaction-costs arguments.)

Management of knowledge flows within and across the organizational boundary is therefore key to strategic success when dealing with multiple competitors and partners. This leads to the second sub-group of firm-specific factors affecting the choice of organizational mode.

Whether a firm will decide to "go it alone" or cooperate with partners, and if so, under what mode of association, depends not just on the intended transaction or on the characteristics of knowledge within a firm, but on the broader structure of the firm and its industry as well. These variables include size and scale, diversification, investment in R&D and training, experience, flexibility, speed, first-mover rewards, and synergies of cooperation. Each of these variables is complex and is not amenable to easy generalizations as to its effects on the modal choice. For example, Gomes-Casseres (1989) indicates that the quest for global economies of scale will discourage cooperative organizational modalities.

Yet, in some sectors, economies of global scale may be captured equally well by quasi-integration across national borders. To capture global economies some firms may grow larger by mergers and acquisitions, or via internal growth; others may join a coalition or network to achieve the same ends, especially if rapid growth is needed for competitive reasons.

How does "knowledge intensity" affect the modal choice? In the manufacturing sector knowledge intensity has been measured by the R&D/Sales ratio. Since hotel companies do not do R&D per se, the ratio of the amount they invest in the training of their personnel, over sales, can provide an alternate measure of knowledge intensity. Gatignon and Anderson proposed that when the proprietary content of products or processes is high the choice will tend towards the full ownership end of the spectrum. For hotels, one can operationalize knowledge intensity by ratios such as "investment in training over sales."

Shane applies agency theory concepts to show that non-equity modes of entry can be efficient substitutes for equity investment. Consider the choice between a fully owned foreign hotel operation, where the global company has to hire its own staff, and a franchise. The so-called "adverse selection" and "moral hazard" problems in agency theory focus on the difficulty of assessing the abilities of foreign employees, and monitoring them for performance. This is more difficult the greater the cultural distance between the firm and the host nation.

Equity owners only have residual profit claims on the remnant of the net cash flow from a foreign operation after costs, including those of employees, are met. By contrast, not only does a local franchisee have the better local knowledge to select and monitor employees, but also promises to the franchisor the "first cut" of cash flow collections. This is because, in franchising, lump-sum fees are paid in advance, and royalties must be paid out of sales revenue collections (regardless of profits). More specific theoretical arguments will be developed later with the hypotheses.

The questionnaire responses listed, for each hotel in a foreign nation, its organizational mode, whether the hotel is a Franchise = 1; Under the company's management in a service contract = 2; Partially Owned (Joint Venture) = 3; and Fully Owned = 4. The dependent variable M is therefore a polytomous measure generally depicting rising levels of equity ownership and overall control. Overlapping categories (e.g., a hotel property under management service agreement and partial equity investment) were dropped, as Discriminant Analysis requires non-overlapping categories. This affected only 6.5 per cent of cases.

Two techniques with different objectives and different methodology were used: Discriminant Analysis as a test of the robustness of the group classification based on independent variables, followed by Ordinal logistic regression using a generalized LOGIT model. Discriminant Analysis tests the validity and robustness of the modal choice categories, but is not concerned about their rank ordering. Regression is concerned about by the ordering of categories within the multinomial measure M. The hypotheses developed below relate principally to the regression analysis.

Independent Variables

A complete picture of the organizational choice question needs a syncretic approach combining transaction-cost and agency theory reasoning, as well as country-specific and firm-specific variables, as Contractor pointed out. This was echoed by Kim and Hwang, and Erramilli and Rao who used all four types of factors in their empirical studies. Even earlier, while operating under the panoply of transaction-cost explanations, Gatignon and Anderson (1988) had used country indicators, such as country risk, as well as firm strategy variables, such as advertising/sales and R&D/sales ratios, and number of employees, as a proxy for firm size.

The first group relates to the country in which the hotel property is located. We will ask how country-specific variables affect the modal choice. The second groups' independent variables describe the size, international experience, and extent of foreign business of the hotel firm. The third groups' independent variables describe responses from hotel executives on the perceived importance of strategy and control variables.

In diverse international operations, the organizational form is sure to be affected by local conditions. Few companies today follow uniform policies across countries. Assume that a global hotel company is willing to consider in each country either an equity investment (fully or partially owned), or a management service agreement, or a franchise. It assesses each situation, and makes the appropriate choice of organizational mode.

Country Political and Economic Risk: Data for this independent variable were obtained from Frost and Sullivan's, International Country Risk Guide, for each nation where the sample hotel properties are located. The composite (i.e., political cum economic) risk rating issued by Frost and Sullivan for the particular nation "i."

Development of this hypothesis rests on four arguments. The first relates to the size of resource commitments in risky nations. Kim and Hwang, Agarwal and Ramaswami, and Madhok propose that, ceteris paribus, higher country risk will favour entry modes with lower resource commitments or ownership. Gatignon and Anderson (1988) and Goodnow and Hansz (1985) also suggest that equity investment modes are less likely when country risk is high. We should recall that in this business, capital investment in real estate is normally high - occasionally approaching $100 million for large resort properties. The second argument deals with "environmental uncertainty" in terms of political and currency volatility.

When volatility is high, franchising is preferred over corporate ownership. Agency theory concurs and suggests that franchising can be an efficient organizational mode in risky markets, where the franchisee is responsible for employee selection and monitoring. Control over the brand name is maintained by the global firm, tempering or eliminating franchisee opportunism. Kim and Hwang use the term "demand uncertainty" and postulate that when uncertainty is high, equity ownership will tend to be low. This is corroborated by Erramilli and Rao. Third, in the international hotel business, management service contracts enable the firm to exercise a high degree of control over the foreign operation without ownership risk.

Franchising involves an even lesser commitment. Finally, the inclusion of royalty-type payments in alliance agreements, where the earnings of the global hotel firm are linked to sales, and not profit of the hotel property, reduce their risk significantly in volatile environments, because royalties are linked to sales and not profits. Sales are far more stable over the business cycle compared with profits. In Buckley and Casson's words, "...as volatility increases so internalization becomes less attractive."

In risky nations then, hotel firms would be more likely to avoid the risks of equity investment and opt for management service contracts or franchising. Hence, our hypothesis:

H1: M (rising levels of equity and control) will be negatively associated with country political and economic risk.

(However, please note that because Frost & Sullivan's "Composite Risk Index" is on an inverted scale of Highest Risk = 0 to Lowest Risk = 100 our hypothesis expects a positive sign for variable CRI).

Cultural Distance: Several studies suggest that "Cultural Distance" between the home base of the firm and the intended foreign market is a powerful determinant of modal choice. There appears to be a consensus in the literature on this topic, namely, that a greater cultural distance between the firm and the foreign nation it is operating in will lead to less equity ownership, and a greater incidence of cooperative modes, ceteris paribus. Gomes-Casseres explains this in terms of needing more help from local joint venture partners in less familiar environments. Fladmoe-Lindquist and Jacque posit that "...cultural distance tends to create costly information requirements which encourage U.S. service firms to use lower-cost governance structures."

At the same time, the risk of cultural misunderstandings is higher, especially in a service industry, and one with a high local labour content. Shane's (1996) adaptation of agency theory makes a congruent hypothesis, namely that local partners ease the "adverse selection problem" in selecting and overseeing staff in culturally distant markets. The global firm needs local partners' help all the more when the culture is unfamiliar. We should distinguish here between cultural distance risk versus political and economic country risk discussed earlier. The two are not necessarily correlated. All in all, ceteris paribus, the higher cost and risk of operating at a greater cultural distance makes the firm less inclined to make large equity investments, especially fully owned ones.

Hence, the hypothesis that:

H2: High equity ownership modes will be negatively associated with increased cultural distance (CUL) between the global hotel firm and the nation where the hotel is located.

Level of Economic Development: How might a country's level of economic development affect the modal choice of prospective investors or entrants? In their study of the hotel industry over a decade ago Dunning and McQueen (1981) proposed the hypotheses that the incidence of equity ownership in the hotels business should be positively correlated with economic development. But they did not test this. Moreover, a priori reasoning tends to give greater weight to the opposite hypothesis, that higher income nations will have a relatively larger share of non-equity modes, such as franchising and management service agreements. Why?

First, the lower "absorptive capacity" of franchisees in lesser-developed nations and the consequently higher costs of adaptation and knowledge transfer would tend to support the idea that franchising would be more prevalent the more developed the nation is. Second, while the global hotel company will try to retain legal control over its brand and other intellectual property, enforcement is weaker in developing nations. Many companies which consider intellectual property protection as central to strategy, have concluded that majority or full equity ownership of developing country operations is consequently necessary.

Thirdly, emerging markets are also characterized by weaker competition, faster growth, and higher returns and profits. Recall that contractual modes, such as franchising or management service agreements, constrain the return of the global hotel company to a royalty-type return (a percentage of sales). This is a less volatile cash flow, but one that is inferior to returns on equity in absolute magnitude. In high profit potential areas, returns on equity investments far outstrip royalties.

Moreover, the contractual organization modes are subject to cancellation on expiry of the agreement, whereas a fully owned equity investment is of indefinite duration, in theory at least. For this reason, we propose:

H3: M (rising levels of equity and control) is negatively associated with the level of economic development (GDPCAP) in the country where the hotel is located.

Foreign Business Investment Penetration In The Local Economy: In an earlier study, Dunning and McQueen (1981) proposed that, other things being equal, in nations characterized by a higher penetration of FDI, the firm will choose higher control and equity-based modes. They stated this as a hypothesis to be tested. Possible explanations involve a "follow the client" abroad hypothesis, based on the assumption that global hotel chains draw an appreciable fraction of their clientele from international business travellers. Hence, in countries whose economies are more open to international investment and trade, there should be a greater incidence of international business travellers who are particularly concerned about quality standards.

To be sure, one can question some of these assumptions. There are no data available per hotel, or per firm, on the fraction of clients who are international businesspersons, so one cannot gauge the extent of their influence. Nor can we assess whether their preferences for quality are different from other classes of customers. However, since Dunning and McQueen's (1981) work is the only other empirical study on global hotels, we thought it worthwhile to test this hypothesis. The penetration of FDI into a host nation is operationalized by the ratio of FDI over GDP.

Three characteristics of the host nation (where the hotel property is located) are said to influence the mode of organization: Country Risk, Cultural Distance, and Foreign Business Penetration. We now turn to firm-specific factors.

Firm-specific factors have been divided into two groups. So-called Structural or Objective factors include Firm Size, International Experience, and Degree of Internationalization. The questionnaire also asked executives in the global hotel firm to give subjective Responses to Strategy and Control Questions. The latter are based on a 5-point Likert Scale (5 = Very Important.....1 = Not Important), covering the perceived strategic importance of Global Scale, Intangible Assets such as a Global Reservation System and Brand, Investment in Training and Ability to Exercise Control over Management and Quality.

How does size of the firm relate to the propensity to choose non-equity and contractual organizational modes? The majority of studies indicate that larger firms are likely to prefer high levels of equity ownership. Smaller firms, which lacked the resources or expertise to venture into foreign markets, would prefer shared control modes. This remains the accepted view, and will accordingly be stated as the hypothesis.

Nevertheless, it should be pointed out, that other studies suggest the opposite, namely, that these assumptions may not apply to several service sectors, especially the hotel business, where the advantages of size may equally well be derived by a global network of partnerships and alliances. Gatignon and Anderson state that "higher control entry modes are less likely for large foreign operations." They base this argument on the notion that the size of global operations in many industries will force even large firms - or particularly the firms that wish to be large - to accept partners to share in the large total investment and large coverage of a global network.

In this strategy, the path to becoming a large global player requires the firm to accept a lot of partners and have lower-control, non-equity relationships (in our case such as franchising). Agency theory suggests that the problems of human resource selection and management may grow even faster than the firm's growth in size, especially in international operations.

We propose to test these contrary views by formally proposing the first viewpoint:

H5: We expect a positive relationship between firm size and M (rising levels of equity ownership and control).

International Experience and Degree of Globalization: More internationally experienced firms have less need for local help in the nation in which they operate and will have a lower tendency to use partners. In longitudinal studies of Scandinavian companies, as well as in Chang's (1995) study of Japanese firms, the company builds its organizational capabilities through sequential experience in overseas markets, initially taking non-equity positions, such as exporting or licensing, and later increasing its equity investment levels.

We may call this the traditional view. (It is worth noting, in passing, that there is a contrary, non-traditional view on the international experience variable namely that with greater international learning, the firm is better able to harness international partners and better assess and utilize the full spectrum modal choices. There is no empirical evidence as to which perspective applies to the hotel business. For testing purposes, the traditional view is stated in the hypotheses.)

We use two independent variables. The first, IEX is the number of years since the firm set up its first foreign operation. This time-based measure, while commonly used as a surrogate for international experience, has some caveats associated with it. For instance, mere length of time in one cultural setting may not prepare a firm for expansion into another country and culture. For another thing, some firms may have expanded internationally faster than others; a time-based measure may therefore be somewhat biased in a cross-sectional study. For these reasons, a second independent variable, GLOP (number of properties outside the home nation of the firm divided by the global total including the home nation of the firm) was introduced as an alternative measure for the extent of globalization of the firm.

For global optimization purposes, a global company had rather not be hampered by the local preferences of local partners. Hence, a firm with a larger fraction of business globally should prefer majority or full equity ownership. IEX and GLOP are different measures. One is a measure of time since the company's first foreign excursion. The other records the proportion of foreign to total business which the firm has actually achieved.

H6: Rising levels of equity and control (M) and the number of years since the first foreign operation (IEX) will be positively associated.

H7: M and GLOP (ratio of foreign over global total number of properties) will be positively associated.

We now turn from objective data on the hotel firms to subjective responses, on a 5-point Likert scale (5 = Very Important.....1 = Not Important), from responding executives, to questions about the perceived importance of the following strategy variables.

Perceived Strategic Importance of Global Scale: One view in the literature is that in order to capture the economies of global scale, a firm is required to have high control and high ownership modes of operation, unhampered by the possibly contrary sub-optimizing concerns of local partners. The executives of such companies would indicate the need for equity ownership-based control in order for the firm to capture the economies of global scale. On the other hand, we also have a diametrically opposite view expressed in the literature: To become global, a firm may be forced to accept many local partners in various markets.

If what we mean by scale economies in the hotel business relates to logistics, supply, common architectural designs etc., which can be shared with a network of franchisees and local partners at relatively low knowledge-transfer cost, then such economies can indeed be gained without ownership, or even managerial presence. Thus Galbraith and Kay's "economies of information" as the key ingredient of multinational strategy may be achievable without high equity investment or control. We thus have two diametrically opposite hypotheses in the literature, and propose to formally test the first strategy view, that:

H8: The perceived importance of scale in global hotel operations (PSCA) will be positively associated with M (rising levels of control and equity ownership).

Perceived Strategic Importance of Control over Management and Quality: management control is a complex and multidimensional concept. We identified Daily Management and Quality Control as one dimension of overall administrative control. The table implied that control by the global hotel firm, in a day to day sense, rises as we go from franchising to fully owned operations.

Hence we would expect, in general, that for executive respondents in the global hotel company, who indicate a greater importance for daily management and quality control (on the 5-point Likert scale), the hotel property in question would be more likely to be under a higher equity and ownership mode, ceteris paribus. This is not tautological. Recall that executive responses indicate the firm's general strategic preferences; but in the "portfolio" of each firm there are likely to be some properties which are fully owned, some under management service contract, some franchised.

The objective here is to test the extent to which the expressed strategy preferences of executives correlates with the actual disposition of each property's management mode, and the strength of this association, statistically speaking as opposed to the influence of the other influences on the choice of organizational mode. We formally propose therefore, that:

H9: The perceived importance of operational control over management and quality (CQ) will be positively related to M (rising levels of equity and control).

Perceived Strategic Importance of Size in Global Hotel Operations: We have already discussed the SIZE variable earlier, based on an objective measure. Here, in the variable PFS, we asked managers to subjectively rate the importance of size as a strategy variable in global hotel operations (on a 5-point Likert Scale). Our reasoning for this variable is the same as for the objective SIZE, namely that executives placing greater importance on a larger size of global operations will influence, for a particular hotel, a higher level of equity investment and greater overall administrative control (i.e., a higher value for M), with better appropriability of rents, ceteris paribus. Hence:

H10: PFS will be positively associated with M (rising levels of equity and control).

(We included both the objective measure ($ Worldwide Sales) and the subjective measure (executive responses on the perceived importance of size) conscious that the two may turn out to be collinear. If so, one would be dropped. More on this issue in the section on Empirical Tests and Methodology.)

Perceived Strategic Importance of Global Reservations System and Brand: These are the two principal codified strategic assets, over which proprietary control is usually maintained by the global hotel firm, regardless of the organizational mode. A global reservation system increases global revenues. In particular, codified assets, such as brands and reservations systems, increase the ability of a firm to have alliances for three reasons. First, codification reduces the "bounded rationality" problem of partners in each nation, who seek to assess the value they will receive from a partnership with the global hotel firm.

Second, by maintaining control over the brand and reservation system, the global firm greatly reduces the opportunism of franchisees or partners in management service agreements, who may be tempted to strike out on their own, on expiry of the agreement. Third, while creation of brand equity and a global reservations system involves large sunk costs, the incremental costs of adding another franchisee, or non-equity partner, is low. Thus, such strategic assets increase the likelihood of alliances in general, and franchising, in particular. Hence, we propose:

H11: PRES (Perceived Strategic Importance of Global Reservations System and Brand) will be negatively associated with M (rising levels of equity investment and control).

Perceived Strategic Importance of Investment In Training: Gatignon and Anderson (1988) indicated that when the proprietary content of products or processes is high (operationalized by the R&D/Sales ratio), the choice will tend towards the full ownership end of the spectrum, since rents from this competitive advantage can be best exploited by full or high ownership modes. The service sector equivalent to "R&D investment" is "investment in training" which upgrades the knowledge and organizational capabilities of the global hotel firm's management and employees.

All hotels, especially the large ones, employ complex logistics, dynamic pricing, marketing and inventory control systems for everything from towels to room occupancy rates. Such management skills and their dissemination throughout the company's organization comprises the basis for competitive advantage. This enables the firm to appropriate higher rents which would lead to a preference for equity, and particularly, full ownership modes.

At the same time, the greater the intensity of tacit knowledge in the firm (here we are not referring to codified strategic assets, but tacit organizational routines) the higher the costs of transferring such knowledge to partners, thereby lowering the likelihood of alliance. This hypothesis was verified by Kim and Hwang. Similarly, we propose that:

H12: M will be positively associated with investment in training (PINV).

Two statistical techniques will be used. Discriminant analysis merely tests the validity and robustness of the classification of the dependent variable M into four groups, and reduces the explanatory variables to a smaller number of factors. Ordinal logistic regression (using a Generalized LOGIT model) enables us to test the above twelve hypotheses, and identify independent variables which most strongly influence the choice of organizational mode.

Two Methodological Issues

Problems in Using Objective Firm Data, such as Dollar Sales in Research Involving Alliances: As we suspected, the objective SIZE variable (measuring Dollar sales revenues of the global hotel firm) turned out to be collinear with other variables, including PFS. But SIZE also has other methodological problems, which often hamper its use in alliance research:

i. The sales of minority joint ventures may not be consolidated into the accounts of some of our sample companies, since accounting conventions used in the reported financial data vary across nations;

ii. Franchise and management service agreement revenues may not appear under the consolidated sales figure of some companies;

iii. Even if they were added to global revenues, this would greatly understate the global total sales of the entire alliance network, because franchise and management service agreement earnings are typically expressed only as a percentage of sales of the hotel property in question. Hence for both multicollinearity reasons, as well as measurement reasons, SIZE was dropped from the subsequent analysis.

The number of usable observations had to be reduced from the 1,131 hotels, to 720, for two reasons. 74 hotel properties were dropped because discriminant analysis cannot accept overlapping categories (typically, a hotel having both part equity investment and a management service agreement). This is a minor loss of only 6.5 per cent of the data. However, another 337 cases had to be dropped because of missing data in various independent variables, but particularly in the cultural distance CUL variable. This variable is constructed from Hofstede's (1980) data on cultural attributes, covering less than 50 nations.

No other similar data exist; nor has any scholar subsequently replicated Hofstede's work, or added to his number of countries. A researcher is thus faced with a dilemma: Either drop the cultural distance variable, considered by many scholars, such as Kogut and Singh (1988) to be a crucial determinant of modal choice, and have a larger data set, or keep the cultural distance variable and work with a reduced data set. In this study we chose the latter option, given the importance suggested for the cultural distance variable. The testing is therefore performed on a data set with n = 720 hotels, which is more than ample for statistical purposes.

Before performing discriminant analysis, Variance Inflation Factors for all independent variables were computed, and their low values (not shown) indicated that the discriminant function coefficients can be interpreted with reasonable confidence. The distances are not inconsistent with the rank ordering of groups within the measure M. The largest squared distance of 4.88 is between categories M = 1 (Franchising) and M = 4 (Fully Owned); followed by the 3.16 squared distance between M = 1 (Franchising) and M = 3 (Partly Owned); followed by M = 1 (Franchising) and M = 2 (Management Service Agreement). The smallest distances are between the pairs M = 3 and M = 4 (Equity-based) and M = 1 and M = 2 (Non-Equity).

The absolute magnitude of the standardized discriminant coefficients enable us (with appropriate caveats) to identify some of the independent variables as being most instrumental in discriminating among groups. In Function 1, IEX (International Experience) and GLOP (Fraction of Foreign to Total Hotels) have the highest coefficients. An examination of group suggests that Function 1 serves to differentiate M = 1 (Franchising) from the remaining groups. With appropriate caution therefore, we can venture to say that international experience and geographic reach of the global firm strongly distinguish the equity investment mode from the franchising mode. The coefficients of other variables in Function 1, such as PRES, GDPCAP and PFS are much weaker, and we should not give them as much credence, although they do meet the cutoff of [absolute value of Coefficient] [greater than].30 suggested by Pedhazur.

It is worth noting that the signs of all the above variables are consistent with the results of the Logistic Regression using Generalized LOGIT, suggesting the convergent validity of results from two separate statistical techniques. Function 2 differentiates the centroid for M = 2 (Management Service Agreement Mode) from other modes. Among the independent variables, PSCA (strategy importance of scale) and PINV (strategy importance of investment in training) stand out as differentiating management service contracts from the rest.

A Posterior Classification was next computed to test the predictive ability of the discriminant functions. Correctly classified cases were 58.88 per cent in M = 1 (Franchising Mode); 73.80 per cent for M = 2 (Management Service Agreement Mode); 37 per cent for M = 3 (Part Equity) and 41.46 per cent for M = 4 (Fully Owned). The overall average correct posterior classification has a 58.75 per cent rate. Given the four groups under the variable M (a priori p = 0.25), the overall classification rate is good.

This is a logistic regression using a generalized LOGIT model, which assumes a common slope parametre for the predictor variable (also known as the "Proportional-Odds" Model). The results show a strongly significant overall Chi-square value of 380.27, and a Somers' D of 0.61. For the overall model, concordant probabilities were a fairly high 79.6 per cent. Seven out of the eleven independent variables are significant at better than.05, and of these, five are significant at better than the.01 level.

Country independent variables CRI (Country Political and Economic Risk), and GDPCAP (GDP per capita) both had results congruent with the hypotheses. The negative sign for the GDPCAP variable confirms the hypothesis that nonequity modes are preferred in high income nations, and equity investment in low income nations, ceteris paribus. This is consistent with other studies which show a positive correlation between country income levels and franchising. In developing nations, the higher knowledge transfer costs to franchisees, and the risks of poor quality, and weaker enforcement of intellectual property rights lead many firms to prefer equity investment and higher control modes there.

The positive sign for the CRI coefficient confirms that, with higher political and economic risk (volatility), non equity modes, such as franchising and management service contracts, are preferred in higher risk environments, where the real estate investment and business risk is substantially on the shoulders of local investors. Moreover, the royalty-type payments, which comprise a substantial part of the contractual arrangements, are inherently less volatile compared with returns on equity, which in risky nations may disappear altogether.

The results for the country risk and income variables may appear contradictory and paradoxical, but they are not. It proposes that equity-based modes are preferred in "low risk" and "low per capita income" nations. Non-equity modes are preferred in high income/low risk countries, as well as in high-risk/low income nations. (Incidentally, the fourth quadrant of the typology, namely high risk/high income naticns ought not to contain too many countries, as a practical matter, and this common-sensical presumption is confirmed in the scatterplot of countries shown in. Since the risk variable CRI was on an inverted scale with 100 = lowest risk, it has been transformed into CRISK = 100 CRI to conform to the typology in.

What explanations apply to for the typology? First of all, in regression, interpretation of each variable is to be taken one at a time on a ceteris paribus basis. On the per capita income variable, virtually every survey of U.S. company global investment by the U.S. Department of Commerce indicates that the profitability of direct investments in emerging and developing nations is considerably higher than in the richer nations. These countries also grow faster. Higher rents are to be had in emerging nations, rents that can only be captured by dividends and returns on equity investment. By contrast, franchising royalties and management service fees, while less volatile, are necessarily constrained to a small, fixed percentage of sales of the hotel property. Therefore, in potentially lucrative markets, a firm may prefer the (unconstrained) higher returns from equity investments, despite the higher risk.

The normal specification of royalties as a (modest) percentage of turnover, compared with the unconstrained nature of returns on equity investment, also explains the CRI (country risk) result. It is axiomatic that royalties, as a fixed percentage of sales, are far less volatile than dividends. In riskier nations (risk ultimately defined by volatility of sales), therefore, franchising and management service agreements would be preferred, ceteris paribus. Fladmoe-Lindquist and Jacque, in their report on international franchising indicated that royalties linked to turnover also provide a better protection to the franchisor from currency risk if gross revenues are indexed to inflation. This echoes the findings of Kim and Hwang, who indicated that in conditions of "demand uncertainty," equity ownership tends to be low.

Hypotheses for CUL (Cultural Distance) and FDITOGDP (FDI to GDP Ratio in the host nation) were not supported. Empirical studies using the Cultural Distance variable have yielded mixed results. Madhok explains these inconclusive results by suggesting that the hypothesis of greater use of partners in culturally distant nations, may be countered by "...the inadequacy of a partner's ability (to absorb knowledge at a high socio-cultural distance) or the incompatibility of his routines." (Parenthesis added).

The objective firm variables IEX (International Experience) and GLOP (Proportion of Hotels Outside the Home Nation) yielded strong support for the hypotheses, that equity-based modes will be preferred by companies with considerable experience and existing geographic reach. These results perfectly echo those of the discriminant analysis.

The results for the Management and Quality Control variable (CQ), support the hypothesis that the organizational mode for a property would be influenced towards more equity ownership, ceteris paribus, in firms whose executives place a higher importance on control over daily management and quality. Incidentally, this finding validates the construction of the dependent variable M.

The sign for the PFS (Importance of Size) variable is opposite to the hypotheses (and highly significant). This suggests that the expressed importance of size, as a strategic factor, is not necessarily correlated to the propensity to use high-ownership modes, and supports the conclusion of Gatignon and Anderson (1988) that "higher control modes are less likely for large foreign operations." The high incidence of management service and franchise modes in this business suggests that many firms have concluded that they can be "big," not necessarily via controlled, equity investments, but by building a network of alliances.

The sign for PRES (Importance of Reservations System and Brand) is congruent with the hypothesis. The results suggests that a global reservations system, and brandname, are crucial strategic assets which enable a global hotel company to build and control a network of contractual alliances. Not only do these strategic assets yield additional income (such as a fee for each reservation made through the global reservation system, or separate royalties for the brand name component), but they also reduce the opportunistic behaviour of franchisees and local (management service) partners because of the threat of withholding of these assets.

The "proportional-odds" model for an ordinal response logistic regression assumes a common slope parametre for the predicting variables. The "Score Test" generates a Chi-square statistic. If the p-value of the statistic is large, then the proportional-odds assumption is valid. However, if the p-value is small (as we found in our case) this does not necessarily mean the proportional-odds assumption is invalid.

In brief, a small p-value for the "Score Test" Chi-square does not mean anything, one way or another.

Nevertheless, we ran the multinomial logistic procedure assuming different slope parametres, and showed the maximum likelihood analysis of variance. The results are broadly consistent (common slope parametre assumption) in that all independent variables except FDITOGDP, CUL, and CRI, have a p-value better than 0.05, and even CRI may be marginally acceptable with a p-value of.095.

Consistency of Results In general, the results of discriminant analysis and ordered logistic regression are congruent and lead us to have a high degree of confidence in the validity of the classification and construction of the measure M, and in the explanatory independent variables.

International management today involves the art of selective strategy knowing where to compete, and where to cooperate. An international firm's collection of business ventures will involve some with a high level of ownership or control. Other ventures will be run on a contractual alliance basis, with franchising being a special case of repeated contracting tending towards a standardization of contractual terms and operating procedures. Management service agreements, whereby global hotel chains manage hotels on behalf of local owners of the property, may today be the single most common organizational mode for global operations. This paper offered a spectrum of alternatives, from franchising to management service agreements, to equity joint ventures, to fully owned investment.

How does a manager know when to choose which mode of organization? This is becoming an important art in the practice of management, since the optimum configuration of global operations is seldom standardized. Until a decade ago, local adaptation by global firms was expressed by varying their business practices and methods in each country, while leaving the ownership and organizational structures fairly invariant across nations. Today, the modal choice issue has gone beyond the "internalize or not" question, and even beyond the "licensing vs. joint venture vs. merger" set of alternatives, to include other types of alliances, such as management service contracts, and franchising. The general modal choice set now includes varying levels of equity ownership, as well as several alliances of various descriptions.

The manager must, today, choose from a larger set of options. This paper offered three groups of explanatory variables: Country-specific variables, variables relating to the international experience and global scope of the firm, as well as perceptual strategy variables, which were shown to influence the modal choice.

The convergent results of discriminant analysis and logistic regression supported the robustness of the model and variables. Higher equity and control modes are preferred by companies with longer international experience and geographic reach. Companies appear to shun equity-based modes in risky nations, preferring to use management service and franchising contracts instead, where royalties and fees provide a surer return compared to dividends.

At the same time, on the per capita income variable, firms appear to prefer equity investments in lower income nations, ceteris paribus. It is an accepted fact that growth in emerging nations tends to be higher, and returns are also higher due to weaker competition in such nations. In all likelihood, this applies to the hotel business as well.

The global hotel business showed results contrary to those found in several manufacturing sectors, with reference to the strategic perceptions of size. In this business at least, high equity and control modes are not seen as crucial for large global operations. In the quest for global reach, hotel firms place considerable reliance on non-equity partners and franchisees. A network of franchisees and hotels under management service agreements enable it to capture some of the economies of global logistics, supplies, architectural design, reservations, training, and brand recognition. It is possible that the findings of this study apply also to other service sectors. This remains an area for further research.

One general conclusion that can apply to other sectors is that contractual relationships can effectively substitute for equity ownership when the fear of partner opportunism is reduced by the global company's ongoing control over key strategic assets. The threat of withdrawal of an international reservations system or brand name moderates the behaviour of local partners in each nation. Moreover, these same strategic assets enable the firm to earn additional royalties (together with royalties for providing management services) in franchising and management service agreements.

Such contract-specified royalties and fees often tip the balance towards alliance-based participation in risky nations, where equity-based investment may be precluded. This study has made a beginning towards understanding modal choice in the context of the dynamic interaction between the risk/ return framework. This remains an area for further research.

What are the implications of this study for theory development? A theory of modal choice cannot rest only on conditions in the country market or host foreign environment. Similarly, the nature of the "transaction," or entry conditions negotiated with a prospective corporate ally, can provide only a partial explanation, Why? Because the global firm is more than a collection of national organizations; it is more than a set of discrete transactions. The global company has an overall long-term strategy. A robust theory of modal choice is therefore necessarily syncretic, and includes country, transaction specific, agency theory, as well as firm strategy factors.

Chapter 4

Hotel Load

A mid-year look at the state of banks' hotel real estate portfolios reveals improved conditions in most regions and good reason for California lenders to exercise caution. Few industries are as closely tied to the economy as the hotel industry is. And there's still a dark cloud over the Golden State's economic landscape. But in much of the rest of the country, the hotel market is heating up. Bankers around the country—and the hotel management companies assigned the task of increasing the properties' value—are now reporting an increase in the number of parties interested in purchasing hotels. Increasing pools of capital, however, are chasing fewer properties.

The scarcity of properties is attributed simply to the fact that far fewer new hotels are being built—and many of the more attractive ones that banks have been trying to unload have already been sold. Today, banks generally have far fewer foreclosed hotels in their real estate portfolios than during the 1990-91 period, when they were swamped with properties. What a difference two years makes. Today, note industry observers, bankers have a better perspective on the prospects for moving foreclosed hotels out of their portfolios.

That's because bankers better understand the business of operating a hotel-that it is a compilation of several businesses, not one that depends solely on rent for income.

"As we've gone through this process over the past few years, everyone has become more educated," notes Len

Wolman, president of the Waterford Hotel Group, Inc., Waterford, Conn. "The biggest example is that when lending on hotels a few years back, lenders thought they were lending on real estate. Now they realize they're lending on management and people – that it's an operating business, not just a real estate assets."

By the same token, lenders and buyers now appreciate the real value of their hotel properties. They are leaving the inflated property values of the late 1980s in the past and now approach purchase negotiations armed with experience and a strong dose of reality.

Who bought what in '92. "Bankers today are more realistic about what the price of a hotel really is and what they will get for it when they sell it," notes Michael Cahill, senior vice-president of Hospitality Valuation Services, a Mineola, N.Y.-based consulting and appraisal firm specializing hotels. HVS has monitored hotel property transactions in excess of $10 million for the past two years. In 1992, 41 such transactions took place, an increase of 78% over 1991, when 23 such transactions occurred. The total value of the 1992 transactions was $1.6 billion, compared to 1991's total transaction value of $773 million.

Analysis of the first quarter of 1993 indicates a continuation of the trend upward in the number of transactions taking place and their overall value. Of the 41 hotel properties included in the 1992 survey, 13 (32% of the total) were sold by banks or thrifts, the remainder by insurance companies, government entities, and real estate and development firms. Of the 39 transactions where a price was given, 12, or 31%, were valued at $30 million or more. Four properties (10%) were valued at $20 million to $30 million, and the majority, 59%, were valued from $10 million to $20 million.

On the buyer side, foreign investors accounted for 44% of the total purchasers, a slight decrease from the norm of 50% domestic and 50% foreign buyers.

Ray Dunn III, vice-president and REO (real estate owned) asset manager for Maryland National Bank's South Charles

Realty Co., Baltimore, traces an increase in buyer interest to the 1992 general election. "Money that may have been on the sidelines emerged at that time, and since then we've seen more serious buyers and more serious offers come forward," says Dunn.

His theory: The election of President Clinton marked a turning point in the commercial real estate market. Investors interpreted the election as a signal that the market had already bottomed out, and it was time to invest while prices were still low.

"That event spurred a lot of activity," says Dunn, "and there has been a lot less resistance from the investment banking community to making funds available for hotel purchases."

South Charles Realty, established by Maryland National to cope with the real estate turmoil of 1990, has so far sold or restructured 14 properties worth well over $400 million, according to Dunn.

"The interest of buyers is much stronger," he insists. "Before hotel properties are even on the market, we have parties wanting to make offers. We're able to choose between offers and better qualify the buyers ahead of time." But not all buyers are in the market they would like to be. U.S. banks are reluctant to extend credit for purchasing hotels, so domestic buyers may have to turn elsewhere for debt financing. "I don't see that changing over the next two to three years," says Cahill of HVS. "Where they're forced to, banks will extend the term of a loan. But the ones that have hotels are so busy providing seller financing on properties they're trying to move that they're not in the market to provide third-party financing for hotels they're not involved in."

Concurs banker Greg Reimers, a vice-president at Bank of New York: "Banks don't want another hotel loan in their portfolio. But if they do extend credit for hotel purchases, then obviously the loan should be better underwritten this time around."

Still, when is it prudent to invest further capital in a foreclosed hotel? Does the bank gain by deferring investing in maintenance improvements or redecorating in the hope that the new owner will assume those costs? Unfortunately, there's no easy answer, because every hotel property has its own story to tell.

A snapshot of today's hotel property scene from the perspective of David McIlroy, vice-president, Neworld Bank, a Boston savings bank, looks like this: "ADRs [average daily rates] are up in just about all Massachusetts hotels, and new hotels aren't being built, so you have absorption of existing properties. The owners of properties that have been foreclosed on—those making $30 to $50 per night per room—have deferred maintenance by and large, and are not putting money into the hotels."

The most vulnerable hotels the next time interest rates creep upward, McIlroy suggests, are those with excessive debt that can't afford to make necessary maintenance improvements. "In the meantime, people are buying those hotels that can afford to make the necessary improvements, and they are building that cost into the purchase price or financing terms," notes McIlroy.

Hotel managers' role. They key to riding out the remaining turbulence associated with hotel real estate holdings is to make the most of existing and future ties to hotel management companies. A necessary part of the hotel real estate scenario, hotel managers are finding themselves in an increasingly competitive business.

Which means they are willing to work harder to garner market share as banks' hotel portfolios are reduced? Today's hotel management companies stress their ability to operate hotels as multifaceted businesses, a necessary ingredient in any management arrangement. But rather than charge banks nebulous fees for a package of services, the norm increasingly is to work on incentive. If a management company you work with doesn't offer such a plan, consider asking why not.

"Awarding a service contract to the lowest bidder isn't always the best way to go," notes Bruce Wiles, executive vice-president of American General Hospitality, Inc., Dallas.

Wiles says that most of his company's base contract fees range from 1.25% to 1.50% of the gross sale price plus from 5% to 10% of the improvements in gross operating profits on a year-over-year basis.

Another hotel manager, Len Wolman, of Waterford Hotel Group, stresses the importance of working quickly to analyze the hotel's balance sheet in order to trim waste and build credibility in the hotel's marketplace. "The first 90 days of taking over a property are critical in terms of staffing and the confidence of the local community," says Walman. Therefore, it's important to stress that booked social functions will occur as planned, capital expenditures will finally be made, and vendors will be paid.

Once that task is complete, suggests Wolman, it's time to examine the hotel's financial picture very carefully.

Waterford's approach: "We first attack the fixed costs," says Wolman. There isn't a property the firm has gone into, he says, where insurance couldn't be reduced significantly. "We went into one hotel where the insurance could be rewritten with the same carrier, and the hotel saved $40,000 per year," says Wolman.

The other fixed cost to concentrate on is taxes. "We took a property where the annual tax bill was $805,000," says Wolman, "and by working with a local attorney, we reduced it to $155,000."

Hotel management companies need to also be adept at consolidating staff.

Cutting back an account staff from five people to two saved one of Waterford's properties under management $150,000 in one year.

Even though banks' hotel portfolios are lightening up, there are still traps for the unwary.

Despite strides in understanding what makes the hotel business tick, it's foreign territory to a large extent, and few bankers yearn to manage hotels.

"One of the biggest pitfalls," warns Michael Cahill, of HVS, "is not realizing that the hotel market will turn around. Selling the property for a price below its intrinsic value is a pitfall a lot of lenders fall into."

Cahill's rule of thumb is to look three to five years out for any potential upside to the property, despite where it is today. "If there's no upside and it's a cash drain, sell it," he advises. "But if there is some upside and it's only breaking even today, then maybe you should hold onto it." Should your hotel loan be restructured?

Strong hotel/strong market:

- Is a candidate for restructuring, but if it is to be sold, it should be marketed aggressively.
- When courting buyers, ensure that the individuals interested recognize that the hotel is a strong property in a strong market.

Weak hotel/strong market:

- Is a questionable candidate for restructuring.
- Require upgraded capital.
- Examine any franchise affiliation for possible additional strength.
- Recommend a bolstering of the hotel's management, and increase marketing efforts.

Strong hotel/weak market:

- Restructure with caution; the hotel could be on the brink of a downward slide.
- Aggressively build market share.
- Diligently control costs, and work to shore up the hotel's net operating income.

Weak hotel/weak market:

i. Not a candidate for restructuring.

ii. Downsize operations to contain costs.

iii. Market to a nontraditional niche buyer, such as a college or university for student housing or a wholesale tour company for discount travellers, Source: Lodging Solutions, Inc., a Boston-based hotel management firm.

Remember the British television series "Fawlty Towers"? In each episode, the chronically incompetent Basil Fawlty (played by John Cleese) would turn inept hotel management into comic art. Fawlty got stuck in the most unfortunate situations, never realizing that his lack of management skills contributed to the disasters that plagued his establishment.

Fawlty's problem was his failure to realize that running a hotel is not child's play. Unfortunately for banks financing hotel loans, life in the hotel industry often imitates art.

Indeed, The Wall Street Journal reports that between 350 and 355 hotel properties have experienced financial difficulties annually since 1980. By the end of 1990, the paper estimates, 1,000 properties could end up in foreclosure. Not so simple. Morris E. Lasky, president of Lodging Unlimited Inc., West Chester, Pa., says the misconception that the lodging industry is an easy field which anyone can enter has contributed to the rising rate of hotel loan foreclosures.

Since its founding in 1970, Lodging Unlimited has revitalized over 130 troubled hotels and motels. These properties, which were valued at over $1 billion in total and were threatened with foreclosure or other serious hardships, are brought to Lasky by both lenders and owners.

In an interview with ABA Banking Journal, Lasky talked about the pitfalls of the business and how lenders can avoid following borrowers into them. ABA BJ: What future is there for the hotel business? Lasky: We surveyed lenders at a recent workshop on hotel loans. We came up with the projection that there would be over 1,000 hotels and motels foreclosed on in the next couple of years.

Last year at this time, in terms of my own personal experience, we were looking at probably five hotel and motel problems a month. This year we are looking at approximately one hotel property per day. ABA BJ: How do you account for the large number of problems in the industry? Lasky: Probably 95% of the hotels that we've taken on were managed by inexperienced operators.

Many investors come from other fields. They were very successful in those fields, and decided the hotel business was "easy" and invested in it. They were obviously very disappointed. ABA BJ: How does a hotel get into trouble? Lasky: The first time three people sit down and decide they want to build a hotel. They usually have no background in the hotel business. They also have a fourth friend who is a lender, and all agree that a hotel could be built and could succeed in that market.

The first mistake the banker makes is that he never asks the obvious question: Who is going to manage the hotel? If the answer isn't a highly experienced management company or a highly experienced joint venture partner, the banker should consider the deal potentially dangerous. ABA BJ: Why is professional management so necessary? Lasky: People from other fields sometimes enter this industry thinking, "I've stayed in a hotel, so I can run one." This could not be further from the truth.

The hotel business is very complicated. Hotels are open 24 hours a day, 365 days a year. They require a massive amount of skill in specialized marketing—establishing sales quotas, establishing relationships with travel agents and the corporate tour and travel departments of major corporations, and more. Specialized management and accounting skills are also called for. ABA BJ: What other danger signs should a lender watch for? Lasky: The next major mistake involves feasibility—whether the market can support another hotel. In order to satisfy the needs of the lending institution, a study by a feasibility company is requested.

However, most people do not ask who in that company will actually perform the study. In our experience, many of the feasibility companies have their least-experienced employee do the field work. That person has probably just graduated from college and doesn't have all the skills necessary to recognize the issues and problems in the market which could negatively affect the feasibility study.

As a result, many studies are glowing—but they fail to consider the question of other new hotel construction in the same market or what brand name should be on the hotel. ABA BJ: What do you mean by "brand name"? Lasky: A large majority of hotels have some national affiliation, either through a franchise or membership relationship.

Generally the investors determine which names might be available in that market and select one. Lenders should consider whether that name is going to produce business for the hotel. The only reason to buy a brand is to produce business, thus a name should be chosen so it can make an impact and create a positive result for the hotel. Studies can be done to determine the effectiveness of a franchise name in a particular market.

A franchise should produce at least 15% total occupancy to justify its existence. A franchise might cost 6% to 8% gross of room sales plus initial franchise fees. As a result, this can have a major impact on the bottom line. ABA BJ: What other trouble signs should lenders watch for? Lasky: Consider the budget for the hotel. We find that most people who don't have experience in building hotels generally understate budgets by 10% to 20%. And this is assuming they know the basics—the cost of building, furniture and fixtures, and debt.

They generally forget the cost of pre marketing a hotel, the cost of prestaffing a hotel, and the cost requirement for operating capital in the early stages of the hotel. They don't realize that operating at a loss for the first year is fairly typical. They also forget the cost of supplies and small equipment, such as the maids' utility carts and their vacuum cleaners. There should also be a fairly reasonable contingency plan for mistakes or delays in construction. In short, a good hotel budget should account for errors in advance.

THE HOTEL-TOURISM INDUSTRY

In the wake of the 1992 urban rebellion and subsequent natural disasters, the Los Angeles Visitors and Convention Bureau unveiled a multimillion dollar ad campaign with a new public relations message, "Los Angeles - Together We're the Best." Throughout the L.A. area, billboards, flags, and advertisements all carry this latest version of civic boosterism. Unfortunately, this slogan masks the widening gap of social and economic inequality in L.A. between the haves and have-nots. There is a growing income disparity between the high-skilled, white-collar professionals, who work in high-rise office and entertainment complexes, and the low-wage, primarily Latino, immigrant workers that keep the service and sweatshop economy operating.

It is not coincidental that a widening gap of poverty in Los Angeles has occurred at the same time as the region became an international business centre and a destination for leisure activities. The purpose of this article is to provide an analysis of one industry, the hotel-tourism industry, a fragile pillar in the construction of L.A.'s restructured economy. The tourism industry thrives on a manufactured image of the region that includes sunny beaches, Hollywood entertainment, and mega-amusement parks.

However, the slick PR campaigns and the glamorized interpretations of social reality hide a dark underside of poverty and racism that will be explored below. The central questions addressed are: What forces fueled the growth and restructuring of the hotel-tourism industry, what were the local effects, and how have immigrant workers responded to the internationalization of the tourism industry?

A paradox in L.A.'s meteoric rise into a global centre is that it also produced an equally alarming growth in poverty among low-wage workers. In the 1960s, a regional centre of finance and other services was constructed by a growth coalition that included oil companies, banks, real estate developers, and the Los Angeles Times newspaper. This coalition was infused in the 1970s by a wave of Japanese and other foreign investment capital that transformed L.A. into a centre of global capital. Besides the construction of office buildings, hotels and leisure entertainment were developed to attract international business and tourists. To staff the burgeoning tourism and service industry, large numbers of low-wage immigrant workers, predominantly from Mexico and Central America, have become the dominant work force replacing African Americans and ethnic whites.

The new immigrant workers have not received the economic and social benefits commensurate with the labour they invested in L.A.'s transformation. For the City and County of Los Angeles, the growth of the tourist industry is an integral part of the region's transition from a heavy industrial and a defence economy into a light manufacturing, apparel, and service economy. Because federal and state funds have dried up, urban centres such as Los Angeles have been scrambling to adopt policies that will create public revenues.

The development of the tourism industry is seen by local government officials as being able to generate needed public revenues through bed and sales taxes. The economic importance of the tourism industry cannot be ignored. Tourism in L.A. provides jobs and entertainment for the more than 22 million visitors each year. First, the tourism industry played a prominent role in L.A.'s restructuring into an international tourist destination and business centre. Second, local government officials actively supported the growth of hotels and tourism into an international industry.

Third, as the L.A. tourism industry became internationalized and corporate decision making moved overseas, problems of accountability to the local workers were exacerbated. Access by workers and other local community elements to the source of corporate power became more limited. In response to the internationalization of the tourism industry, the Hotel Employees and Restaurant Employees, Local 11, in L.A., has used what Johnston (1994) calls social movement unionism(1) to build campaigns that include locally based groups and public officials to pressure transnational corporations for justice for hotel-tourism workers.

Evidence to substantiate these propositions comes from a variety of sources, including interviews with HERE union leaders and staff members, community activists, and public officials that were conducted over the past several years. In addition, research was conducted on the decisions of the Los Angeles Community Redevelopment Agency (CRA), the Los Angeles City Council, and the L.A. real estate and tourism industries.

To facilitate a thorough analysis of international growth and local effects in the hotel-tourism industry, this article will be organized into four sections: an analysis of the commodification of L.A. as a tourist attraction, the development of the hotel-tourism industry, including the role of immigrant labour, the role of local government in the construction of the tourism industry, and a case study of HERE Local 11's efforts.

Travel and tourism industries employ over 200 million workers worldwide. One in every nine workers worldwide is employed in the tourism industry (Westin Bulletin, Spring 1994). The hotel-tourism industry provides a complex web of products and services for travel, including leisure/vacations, travellers for business, and convention travel. During the 1980s, in the U.S., pleasure travel accounted for 40% of the travellers and business increased to 17% of the total travel volume. Under the laws of supply and demand, the need or desire for a product is what attracts the visitor (consumer) to a place; in this case, it is the urban landscape and events available for use by locals and visitors.

Places are marketed as part of the new culture of consumption, thus creating fierce competition for business. Both domestic and international tourists travel to L.A. to visit an "image" of sun and fun promoted by the tourism and entertainment industry. Urry (1990) describes the attraction of a place where a tourist can "gaze" or observe particular objects that are not normally seen in their typical daily experience.

The mythology of Southern California as a tourist destination began in the 1880s and expanded in the 1920s and 1930s as the Hollywood entertainment industry promoted Los Angeles as a glamorous "island on the land". The construction of Disneyland in 1955 marked the beginning of postwar mass consumption and the commodification of Southern California. As Zukin (1991) notes, the traditional amusement park was transformed into a "landscape of social power," whereby several different landscapes, some imaginatively recreated, and others purely imaginary, were conceived in a controlled environment. The Hollywood entertainment industry, based in L.A., contributes to this manufactured image of L.A. Sanitized images of L.A. are created through television shows such as "Beverly Hills 90210," "Melrose Place," and "Baywatch," as well as harder-edged cop shows like "LAPD."

Recent films such as L.A. Story, Boyz N the Hood, and Grand Canyon depict L.A. as an urban area composed of a fragmented landscape divided into multiple identities. Place-specific films and television shows create fantasy by promoting images of particular locations. The entertainment industry is able to capitalize off positive and negative images to profit financially by using L.A. as a place to be marketed and sold as a commodity.

Los Angeles is marketed as a place for consumers to enjoy, but only in preselected places. Other parts of L.A. are never visited by tourists. The communities where the tourism industry workers live and raise their families are not on the tourists' map. These are the areas that went up in smoke during the 1992 urban rebellion. There is a duality to L.A., one of leisure and business, and another as a location of fear and avoidance. Although both images can be used by the entertainment industry to profit from L.A. as a place commodity, for the tourism industry though, only positive images of L.A. are promoted. Major social problems and negative images can quickly threaten the viability of tourism as a profitable industry. In the aftermath of the 1992 riots in Los Angeles, tourism plummeted. Paradoxically, two of L.A.'s fastest growing industries are seemingly in conflict when it comes to how to promote L.A. as a place commodity. The development of a tourism industry has been constructed by a combination of local real estate interests, global capital, and local political actors.

Capital Investment in the Hotel-Tourism Industry

There are several factors that combined to create L.A.'s restructured economy, including the closure of large segments of the durable goods manufacturing industry (all auto, steel, and rubber plants were closed), defence industry cutbacks following the end of the Cold War, and corporate downsizing that reduced the work force in numerous service and retail industries. These globally based processes have meant that L.A. has had to become increasingly dependent on other industries to generate jobs and revenues. Beyond the growth of the financial and real estate sectors, hotels, entertainment, and tourism have also become key pillars of the L.A. economy.

In particular, the steady flow of visitors into L.A. has become vital for the local economy. In 1994, 22.2 million tourists spent $9.5 billion, which translates into a total economic impact of $22 billion in revenue generated by the tourism industry in L.A. County. The tourism industry is a large job generator, including 50,000 hotel workers, 227,000 in restaurants and bars, plus an additional 50,000 workers at amusement parks, recreation, and race tracks (many of these workers cater directly to tourists).

This is a grand total of 337,000 employees in the L.A. hotel and tourism industry. In the entire tourism industry, fewer than 10% are unionized workers. Most of the unionized workers are employed at hotels, amusement parks, sporting venues, and race tracks, while most restaurant and bars are nonunion.

The global restructuring of the hotel and tourism industry in Los Angeles is most apparent in the growing internationalization of capital and labour. The investment of international capital has come in two waves. The first wave began during the 1970s when Japanese capital, in conjunction with Canadian, European, and U.S. capital, fueled the growth of the built environment in downtown L.A. and other sub-regional centres. The first stage represented the growth period, when the local growth coalition focused on construction of the corporate downtown headquarters.

The second stage began in the 1980s as other international players began to invest in the L.A. real estate market. This created a high demand for real estate that resulted in the inflation of market values. Labour migration to L.A., since 1965, also came in waves as immigrants from Asia, Mexico, and Central America fueled the growth of the service and light manufacturing industries.

The foundation for rapid growth in downtown L.A. began in the 1950s. L.A. corporate, media, and political leaders recognized the need to utilize federal funds to rebuild the central city area into a major corporate headquarters. Davis (1992) discussed how L.A. city government embarked on a major urban renewal project that covered most of downtown L.A. Needing additional sources of capital investment, the local growth machine established a local redevelopment agency that obtained federal funds. In addition, foreign sources of capital were sought to supplement domestic capital resources. The combination of domestic and foreign investment capital enabled L.A. to make the transition into an international global Financial centre and corporate headquarters.

Circuits of Capital Investment

Global capital investment is critical for the development of cities. Capital contains several circuits, or levels, of investment. The first (primary) circuit is the investment of money and credit capital into raw materials, equipment, labour, and transportation. The secondary circuit of capital contains the flow of capital into land and real estate, including the "built environment" of office buildings, shopping centres, and factories.

In the early 1970s, the international economic crisis of profits in the primary circuit of manufacturing capital prompted a dramatic increase in the secondary circuit of capital within the built environment, as many investors sought alternate locations for investment. Capital investment has come from two sources: the surplus profits gained in the primary circuit such as the flood of Japanese and OPEC oil money in the 1970s and from local economic actors seeking to profit from real estate investment.

This second group includes commercial real estate brokers and investors. The flow of investment capital into the real estate market fueled the growth of L.A.'s downtown and sub-regional centres. Speculative investment by developers involves a complex process whereby local and international construction companies, architectural firms, and city government officials utilize financial capital to develop offices, hotels, and retail malls. The sources of venture capital generally are financial capital in the U.S. and foreign banking institutions.

Since the 1970s, global investments in the secondary circuit of real estate have rapidly expanded. This study focuses on Asian capital investment in the L.A. tourism industry. Japanese capital investment played a crucial role in L.A.'s economic growth. In the late 1960s and 1970s, Japanese venture capital invested the surplus profits gained in post-World War II Asia and the U.S. in overseas real estate properties. Japanese corporate interests, looking for a way to enter the U.S. real estate market, obtained prime urban sites in San Francisco, Los Angeles, and other cities.

Overall, Gerlowski, Fung, and Ford found that Japanese real estate investment in the U.S. was overwhelmingly based in California. The first Japanese involvement in the real estate market took place in the traditional Japanese enclaves known as "Little Tokyo" in L.A. and "Nihonmachi" in San Francisco. These investments were considered relatively safe risks. However, to obtain the properties they needed in Los Angeles and San Francisco, Japanese capital forced community residents to leave their traditional communities. Local community residents were replaced by hotels, office buildings, and shopping centres for Japanese tourists and businessmen. In L.A., low-income residents and small businesspeople, after years of mass community protests, were forced to relocate out of Little Tokyo.

For many residents of Japanese descent, this was the second forced evacuation from their community, as many residents were forced into Japanese relocation centres during World War II. The Kajima Corporation, a billion dollar construction company with close ties with the Sumitomo Group in Japan, was the first major Japanese developer in L.A. Kajima first developed an entire block in L.A.'s Little Tokyo in the early 1970s. Kajima acquired extensive financial resources through connections with Japan's largest banks. Kajima outbid other local developers to build the New Otani Hotel. The Kajima Corporation was able to purchase land valued at $1.5 million for a little over one million dollars from the Los Angeles redevelopment agency.

After beginning in Little Tokyo, Japanese capital began to expand their investments. Japanese investors figured prominently in the building of the Bonaventure Hotel. The Mitsubishi Corporation, Japan's largest real estate company, helped finance the construction of this hotel. The Bonaventure Hotel was designed to anchor the redevelopment of downtown L.A. and signaled to other Japanese investors that the downtown area was an important place to construct and purchase existing office buildings.

The construction of the Bonaventure and the New Otani hotels in the 1970s marked the entrance of Japanese capital into the L.A. hotel market. By 1995, Japanese ownership was 40% of the L.A. luxury hotel market, nearly double the percentage under U.S. ownership.(2) In one widely publicized purchase in 1989, the Bel Air Hotel, an exclusive hotel in L.A.'s exclusive westside area, was purchased by the Sazale Group of Japan. The property sold for $110 million or $1.2 million per room.

Investment by Japanese capital also extended into the real estate sector; for example, the Shuwa Investment Company purchased the Arco Plaza in downtown L.A. for $620 million in 1986. This large an investment by direct foreign investors was unprecedented in L.A. and demonstrated the rapid growth of international capital at the local level. By 1990, Japanese owned 27% of downtown L.A.'s real estate market.

New Stage in Hotel-Tourism Development

In the late 1980s, as part of the global restructuring in the hotel-tourism industry, new investors entered the L.A. real estate market from the developing nations in the Pacific Rim. This second stage involved a relatively limited amount of new construction; instead, existing properties have been purchased and then resold to new investors. In the 1980s, Japanese investment began to diversify, particularly into the entertainment field and in other real estate investments.

For example, the Sony corporation purchased Columbia Pictures and the Matsushita conglomerate purchased MCA, which included Universal Studios, a major L.A. tourist venue. Korean and Taiwanese capital interests also invested overseas and the U.S. was one of the major investment destinations. Since 1989, three hotels in L.A., including the Westin Bonaventure, were sold to Taiwanese corporations. Korean capital interests recently purchased two hotels. The L.A. Omni (formerly known as the L.A. Hilton) in downtown L.A. was purchased in 1989. In 1991, an L.A. Hyatt Hotel was sold to wealthy Korean investors.

What stands out about L.A. is the rapid diversification of different sources of growth in foreign investment. Of the 24 major L.A.-area luxury hotels (excluding Santa Monica and Los Angeles Airport that are part of another HERE local's jurisdiction), 75% are owned by non-U.S. investors. In addition to Korean, Taiwanese, and Hong Kong investment, the Sultan of Brunei, who is worth an estimated $30 billion, owns the opulent Beverly Hills Hotel.

Investment in hotels is highly speculative. Real estate values rise and fall rapidly due to a number of economic factors. In addition to long-term players in the tourism industry, there are investors who seek to make a quick return on their investment through the buying and selling of property. This creates rapid swings in property values with boom-and-bust cycles becoming a common occurrence. The dizzying pace of property transference is exemplified by the following two examples.

The Bonaventure Hotel was built in 1977 for $110 million. In 1989, it was offered for $290 million to potential Japanese investors during the last Japanese buying binge of U.S. real estate. In 1994, the original owner went into bankruptcy due to a collapse in the domestic commercial real estate market during the 1990-1992 recession. The hotel recently sold for $50 million to a Taiwan-based company (interview with HERE researcher). The Bel Air Hotel was sold in 1995 for a reported $50 million, less than one-half of what it was sold for in the late 1980s.

The boom-and-bust cycle of real estate speculation in L.A.'s hotel industry cannot be explained solely by the local context of the real estate market. Most investment decisions regarding a particular property take place at the global level by international speculators. Investment decisions may be influenced by a variety of factors. Aoyama (1990) examined the reasons for Japanese investment in the L.A. real estate market and found that the limited availability of real estate property in Japan creates steep land prices and is very rarely sold.

Investment in real estate overseas is motivated by differences in return on investment; for example, in Japan the return on equity investment is between two per cent and four per cent. In the U.S. during the 1980s, however, return on equity was between five per cent and eight per cent on real estate properties (Ibid.). Japanese capital left the country due to the lack of investment opportunities and was pulled toward the higher yields of L.A. properties. An additional pull factor from L.A. is that there is a strong presence of Japanese manufacturing and banking sectors that are based in Southern California.

At the local level, commercial real estate interests play an important intermediary role. They assist global capital in the complicated process of buying and selling hotels as well as other properties. Their clients are primarily international investors. Ownership in the L.A. hotel industry is primarily based overseas. The hotel management companies, on the other hand, have historically been based in the U.S. This group includes well-known corporations such as Hilton, Westin, and Marriott. This pattern of ownership and management is changing rapidly.

There is a blurring of any clear pattern in the globalized hotel industry. It is common to fin l a U.S.-based management company operating a hotel for a partnership of foreign investors that is financed by a Japanese lending institution. Determining ownership and accountability has become increasingly difficult. Many companies use offshore dummy corporations located in corporate tax-free places like the Grand Cayman Islands to conceal investments and profits.

Management, financing, and ownership are integral components of the increasingly diffuse global hotel and tourism industries. Generally, foreign owners tend to stand aloof from the local area and their involvement with the daily operations of their U.S. investments is minimal. How has the growth of foreign ownership affected the lives of tourism workers?

Tourism Profits from Immigrant Labour

Coupled with the rapid investment of international capital in the L.A. hotel-tourism industry, there has been a corresponding growth in immigrant labour. In 1960, 35 years ago, the population of L.A. County was 85% white. By 1990, Latinos comprised 37.8%, African Americans 11.2%, and Asian 10.8% of the population. This dramatic demographic change was spurred on by the loosening of immigration restrictions in the 1965 Immigration Act, to accommodate the needs of capital for inexpensive low- and high-skilled labour from the developing world. L.A. became a magnet for immigrants from Asia and Latin America, including a massive influx of workers from Mexico seeking jobs and a more economically secure way of life, and from Central Americans fleeing from war and deteriorating economic conditions in their own countries. By the 1980s, Latino and Asian immigrant workers had become the dominant sector in the local work force in the service and light manufacturing industries.

As a result of the economic and political calamities in Latin America, coupled with the relaxation of immigration restrictions, millions of young Latino/a workers have moved north to work in L.A.'s restructured economy. Unlike some of the older highly industrialized cities where high rates of poverty are associated with joblessness, in Latino and low-income Asian communities in L.A., poverty is related to the quality of employment. Labour-force participation rates are relatively high, as demand has been consistently heavy for low-wage workers, but poverty rates are also extremely high in immigrant communities, with 75% of the poor in L.A. spending half their income on rent.

The restructuring of L.A. with low-wage immigrant labour has meant increased profits for the corporate community, but limited economic mobility for the service workers who keep the system functioning day to day. The restructuring process helps create the conditions for the widening gap of poverty in L.A. The effect of labour migration is illustrated by an examination of the tourism industry. In the 1980s, Latino immigrants became the largest segment of the tourism industry in L.A. Foreign-born room cleaners rose from 34% to 62% of all cleaners in the hotel industry between 1980 and 1990.

The hotel industry is composed of large numbers of first-generation immigrants, with the ethnic composition being 70% Latino, 10% Asian and Pacific Islander, 10% African American, and 10% white. Besides the high percentage of immigrant workers, another characteristic of the L.A. tourism industry is that wage levels are extremely low. Wage levels among room cleaners and dishwashers are barely above the minimum wage in nonunion places. What these low wages translate into is large numbers of workers being forced to live in poor working-class communities, including Pico Union, East Hollywood, East L.A., and South L.A., which surround downtown. Many hotel workers, unable to afford high rents, are forced to share apartments with other families. Numerous hotel workers work two and three jobs at the same time, juggling work and family responsibilities.

The lack of medical benefits also forces nonunionized workers to utilize the county public health-care system. Currently, there are over two million uninsured Angelenos who use the public hospitals. This creates an even greater strain on the county hospitals that are overflowing with an unemployed, underemployed, and low-wage work force that can't afford private health care.

The increase in the prevalence of low wages, inadequate health care, and poor living conditions for low-wage Latino workers corresponds to the expansion of the tourism industry. International capital, seeking to maximize return on investment, has increased the inequalities in the tourism industry by hiring low-wage Latino labour and added to the social and economic inequalities in L.A.

Support for Hotel-Tourism Growth

In addition to global capital investment and labour migration, local government in L.A. represents the third component in the growth of the hotel-tourism industry. In recent years, various scholars have debated the role of local government in the economic development of cities. Peterson (1981) argues that cities are constrained by fiscal crises and have limited influence in the investment decisions of capital.

The "unitary" interest of cities is to seek and attract capital investment. In contrast, I argue that local politics matter in economic development decisions. Local politicians and officials do influence the investment decision-making of corporate interests through the use of public funds to encourage capital investment. Regalado (1992) discussed how local government actors, acting on behalf of corporate interests, played an important role in securing investment in downtown development.

The efforts of local government officials to assist corporate investment do not go unrewarded. L.A. Mayor Tom Bradley, for example, received $100,000 in campaign contributions from Shuwa Investment Company, after Shuwa purchased the Arco Plaza in downtown L.A. in 1986. The cozy relationship between corporate interests and local politicians suggests that the city government of L.A. has not been a neutral observer in the process of the internationalization of the hotel-tourism industry. Local political leaders helped shape the flow of public capital. They provided subsidies and tax incentives to entice economic development, particularly international corporate capital, to transform L.A. into a global city.

Besides facilitating urban real estate development, local political leaders have sought to increase the financial resources of the city. Property, sales, and corporate taxes pay for the costs of running the city and by attracting new investments they boost revenue sources. For example, the Los Angeles Community Redevelopment Agency (CRA), using federal money, forced the removal of local residents in downtown L.A. and then provided land at below market prices to developers.

Wealthy investors then purchased the land, and built hotels and offices, as well as fancy condominiums for white-collar professionals. The L.A. CRA used tax-increment financing to gain control of property tax revenues that otherwise would be split with other governmental agencies. L.A. became a global city because local governmental officials were active in the growth coalitions' efforts.

In the 1980s, there was a rapid increase in property values in California. This inflationary trend was spurred on by wildly speculative purchases by domestic and international investment interests. Downtown L.A., designated as a redevelopment area, had overinflated property prices. These properties continue to bring the L.A. CRA hundreds of millions of dollars annually in tax increment revenues that were used to purchase additional land and properties. In the 1980s, after years of community pressure, some of the tax-increment revenues began to be used to build low-cost housing in conjunction with nonprofit community organizations or private investors.

An important facet of the tourism and travel business is the revenues generated by convention business and major events. The significance of local context is critical for the tourism industry, which sells images and specific locations as places of consumption. In the 1980s, the city of L.A. embarked on a costly effort to lure large conventions to the city by expanding the L.A. Convention Centre. Conventions of large groups of businesses and trade associations produce multibillion dollar business for cities. Cities compete with each other to attract the most lucrative conventions.

The biggest conventions and events can generate tens of millions in revenues in a matter of days. For example, the 1993 Super Bowl, held at the Rose Bowl in Pasadena, a suburb of L.A., generated over $100 million dollars for the region in a matter of days. Also, the World Cup Soccer Finals held in L.A. in 1994 generated one billion dollars in revenues along with one million visitors to the L.A. area. In addition, the City of Los Angeles economically benefits from conventions in that it charges a 14% room tax on each hotel room rented, which generates $67 million dollars a year in revenues.

In 1983, in the midst of a tourism and business traveller boom, L.A. city officials decided to expand the existing convention centre. A study, commissioned by the city, anticipated an indefinite increase in hotel occupancy rates of six per cent per year. Over the next several years, $500 million dollars in city bonds were sold to fund construction of the expansion. Between 1987 and 1994, hotel occupancy rates fell 10% (from 71 to 62%) as recession, the L.A. riots, rising crime, and natural disasters combined to push the L.A. hotel industry into a near financial crisis. Due to construction delays, the convention centre opening was pushed back to 1994.

Major conventions need four to five years lead time to book their conventions. Many of the convention groups chose other locations to hold their events due to the uncertainties of the convention centre completion date and L.A.'s image problem. The convention centre is now severely underbooked through 1998.

L.A.'s convention centre is in stiff competition with Anaheim, San Diego, San Francisco, and Las Vegas for business. All of these cities have invested heavily in their tourist convention facilities. Meanwhile, L.A. taxpayers will spend 47 million dollars per year, for the next 30 years, to pay off the costs of constructing the convention centre expansion. In summary, the L.A. city government not only financially assisted the efforts of private capital in the economic development of L.A., it was also proactive in generating public capital and in expanding the convention centre so that the city could compete as a tourist and business destination.

The next will critically examine the strategic thinking and actions of HERE Local 11 to affect the globalization of the hotel-tourism industry. The history and background of HERE Local 11 are analyzed and then a theory of social movement unionism will be applied to the practice of Local 11 to observe the applicability of this theory to a contemporary U.S.-based union.

HERE Local 11 is a local of the International HERE Union. The 100-year-old international union has numerous locals throughout the U.S., Puerto Rico, and Canada. Local 11 was formed after a merger of several craft locals following World War II. During L.A.'s rise into a financial and global headquarters city, Local 11 was run for 23 years by officials unwilling to confront the rapid changes in the hotel-tourism industry and organize the membership to win the best possible contracts.

Instead, a handful of white males controlled the local. As the demographics of the work force changed to predominantly Latino workers, they demanded bilingual materials and translation. The local leaders prevented meetings from being translated into Spanish and other languages necessary for the full participation of workers. The workers ultimately sued their own union for discrimination for refusing to translate meetings into Spanish.

As new hotels were built in downtown L.A., the union assumed that the new hotels would automatically sign up with the union. Before 1970, all the major hotels in L.A. were union houses. The New Otani Hotel was the first luxury hotel to resist efforts at unionization in downtown L.A. and, in the 1980s, the Sheraton Grande also opened nonunion. In both cases, HERE failed to mount an effective response to the growth of nonunion hotel construction. Without a strong union presence, hotel owners felt little pressure to negotiate for improved wages and benefits during the economic uncertainties of the 1970s and 1980s.

As noted earlier, a key aspect of the local context is that L.A. has become a "Third World city" with an almost unlimited immigrant labour supply of Latino and Asian workers. Hotel management used the threat of firing workers and replacing them overnight with others to keep immigrant workers from organizing their hotels. Furthermore, management employed sophisticated union-busting tactics to further intimidate and fire union activists.

Hotel owners also took advantage of a situation where the union was weak and did not organize its membership. The union relied on collaboration with owners rather than on militant confrontation in their approach to negotiations. Since hotel contracts are negotiated at the local level, not at the national level, the ability to achieve a good contract is based on the local conditions. The local conditions are determined primarily by the strength of the local union's power vis-a-vis the hotel industry. By the late 1980s, less than 50% of the hotel industry was organized. HERE Local 11 was lagging far behind the wages and benefits of hotel workers in other cities.

The combination of a long history of anti-union efforts by private companies, the internationalization of the tourism industry, and the lack of local union strength has resulted in the L.A. area in the lowest wages paid to hotel-tourism workers relative to tourism workers in other large urban and tourist centres on the West Coast. For example, L.A. housekeepers averaged $4.87 per hour in 1990 and $7.27 in 1996, whereas unionized San Francisco housekeepers were paid $8.02 in 1990 per hour, and $12 in 1996. The key to understanding these large wage differentials in cities similar in other respects is the beneficial effects of unionization on the labour markets.

Many of the same management companies who operate hotels in L.A. also operate hotels in other cities. What is different about San Francisco, Las Vegas, New York, and Hawaii is that the majority of major hotels in those cities are unionized. Militant strikes by various locals of HERE have beaten back efforts to force their salaries downward. HERE conducted strikes in San Francisco in 1981, Las Vegas in 1987, and Hawaii in 1992. Although the union did not win all its demands, they did effectively disrupt business during their strikes and won many of their demands.

Rank-and-file workers, outraged at the weak contracts and poor wages, forced the removal of the HERE Local 11 leadership in 1987. In the past eight years, the local has been revitalized under a new local leadership composed of veteran rank-and-file leaders, primarily Latino immigrants. The local is led by President Maria Elena Durazo, the first Chicana to lead a HERE local. The here international union has also provided strong support to help rebuild the local.

They have provided experienced organizers to assist staff members. The local has consciously promoted shop floor leaders to rebuild the local. This is critical since Local 11 saw its membership plummet from over 20,000 in the 1970s to 8,000 by 1995. The combination of a unified membership, a strong, empowering local leadership, and a supportive international union is viewed as an antidote to stop the union's decline and to rebuild it into a strong union.

For the union, it has successfully evolved from a typical "business union" that maintained a cozy relationship with hotel and tourist attraction operators to a union that has successfully challenged major international tourist corporations. This transformation on the part of HERE is a multifaceted process brought about by international economic restructuring and rapid labour migration that required a change in the organizing philosophy by the union.

HERE envisions itself as a movement for economic and social justice. This perspective is radically different from traditional unions that bargain solely for the economic benefits of their members. Local 11's vision expands the definition of a union to what Lambert and Webster (1988) call social movement unionism. This form of unionism "attempts to link production to wider political issues. It is a form of union organization that facilitates an active engagement in factory-based, production politics and in community and state power issues."

This approach is similar to some autonomous trade unions in the developing world that are radical agents for social change. HERE is at the leading edge of U.S.-based unions that are attempting to organize entire industries of workers by building movements for justice that combine sophisticated corporate research, militant confrontational tactics, and the building of solidarity with other social movements.

An example of the union's approach of building local community support as a key component of their organizing efforts was a 10-month boycott campaign against the Koreana Hotel. This hotel was purchased by a wealthy family from Korea in late 1991 and the 180 union workers were fired on

New Year's Eve. The hotel then reopened after hiring an almost completely new work force at reduced wages and benefits. The union launched a community campaign to boycott the hotel.

The union was able to build support among a diverse cross-section of Angelenos, including several L.A. city council members, who actively supported the boycott and demanded that foreign companies conducting business in L.A. respect the rights of workers. Many Korean community members and the Asian Pacific Islander community in Southern California also pledged not to use the hotel for events and meetings. Community support was backed by a daily picket and boycott of the hotel by the fired workers. Numerous demonstrations culminated in a militant sit-in at the Korean Consulate.

Finally, after 10 months the new owners were forced to sign a contract with HERE. Following in the wake of the 1992 civil unrest in Los Angeles, Korean capital was particularly vulnerable to negative publicity regarding their labour practices toward primarily low-wage Latino immigrants. Faced with a determined union conducting dally picketing outside the hotel, the hotel's owners finally agreed to hire back the fired workers and sign a union contract.

Local 11 has also utilized corporate campaigns and boycotts to pressure international corporations to negotiate with the union. Currently, Local 11 is supporting the three-year effort of workers to unionize at the New Otani Hotel. New Otani is owned by the Kajima Corporation, the second-largest construction company in the world. Given the importance of building support among the large Asian Pacific communities in Los Angeles and in the host countries of corporations, HERE and Asian community activists have jointly formed the New Otani Hotel Workers Support Committee.

Through this support committee, the large Japanese community in Los Angeles, along with other Asian Pacific communities, has become directly involved in the unionization campaign. Local Asian Pacific American community organizations are actively encouraging their respective ethnic constituencies to boycott the hotel for refusing to recognize Local 11.

Local 11 has also made international contacts with minority-group rights activists in Japan. These Japanese activists are attempting to force Kajima to pay claims made by elderly Chinese workers who were brought against their will to Japan during World War II as slave laborers. Many of these workers were tortured and murdered. The issue of Kajima's war crimes and its contemporary anti-worker policies in United States has generated media attention in Japan. Kajima has also been charged with bribing Japanese government officials to secure contracts. Worker and union-based labour internationalism across national boundaries will bring more pressure on the hotel ownership to negotiate with Local 11. Also, international labour solidarity has been a critical component of other social movement unions.

In contrast to a traditional union that presents itself as a business with a product to sell, HERE Local 11 has a different vision of how it presents itself in organizing workers. The union's message to workers is to join a movement to organize the entire hotel-tourism industry. The goal is to make the city a place where workers are empowered in all facets of their lives on the job and in the community. In the aftermath of the L.A. uprisings in 1992, Local 11 believes there is one way to prevent future disturbances: to improve the lives of the working poor and unemployed youth in the city.

To make L.A. a place where tourists and business travellers will want to come will require developing livable wages and benefits for the workers who make the economy run. HERE thus views their current campaign as closely fled to rebuilding L.A. into a multicultural centre for commerce and cultural exchange.

Local 11's vision is that given the right set of circumstances, working people will act to improve their conditions of racial and class inequality. Using a combination of shared Latino consciousness arising out of a common mistreatment as Latino immigrants and a class inequality paradigm, the union is training a generation of experienced rank-and-file leaders in the hotel and tourism industry to fight for their rights. As a solid majority of hotels citywide become union, the HERE union can demand that the hotel owners citywide increase wages and benefits to levels similar to other unionized cities on the West Coast.

The dynamic growth of tourism has become a new form of capital accumulation and exploitation in L.A.'s restructured economy. In the 1960s and 1970s, as heavy manufacturing closed down or fled the area in pursuit of greater profits elsewhere, an economy of light manufacturing and service industries emerged in the L.A. region. During the same time, a massive migration of workers, drawn from Asia and Latin America, filled the new jobs created in L.A.'s growing service economy.

Collaborative efforts by private and public interests were employed to transform L.A. into an international business/ tourist destination and to generate new sources of revenues. A critical part of this joint process was the construction, by civic leaders and the hotel-tourism industry, of a sanitized image of L.A. of movie stars, amusement parks, and sunny beaches. However, this imagery is only a partial cultural and social interpretation of L.A.

In reality, there is a stark duality of immense poverty in the midst of great wealth in L.A., which is also reflected in the hotel-tourism industry. Beyond the manufactured "fantasyland" image of L.A., there is the actuality of hundreds of thousands of new immigrant workers in the tourism industry who labour for subsistence wages and face extreme economic hardships.

These two faces of tourism pose a paradox. Tourism is needed to generate revenues for the tourism industry and local government, yet the growth of tourism has not substantively benefited the workers whose labour creates the wealth in the industry. Instead, a widening gap of poverty has been created between the international corporate ownership and the new immigrant work force in the tourism industry. To reduce the growing inequality, unions such as HERE Local 11 are striving to build social movement unionism.

They are demanding that the tourism industry, politicians, and local government institutions contribute to resolving the basic problems facing L.A.'s working poor. They are dedicated to transforming not only the conditions of the tourism industry, but also their own identity from individual immigrants into a social movement of workers of colour with the power and organization to make dramatic social and structural change at the local level.

Chapter 5

Globalization in the Hotel and Catering Sector

GLOBALIZATION AND CATERING

The issues of globalization, employment and human resources development in the hotel, catering and tourism sector are linked to the strategic objectives of the ILO that were decided at the International Labour Conference in June 1999: to promote and realize fundamental principles and rights at work; to create greater opportunities for women and men to secure decent employment and income; to enhance the coverage and effectiveness of social protection for all; and to strengthen tripartism and social dialogue. The report points to recent developments in the hotel, catering and tourism sector and highlights factors driving the internationalization of tourists' travel and of tourism services, including information technologies, as welt as the internationalization or hotel and tourism enterprises.

Without neglecting the huge subsector of small and medium-sized enterprises, it describes typical features related to the composition of the labour force and to working conditions. It raises questions concerning the difficulties faced by the sector in attracting and retaining skilled workers and in enhancing the skills of newcomers to the labour market in order to stabilize the sector's labour force, while increasing the productivity of enterprises and the quality of services. Particular emphasis is put on new forms of management entailing new skills requirements, with a general tendency towards increased worker responsibility in an environment of flat hierarchies, multi-skilling and teamwork.

As to social dialogue in this sector, a description is provided of certain institutions, achievements and shortcomings in this respect, but in a way that also points to opportunities for increasing its scope and effectiveness. The causal relationships between globalization, employment and human resources development are examined on the basis of the information available, and other factors such as advances in technology and training, and changes in tourism demand are also highlighted.

Hard data on the hotel, catering and tourism sector are not easy to come by as they are rarely singled out from the services sector in general. Data specifically on tourism depend on a form of accounting that covers a broad range of economic activities geared towards tourist consumption. Only a few countries can provide systematically collected data on tourism and little attention is given to labour issues. The report draws on a wide variety of sources for information, including government institutions, intergovernmental organizations, trade unions, employers' organizations, companies, international non-governmental organizations, and individual scholars. The sources used are certainly not exhaustive but are probably fairly representative.

SOCIAL RESOURCES

Small-business ownership among persons of Asian ancestry grew quite rapidly in the U.S. during the 1980s. Gross revenues of Asian-owned small businesses, according to the Census Bureau, nearly tripled from 1982 to 1987, and the number of active firms grew from 187,691 to 355,331 – an 89.3% increase. Rapid Asian business growth has been immigrant driven: of the Asian small businesses operating nationwide in 1987 that were started since 1979, nearly 80% of them were immigrant owned.

This study examines the performance of recently formed Asian immigrant-owned small businesses, focusing upon owner characteristics as well as firm traits; survival of firms operating in 1987 is traced through 1991. Recent studies suggest that Asian immigrant entrepreneurs have achieved success operating in low-growth or declining industry sectors; inner city areas have been the site of considerable business activity and minority clienteles have often been the targeted customer base. Waldinger found extensive firm development and growth among Chinese immigrants in a declining industry segment -garment manufacturing in New York City. Bonacich and Light report that Korean-owned businesses in Los Angeles have established a major presence in low-income Latino and African American communities, particularly in smallscale retailing.

Stressing the relevance of cultural factors, Waldinger, Light, Bonacich, and others have treated immigrant firm ownership and operation as a group phenomenon, heavily dependent upon social resources available from group support networks. This view is contrasted to the perspective that owner "class" resources – human capital and financial capital investments – explain smallbusiness behaviour.

Recent studies of minority entrepreneurship have often focused upon immigrants operating businesses in one specific location – Koreans in Los Angeles or Chinese in New York. Among recent Korean immigrants, Bonacich and Light note the effective use of family resources such as unpaid labour to develop successful small businesses (1988). These immigrant entrepreneurs, however, also tend to be highly educated persons with white-collar work experience, and many of them possess substantial personal wealth.

Qualitative studies of immigrant entrepreneurs operating at one geographic location are often provocative and interesting, yet generalization of the resultant findings is difficult because these studies rarely use sophisticated statistical methodology to sort out and establish cause-and-effect relationships between individual or group traits and business performance. Data sources such as the Census Bureau's Characteristics of Business Owners (CBO) data base

– examined in this study -provide evidence that is not consistent with specific social resources explanations of minority business behaviour.

An alternative explanation of Asian immigrant business patterns, put forth in this study, stresses education, skills, and financial capital resources. The success and survival patterns of Asianowned firms, this study concludes, are shaped by the very substantial investments of financial capital and the impressive educational credentials of the business owners.

Self-Employment Patterns

The focus of this study is upon a nationwide sample of firms formed by Asian immigrants over the 1979-87 period. Firms operating nationwide are owned by Asian immigrants; this sample is representative of the relevant universe of firms entered since 1979 that filed small-business income tax returns in 1987. Firms owned by nonminorities constitute the small-business norm in this country, in the sense that such firms account for over 90% of the small-firm universe by number and 95% by total sales. A representative sample of nonminority-owned firms is presented as a comparison group.

Businesses formed between 1979 and 1987 by Asian immigrants and nonminorities and highlights underlying hypothesized causes of Asian business success. First, we see that 57.8% of the Asian entrepreneurs of Asian business success. First, we see that 57.8% of the Asian entrepreneurs were college graduates (bachelor's degree holders), versus 37.5% of the nonminority business owners. Professional services – the field in which both owner educational attainment and average self-employment remuneration are highest – accounted for 11.5% of the Asian business start-ups, versus 8.7% of the nonminority firm formations.

Second, the average financial capital investment at the point of business start-up was $53,562 among the Asian immigrants, versus $31,678 for nonminority firms. Owner equity investment – derived almost entirely from household wealth holdings – averaged $26,345 among the Asian immigrant business entrants, 88.0% higher than the corresponding nonminority figure of $14,014. Bates and Dunham report that self-employment entry is very strongly and positively associated with possession of household net worth exceeding $100,000. Further, a higher proportion of Asian households nationwide were in the $100,000 plus household net worth category than nonminorities.

Theories of entrepreneurship developed by sociologists have been rooted in their efforts to explain the success of Asian immigrants who pursue self-employment. The entrepreneur is seen as a member of supportive kinship, peer, and community subgroups. These networks, in turn, assist in the creation and successful operation of firms by providing such social capital as sources of customers, loyal employees, and financing.

What precise forms do these social resources take and how do they assist business operation? Social capital in the form of a captive market, according to Light (1972), derives from the culturally based tastes of ethnic minorities that can only be served by co-ethnic businesses. Ethnic businesses offer co-ethnics the comfort and security of conducting transactions in their own language. Also, the information costs in ascertaining consumer preferences among co-ethnics are lower for ethnic entrepreneurs than they are for potential competitors from the "outside".

Of the various forms of social capital associated with immigrant entrepreneurs, the protected market concept has been the most controversial. The very low incomes of most recent immigrants constrain the attractiveness of this protected market. The immigrant business that limits itself to the ethnic market sharply reduces its growth potential. Fratoe reports, for example, that Asians are much less likely to sell to a minority clientele than black- or Latino-owned firms (1988).

Yet reliance upon co-ethnic markets may nonetheless be pragmatic during early stages of firm development, providing an operational base from which later expansion can begin. The co-ethnic market may support immigrant entrepreneurs "in assembling a skilled labour force and gaining efficiency and expertise, qualities that are gradually allowing them to edge out into the broader market".

The Asian immigrant entrepreneurs differ systematically regarding sales, profitability, owner financial investment, and discontinuance rates when they are divided into two groups: those serving a clientele that is 50% or more minority, versus those whose clientele is either racially diverse or largely nonminority. It is the very youngest among immigrantowned businesses that appear to benefit most from serving clients in the broader, largely nonminority marketplace.

Among those in business for two years or less, the Asian firms catering to a predominantly minority clientele are twice as likely to discontinue operations by 1991; they are smaller, less profitable, and attract lower owner financial investments than cohort firms competing in the broader economy. Among the firms that have been in operation from three to eight years, survival rates and mean sales levels are quite similar among the minority clientele and the broader market subgroups of Asian immigrant-owned businesses.

Thus, the hypothesis that immigrant firms may benefit from initial avoidance of the broader, largely nonminority marketÐ place is completely inconsistent with our evidence. Note, however, that the very young Asian immigrant firms catering to a minority clientele are weaker in the sense of being run by owners who are, on average, less educated, and financial investment levels are quite low ($35,232) relative to the broader economy firms ($81,926). This issue is investigated econometrically later in the study. Finally, an alternative definition of what constitutes a "predominantly minority clientele" was investigated by examining firms in which the clientele was 75% or more minority; results of this exercise were highly consistent with the findings.

One problem with using data as a test of the protected markets thesis is the fact that Korean merchants often specialize in selling nonethnic products in minority markets. While Korean firms tend to be broadly dispersed geographically – often in Latino or African American neighbourhoods – the concept of protected markets envisions ethnic businesses located in neighbourhoods where co-ethnics are concentrated. As newly arrived immigrants cluster together spatially for mutual support, they establish a critical mass of customers needed to support the businesses that cater to their distinctive ethnic tastes.

For example, Chinatown in Manhattan was centreed in four contiguous tracts in 1980 with populations more than one-half Chinese. This concentrated population "made Chinatown a hotbed of ethnic commerce, both large and small". Agglomeration economics may occur when ethnic firms proliferate and the size and diversity of the ethnic marketplace attracts additional customers. Thus Chinatown becomes a regional ethnic shopping centre.

The niche attracting Korean merchants to minority clienteles has often differed from the above Chinatown portrait. The Korean population of Atlanta, for example, is too small to support an ethnic Korean small-business enclave: almost 60% of Korean firms in 1982 were found in the inner city or in areas that were at least 50% black. According to Min, Korean business owners in Atlanta said that they would have much more difficulty competing in white areas than in black neighbourhoods. The attraction of black communities was the reduced competition stemming from the paucity of mainstream business competitors.

Yoon reports that Koreans often prefer to locate their businesses in black residential areas of Chicago because of lower discrimination and hostility from local residents, in comparison to white neighbourhoods. Moreover, store rentals in black communities are less costly than in white areas and a limited knowledge of English is often sufficient. "Besides the light requirements for capital and managerial skills, the absence of competition from local black businesses lowers barriers to entry in black areas".

In Los Angeles, half of the Korean businesses located outside of the Korean enclave were concentrated in the black and Latino areas of the county. Thus, catering to a minority clientele – while possibly beneficial for both Korean and Chinese businesses – entails serving co-ethnics relatively more frequently for Chinese merchants, less so for Koreans. Yet recalculations – first, excluding Koreans and, secondly, including Chinese only – do not alter the finding that very young Asian immigrant firms (and firm subgroups) are smaller, less profitable, and more prone to failure when they serve a clientele that is predominantly minority. Solely among Chinese, for example, the survival rate through 1991 of firms operating in 1987 was 78.3% among those catering to a minority clientele versus 88.7% among those operating in the broader economy.

Waldinger argues that social capital in the form of loyal, low cost co-ethnic employees may explain why self-employment is advantageous to Asian immigrants (1986). New arrivals often seek employment in an immigrant firm where they can work in a familiar environment with others who know their language. Bonacich and Light reported that Los Angeles Korean-owned businesses – operating often in low-income, nonwhite neighbourhoods – were very effective at generating jobs for co-ethnics: "about 62% of Koreans found employment in the ethnic economy".

Ethnicity provides a common ground on which workplace rules are negotiated. "Authority can be secured on the basis of personal loyalties and ethnic allegiance.". The relevance of this form of social capital may be constrained, however, by Fratoe's finding that Asian small businesses are considerably less reliant upon minority employees than blacks and Latinos (1988). Using the data examined in this study, Bates and Dunham found that Asian immigrantowned firms hire minorities predominantly, but less so than African-American employers.

Nevertheless, the CBO data base cannot be used to test Waldinger's hypothesis on the low-cost, co-ethnic labour force directly, because minorities are not identified by ethnicity, but rather by "minority" and "nonminority" employee groupings.

Family members may be another possible source of cheap, reliable labour for Asian immigrant firms. Small-business owners face the possibility that their employees will shirk on the job. Married business owners can diminish this risk by hiring their spouses, since spouses presumably have identical incentives -maximization of family income. Borjas reports that married Asian immigrants are more likely to pursue self-employment than their unmarried Asian cohorts.

Yet the evidence on this point is mixed. Boyd uses six different measures of family and extended family in logistic regressions explaining Asian involvement in self-employment: five of the six measures were insignificant statistically as predictors of self-employment among Asians in the U.S. Chan and Cheung (1985) report that most Chinese-owned firms in Toronto had no family members as employees. Impact of labour sources as well as minority clientele, owner educational background, financial investment in the firm, and other factors upon firm survival and discontinuance are further investigated below.

Small-Business Longevity

Over the period from 1987 to 1991, 18.5% of the Asian immigrant firms described discontinued operations. Firms sold to a new owner, merged, or otherwise altered are not counted as discontinued if they continued to operate. Logistic regression equations are estimated in this section to explain small-business longevity. Independent variables used to explain longevity among Asian immigrant firms include measures of owner characteristics, firm traits, and social capital proxies. While longevity is the primary business viability measure under consideration, profitability is analyzed later in this study to test for the consistency (robustness) of the observed relationships between the explanatory variables and firm viability.

Based upon the findings of past econometric studies explaining small business longevity, greater owner investments of human and financial capital are expected to be related positively to the survival chances of Asian immigrant owned small business. Quality of owner human capital is measured by two variables, level of formal education and presence of managerial experience prior to small-business entry. Labour input quantity is measured by owner hours spent working in the business, as well as marital status and number of paid employees.

Married persons living with their spouses are expected to benefit from the availability of family labour, which potentially increases labour input quantity. Applicable demographic traits include owner age and gender. Greater owner age, a broad proxy for work experience, is expected to benefit firms until diminishing effort associated with old age sets in. To test the social capital hypotheses examined earlier in this study, the minority composition of the firm's clientele is introduced as a contributory factor, and labour force composition is investigated as a longevity determinant for employer firms.

Binary variables identifying major Asian ethnic groups are introduced into the log it analysis of firm longevity as control variables. An owner ethnicity frequency distribution reveals that three groups – Chinese, Korean, and Asian Indian – dominate the Asian immigrant entrepreneur sample described previously:

Ethnicity	*Per cent*
Chinese	26.7
Korean	22.6
Indian	20.5
Vietnamese	9.8
Filipino	8.5
All other	11.9

Finally, an agglomeration variable is introduced to test for possible impacts on firm longevity of the intense clustering of Asian immigrant businesses in several large metropolitan areas. Nearly 43% of the Asian immigrant firms analyzed in this study operate in either (1) the Los Angeles county, Orange country megalopolis, (2) the New York City metropolitan area, or (3) the San Francisco Bay region (including Oakland, San Jose, San Francisco, and surrounding suburbs).

Large co-ethnic Asian populations reside in each of these three areas. Yoon (1991) argues that the presence of complementary suppliers owned by coethnics facilitates successful business operation, providing "extended credit terms, lower prices, and easy access to information". A downside to concentration in geographic areas such as Los Angeles and New York is the prevalence of severe intraethnic competition: "eighty per cent of respondents (all Koreans) refer to Koreans as their primary business competitors".

The dependent variable in each of the logistic regression exercises is whether or not the business that was operating in 1987 is still functioning in late 1991. Businesses still operating are considered active firms; those that have closed down are considered discontinued. Logistic regression equations delineating active from discontinued businesses, first, for Asian immigrant firms that were entered (started) in 1986 and 1987 only.

The very high discontinuance rates of these young firms, particularly among those serving minority clienteles, relative to the businesses started in the 1979-85 period. Examination of the 1986 and 1987 entrant subsample permits further consideration of the hypothesis that very young Asian immigrant firms may benefit initially from operating in a minority market niche. Secondly, the employers only group of firms is analyzed in the impact of labour force minority composition on firm survival, and secondarily, to analyze the stability of the explanatory variable regression coefficients when larger small businesses only (the employer subset) are examined.

The firm sample size for all Asian immigrant firms formed in the 1979-87 period is 4,208 in the logit analysis; the sample size drops sharply to 2,623 for employers only, due to the zero employee firm deletion. Finally, all 4,208 Asian immigrant firm observations are analyzed to provide a context for interpreting how very young firms and employers only may differ from the broader Asian immigrant business universe.

In analyses of Asian immigrant firms that were operating in 1987, positive coefficient values are associated with firms still operating in 1991, and vice versa. Five types of explanatory variables are particularly strong for explaining survival and discontinuance patterns for the Asian immigrant firms started up since 1979. The surviving firms that are active in 1991 are disproportionately those started with the larger investments of financial capital, the older firms, those serving a clientele that is not predominantly minority, and those headed by owners who have attended college.

Firms using greater labour input – both the input of the owner as well as the number of employees – finally, were more likely to survive, particularly in comparison to the zero employee firms and those headed by owners working only part-time in self-employment. The very youngest firms – those started in 1986 and 1987 – were most vulnerable to discontinuance, which is consistent with past findings. The strong result that the better capitalized firms at start-up are more likely to stay active, other factors constant, is also highly consistent with past findings.

Thus, the same factors found to explain firm longevity among small businesses generally are important to explaining survival among Asian immigrant firms. Among the very youngest Asian immigrant-owned firms (those started in 1986 or 1987), the negative impact of serving a minority clientele was most pronounced. While the young firms serving a clientele of over 50% minority customers were generally those started with lower financial investments and using fewer employees, other factors constant, that Asian immigrant firms serving a predominantly minority clientele are much more likely to go out of business than cohort firms that operate in the broader marketplace.

This finding is inconsistent with both the Light/Waldinger hypothesis regarding the benefits of serving co-ethnics and the Min/Yoon hypothesis that low income minority clienteles generally offer attractive operating environments to Asian immigrant firms due to ease of firm entry and paucity of competition.

In the employer subset of firms, those having a high percentage of minority employees were more likely to remain active firms, but this relationship was not statistically significant at conventional significance levels. A More precise explanatory variable capable of identifying the percentage of co-ethnic (as opposed to minority) employees might have produced a different empirical result supporting the hypothesis concerning the beneficial impacts of a co-ethnic workforce. But this very hypothesis – if valid – certainly suggests that minority employees at Asian immigrant firms would be overwhelmingly co-ethnics.

Why would minorities other than co-ethnics be employed by Asian immigrant firms in significant numbers if, indeed, co-ethnics were in fact loyal, low-cost workers? Among the immigrant entrepreneurs under consideration, the Asian Indian subgroup relies least on minority employees and clients, while the Vietnamese rely most heavily. The Asian Indian firms as a group have the lowest rates of discontinuance; the Vietnamese, in contrast, have the highest firm closure rates among the Asian subgroups.

Thus, use of social resources may be negatively associated with firm survival patterns. A more likely explanation for survival rate differentials among Asian immigrant ethnic groups is found in patterns of financial and human capital use. Among the Asian Indian- owned firms, for example, mean financial capital at start-up was $70,517, versus $27,812 among the Vietnamese.

In the context of the logistic regressions explaining firm survival, ethnic group, by itself, generally exhibited little explanatory power. While Koreans were somewhat more likely to see their firms discontinue, other factors constant, this relationship did not characterize the larger scale, employer group of firms. The agglomeration factor, finally, exhibited a consistently negative, although statistically insignificant relationship to firm survival patterns, suggesting that major concentrations of Asian immigrant-owned firms in the New York, Los Angeles, and San Francisco areas may simply mirror broader patterns of residential concentration.

The logistic regression exercises offer several other insights into the survival and discontinuance patterns among firms owned by Asian immigrants. Being married and living with one's spouse, first positively and then negatively (employers) related to firm survival, was statistically insignificant, suggesting that the access to family labour potentially available to married business owners may be of minor importance. Entry into self-employment by purchasing an existing (ongoing) firm is much more common among Asian immigrants than among their nonminority cohorts: 24.1% of the former and 17.7% of the latter bought ongoing firms.

Entry into self-employment by purchasing ongoing firms, other factors constant, is negatively associated with firm survival and this relationship is statistically significant among the larger scale employer firms. Purchasing an existing business is never easy: owners may "cook" the books to make things better than they are. Buyers are often naive, particularly if they have not been previously self-employed; people frequently end up buying a firm that is well on its way to failure.

Asian immigrant firms generally and the employer subset specifically were broadly similar overall, regarding traits that are associated with longevity. The well-capitalized, established firms headed by college-educated owners are the businesses that are more likely to be active in 1991, particularly when their clientele is not predominantly minority. The larger scale firms (measured by employment) and those whose owners work full-time in the business are the ones with the greater survival prospects. These same traits accurately predict small-business longevity among nonminority entrepreneurs.

Firm viability is a multidimensional phenomenon: small businesses that keep operating through time tend to be the larger scale, more profitable firms; high levels of profitability not only serve to motivate the present owner to remain self-employed: profitable operations also make small businesses potentially salable to new owners when the present owner chooses to retire or move on to other pursuits.

The logistic regression equations explain firm discontinuance and survival served as the basis for a complementary set of OLS regression exercises that analyzed the log of the dollar amount of before tax profits (dependent variable), using the same data and explanatory variables used. This reanalysis of the Asian immigrant groups of (1) all 1979-87 start-ups, (2) 1986, 1987 start-ups only, and (3) employers only – using the log of the dollar amount of 1987 before tax profits as the dependent variable – was conducted to test the robustness of the logistic regression findings.

Inherent difficulties in the analysis of small-business profitability are rooted in the reality of widely varying accounting conventions regarding depreciation methods, inventory valuation, and so forth. Dollar measures of profitability, therefore, are apt to possess much more randomness than the previously examined small-business dependent variable, longevity. In the CBO data base, furthermore, nonresponse problems on the initial survey questionnaires were greater for the question regarding owner estimates of before-tax profit amounts than they were for any other questionnaire item.

The OLS regression equations explaining profits for Asian immigrant-owned firms, nonetheless, produced clear-cut results that are broadly consistent with those previously reported logistic regression findings. The actual equations – not reported here – appear in a companion study. The portrait of the Asian immigrant businesses generating the higher profit volumes is one of owners working full-time in their firms, being highly educated, and being in business for four or more years. Relative to the findings of the firm longevity analysis discussed previously, the owner human capital variables emerge as consistently positive, statistically significant determinants of firm profits.

The fact that human capital measures such as owner education and managerial experience are more consistent determinants of firm profitability and more erratic determinants of longevity may be noteworthy. High rates of Asian immigrant business ownership coexist with a narrow industry base as well as annual sales and profits that are low, on average, relative to those reported by the dominant nonminority small-business sector.

Waldinger (1986), for example, observes that Asian immigrants pursue self-employment less as a matter of preference and more as a matter of blocked mobility: impediments to more attractive alternatives include poor English language facility and inappropriate skills. Kim, Hurh, and Fernandez argue that American employers often do not recognize the education and work experience that immigrants have accumulated in their native countries.

The lower rates of business discontinuance observed among Asian immigrants may reflect their paucity of alternatives rather than their success in business. If this is true, then highly capable owners (profitability notwithstanding) may exit self-employment when better opportunities arise.

Asian immigrants are very heavily crowded into several industry groups -particularly retailing – and within industries, they are often overrepresented heavily in several of the smaller-scale lines of business. Manufacturing, for example, is one of the larger scale industries where small business is active. Yet Asian manufacturers are concentrated in several of the small-scale lines of nondurable goods manufacturing: garments, food processing, and printing. In retailing, Asian immigrants are overrepresented in restaurants and food stores but they are underrepresented (relative to nonminorities) in larger scale retailing fields such as building materials, new car dealerships, and appliance stores.

Based on CBO data, mean 1987 sales in major industry groups are presented below for the Asian immigrant and nonminority business samples previously described:

	Asian Immigrant	**Nonminority**
Manufacture (dollars)	173,240	381,740
Wholesale (dollars)	417,543	520,223
Retail (dollars)	167,583	266,873
Services (dollars)	85,462	91,930

Mean 1987 firm profits in two of the above major industry groups were substantially lower for the Asian immigrant firms, in comparison with those reported by nonminority-owned businesses. Overall, the groups of Asian immigrant and nonminority small business summarized reported mean profits of $9,970 and $20,519 respectively. Operating marginally profitable small scale firms may be a form of underemployment for many highly educated Asian immigrant entrepreneurs.

If applicable barriers to upward mobility can be overcome, many of these self-employed persons could achieve a fuller use of their human capital either by (1) moving into managerial or professional salaried employment or (2) shifting into more skill-intensive, larger scale lines of small business.

The social capital explanations put forth by Light, Bonacich and Light, Waldinger, Aldrich, Waldinger, and Ward (1990), and others to explain the success of the Asian immigrant-owned small-business community rest, in fact, on an uncertain empirical foundation. The term success may be inappropriate given that Asian immigrants generate substantially lower sales and profits than cohort nonminority-owned small businesses, in spite of their much larger investments of human and financial capital into their firms.

Success may indeed typify the firms owned by immigrant Asian Indians; Fratoe and Meeks (1988) in their analysis of self-employment among individuals associated with the fifty largest ancestry groups in the U.S., found that Asian Indians ranked highest, overall, in mean self-employment income. Asian Indian small business owners, however, are the Asian immigrant subgroup that is least oriented to serving a minority clientele and least likely to employ a predominantly minority labour force. That is, they are least likely to use the forms of social capital discussed above.

Vietnamese firms, in contrast, are the group that most heavily serves a minority clientele and relies most upon minority workers. Relative to their Asian cohorts, Vietnamese run the smallest firms and suffer the higher firm discontinuance rates. Among Asian Indian and Vietnamese firms active in 1987, 14.9% of the former and 22.1% of the latter had shut down their businesses by 1991.

In defence of the sociological approach, note that the quantitative analyses pursued in this study are too broad to reject the results of very specific studies of immigrant groups operating in individual industries or cities. Waldinger, for example, focused upon Chinese immigrants operating in one industry (garments) in one city (New York). Waldinger's analysis may be on the mark; a legitimate concern, however, is that it is risky to draw generalizations from such specific analyses about the behaviour of Asian (or minority) business ownership nationally.

In their analysis of "the underdevelopment of black business," Aldrich and Waldinger point to "the lack of a large protected market, and the fragmented social structure of black communities, which inhibits resource mobilization" and Fratoe present other findings that seek to explain the state of the black business community by noting its limited ability to generate social resources from supportive networks of co-ethnics.

The findings of this study call into question the validity of seeking to explain success in self-employment by observing use of social capital forms such as protected markets and loyal co-ethnic employees. Variations in owner human capital endowments and financial capital investments in one's firm, in contrast, explain patterns of small-business viability.

Many Asian immigrants have achieved success in self-employment in the U.S.; business owners who were educated and affluent prior to self-employment entry have been particularly successful.

Chapter 6

Rethinking Catering Business

TROUBLED RELATIONS

The under representation of women in the activities and leadership of the U.S. labour movement has been a long-standing problem shared by virtually all unions. In the early decades of the twentieth century, men even officered organizations that boasted a majority of female members, such as the International Ladies' Garment Workers' Union. The patterns of male dominance survived the rise of the industrial union movement in the 1930s and 1940s and the influx of women into unions during World War II. In 1986, researchers could still report that despite the growing ranks of women in unions, the number in higher levels of leadership (both elective and appointive) had increased only slightly.

Because of this poor aggregate record, feminist scholars initially dismissed unions as vehicles for female activism, arguing that unions historically operated as patriarchal institutions, steeped in masculine culture and tradition.

Many deemed the structure and philosophy of the U.S. labour movement inhospitable to female empowerment and held male union officials responsible for women's low rate of unionization and participation. The harshest criticism was directed at the American Federation of Labour (AFL) and its affiliates. The conventional notion has been that their elitist "craft" ideology and organizational practices acted as almost insurmountable barriers to the mobilization of women. This skeptical perspective also predominated among practitioners of the new labour history, many of whom located worker militance outside the bureaucratic structures of trade union institutions. Trade unions were viewed as "confining institutions, designed to hold workers in check rather than to liberate them."

Despite their anti-institutional sentiment, these writings have been important in countering earlier analyses which posited women as inherently less militant than men and less concerned with economic justice and workplace representation. Clearly, the gender gap in labour activism resulted from situational factors as much as psychological attributes purportedly shared by women as a sex. The new scholarship documented numerous instances where male workers enhanced their own status by excluding and subordinating women; similarly, it uncovered situations where unions reflected male cultural values and habits – by holding their meetings at night or in a local saloon, for example – and hence thwarted female participation.

Yet, as Ruth Milkmen and Carole Turbin have emphasized in their most recent works, the "wide range of historical variation in union behaviour toward women" and the specific conditions under which unions have been effective vehicles for female collective action and empowerment have received less attention. Moreover, the most systematic treatments of female union activism have focused on situations in which mobilization has been sporadic or short-lived; we know even less about the circumstances necessary for sustained activism among women workers.

The impressive record of participation among union waitresses in the AFL-affiliated Hotel Employees and Restaurant Employees International Union offers the researcher an opportunity not only to specify the conditions which facilitated long-term activism but also to reevaluate craft unionism as an arena for female mobilization. Among those unions in which female leadership has been documented, HERE ranks at the top in the proportion of women among its leaders, even though women were a minority of its membership. HERE waitresses also evidenced a high degree of participation in union activities and, in marked contrast to the traditional portrait of intense but short-lived mobilization among women workers, they maintained their heightened level of activity from the early decades of the twentieth century into the post-World War II period. Yet the achievements of HERE women have gone unrecognized.

Manufacturing unions, such as the ILGVVU or the United Auto Workers, have received the preponderance of attention. The few reports that include service workers have focused solely on the national level – thus bypassing the activism of HERE women on the local level – or on unions with a majority of female members. Relying on previously untapped records from food service locals across the country, this essay will rectify that neglect by first detailing the impressive degree of activity among AFL waitresses.

But once the extensive record of waitress activism is established, how is it to be explained? Previous researchers have credited separate female locals and other structures, such as women's departments and women's committees, with a key role in augmenting the activity of women in the labour movement. Separatism has not been viewed uncritically, however. These same writers acknowledge that separatism has been a problematic long-range strategy for women, capable of sustaining women's leadership in some situations, yet undermining female equality and authority in others.

Separate female structures, played a critical role in stimulating leadership among waitresses. Beginning in 1900 with the founding of the Seattle waitresses' union, female waiters established their own all-female locals in Chicago, San Francisco, St. Louis, Los Angeles, and other communities across the country; they also joined mixed culinary locals of waiters, cooks, and bartenders. By the early 1950s, the apex of HERE strength numerically, union waitresses had expanded their ranks to one-fourth of their trade. The participation of waitresses within their international union, however, reached its peak in the 1920s when the greatest number of waitresses belonged to separate-sex locals; similarly, the decrease in waitress activity from the 1930s onward closely paralleled the decline of female locals.

Yet separatism alone can not fully explain the remarkable extent of waitress activism. After all, women garment workers, launderers, and bookbinders, among others, set up separate female structures, and waitress leaders rose from thoroughly integrated culinary organizations as well as from the separate locals and women's divisions. An adequate explanation must move beyond separatism per se to recognize the particular character of sex separatism in the food service industry.

Unlike women's locals in other industries which included women from many different trades, waitress locals had an "occupational homogeneity" and a legitimacy as a craft-based organization. Because the sexual divisions were also perceived as "craft" divisions, waitress locals received the same treatment and were ac corded the same benefits as any other craft-based local. They had equal voting rights with waiter or bartender locals on the Local Joint Executive Boards, and, like every other local, they elected delegates to HERE conventions based on the size of membership. Their institutional legitimacy as craft organizations also helped waitress locals survive the vagaries of male opinion regarding separate gender-based structures.

Thus, in contrast to the situation of "Ladies Branches" or "Women's Committees," waitress locals enjoyed an autonomy and a separate institutional status that augmented their political power. Yet because the locals were all female, they could function to increase gender consciousness, build leadership skills among women, and voice the special concerns of women workers. In other words, the autonomy and craft legitimacy of the waitress locals ensured that the "ghettoizing" impact that can accompany separatism was minimized and the positive aspects of female institution building were maximized.

But to fully understand the proclivity for activism among waitresses, one must also examine the particularities of their work situation and their household arrangements. Recent research shows that many groups of women workers developed work cultures that were expressed through informal organization at the workplace. Waitresses, however, were one of the few female dominated work groups to institutionalize their informal workplace practices and build permanent labour organizations. They created a work culture that nourished union building and participation. I will argue that this activist-oriented culture derived from particular values waitresses brought to the workplace from their families as well as those engendered by the nature of food service work itself.

THE EXTENT OF WAITRESS ACTIVISM

Waitresses first joined with other culinary workers in forming local labour organizations in the 1880s. Many of these early locals affiliated briefly with the Knights of Labour, but by the 1890s most either disbanded or cast their lot with the newly charted AFL union, HERE. HERE membership hovered around 40,000 — with the exception of the World War I period — until the unprecedented growth of the 1930s and 1940s. By the early 1950s, HERE represented more than 400,000 food service workers, and in labour strongholds such as San Francisco, New York, and Detroit, unionization approached 80 per cent.

Women were never a majority of HERE membership in this period, but their numbers jumped from approximately 2,000 (5 per cent of the total) in 1908 to about 181,000 (45 per cent) in 1950. The rise of HERE female membership paralleled the expansion and feminization of the hotel and restaurant industry. In 1900, barely a hundred thousand workers worked in commercial table service and the majorities were male; by the 1950s, food service was one of the leading retail industries in the United States and 80 per cent of all waiting work was done by women.

Despite their persistent minority status, female food servers sat on the General Executive Board (GEB) of their

International from 1909 on and participated vigorously in its international conventions, state bodies, LJEBS, and local unions. Waitress activists also took on paid work as full-time labour officials, and many became lifetime "career" labour leaders. Although their dynamism did not always secure favourable policy decisions, they played a decisive role in shaping the character of their union.

After the first female delegate broke the ice at the HERE convention of 1901, women attended every succeeding convention. Significantly, female participation in convention life was greatest from World War I to the early thirties, coincident with the flowering of the movement for separate female locals. In 1919, when women were approximately one-tenth of the total membership, one-tenth, or 231, of the delegates to the HERE convention were women. And in the late twenties and early thirties, when women represented one-fifth of the membership, they occupied between 21 and 26 per cent of the delegate slots. Female representation at HERE conventions dipped in the 1930s and 1940s as more women joined mixed organizations, but even in this later period, waitress activity was disproportionately high when compared with women in other unions.

HERE women were also elected to convention committees in disproportionately high numbers, and beginning with the 1911 convention, they secured representation on the GEB and maintained it throughout the twentieth century. At various periods in the history of the union, women occupied two and sometimes three seats on the GEB, a board whose total membership averaged fifteen. Of the women serving on the GEB, only one, Detroit's Myra Wolfgang, was from a mixed local. The other women – Elizabeth Maloney, Kitty Donnelly, Kitty Amsler, Bee Tumber, Olivia Moore, Gertrude Sweet, Fay Rothring – were all from separate locals. Indeed, most waitresses who rose to national prominence came from separate locals. In a 1940 tribute to significant women culinary leaders of the past and present, the editor of the Catering Industry Employee, the national journal of HERE, listed twenty-six outstanding women; twenty were from separate locals.

Waitress leadership in male-dominated mixed locals and LJEBs was impressive, however. Cooks and Waiters' Local 550 in Bakersfield, California, survived the Depression because of the "ines timable fortitude and perseverance" of its secretary-treasurer, Josephine Perry Rankin. Originally a member of Waitresses' Local 639, Rankin "loaned her guiding influence" to Bartenders Local 378 and was "so effective" that Bakersfield bartenders achieved 100 per cent organization. Rankin was not an isolated case. Teresa Wolfson, writing in 1926, estimated that nationally at least forty-three culinary locals had female "secretaries."

Although she thought that more women should have been elected president instead of secretary – a position she considered stereotypic for women – in reality, labour organizations often deemed the secretary their chief officer. Beulah Johnson, secretary and principal officer of Local 324 in Glendale, California, proudly told of her research on California female leaders in the March 1944 Catering Industry Employee. Out of seventy-five culinary locals in California, twentyone had women secretaries. Only three of these were composed exclusively of women, Johnson added; the rest were mixed locals. Gertrude Sweet, a carpenter's daughter who became International vice-president for the Northwest region, recalled that "in Oregon, Washington, and Montana, we had more women officers in the union than we had men [officers]. I find that the women did work and talk and did as good a job as did the men."

From heading up mixed and separate-sex locals, waitresses moved into prominence on male-dominated joint culinary boards. Amanda Keleher took over the top slot of the Salt Lake City LJEB in 1923; in 1946 she still maintained a firm holds. In Oakland, California, Ruby Hall, secretary-treasurer of Culinary and Bartenders' Local 832, acceded to the presidency of the LJEB in 1947; and across the bay, Jackie Walsh, elected president of Waitresses' Local 48 in 1942, captured the San Francisco LJEB presidency in 1950 after a bitter struggle. She retained her power for over two decades. In 1940, the Catering Industry Employee reported that nationwide approximately nineteen LJEBs had women as their chief officers.

Waitresses held their own in the state culinary alliances as well. At the sixth annual convention of the California State Council of Culinary Workers, Bartenders, and Hotel Service Employees, held in 1949, about 30 per cent of the 185 delegates, 37 per cent of the committee members, and 25 per cent of the executive board were female. The president of the council, Frankie Behan, was a San Francisco waitress from Local 48. In the 1930s, the council had also been led by a woman, Bee Tumber, a veteran waitress organizer from Southern California. The picture in Oregon, Washington, and other states with strong separate-sex locals was no different.

Strategies for Representation

These accomplishments in part grew out of waitresses' own keen sense of the importance of equitable female representation. The means by which to achieve this equality were not so self-evident, however, and waitresses debated amongst themselves over the proper strategies for enhancing female participation and power. On a local level, the majority of waitresses favoured sex separatism, at least until the 1930s. After that, most newly organized waitresses adjusted to the new industrial structures of the union. Even in mixed locals, however, waitresses sought a sphere of autonomy by creating women's committees and councils. Both strategies proved problematic, each in its own way, but the separate-sex route granted a degree of organizational power that the women's committees could not duplicate.

Waitresses who preferred separate locals gave many reasons, but one recurring rationale involved the effect such organizations had in developing women's leadership. Separate locals ensured that women would hold responsible positions within the union and that the knowledge required running a local – from grievance-handling and negotiating contracts, to public relations and parliamentary procedure – would be learned by women. Female participation was neither expected nor encouraged in mixed organizations, but in separate locals, women had no choice but to participate, even if the activities struck them as unappealing and unfeminine. Alice Lord, twenty-five-year officer of the Seattle waitresses' union understood this principle. "In a mixed local," she wrote to the editor of the January 1906 Mixer and Server, "the girls do not take the interest that they should; they always leave the work to the boys,... but if the girls know that the success of the local depends on their efforts, they will put their shoulders to the wheel, and most invariably they will come out ahead, as the few waitresses' locals which are in existence prove that such is the case."

Waitresses also recognized the role of separate locals in creating the proud history of waitress representation. "A great deal has been said about having one local union for waiters and waitresses," Carrie Alexander of Chicago's Local 484 began, when the issue of merging the waiter and waitress locals at the 1927 HERE convention was raised, but "if the waiters and waitresses were in a local union, we would not have 51 delegates at this convention." After the applause died down, she underscored her point: "What is the matter with the local union... in New York? They have waitresses..., but there are no women here." She closed her speech with a final appeal for separate locals. "Let me tell you that the women will have to get up and fight for their own and stay in their own local. I hope no delegation here will consider amalgamating with the men because I believe it would be the elimination of the waitresses."

Waitresses took pride in the accomplishments of their all-female organizations and in their ability to take on jobs that the culture deemed inappropriate or too difficult for women. In 1906, Lord encouraged the press secretaries of female locals across the country to write letters for the opinion column of the national journal by pointing out the similarity between writing for the public audience – an unfamiliar task – and talking with each other in private, a common, everyday activity. "Now, girls, I would like to see an article every month in the Forum from one of our number. Do not be afraid, or imagine you cannot do so. Write just as you would talk to one another, even if it is not just correct. I am sure our broad-minded editor will find space for it."

Local 48 of San Francisco bragged of being "completely officered by women and [of constituting] an outstanding example of women's ability both as executives and administrators." In the 1950s, the Los Angeles waitress local printed the following slogan on the back cover of their bylaws: "Who Says 'Women are the Weaker Sex.?' We are the largest culinary craft union in the World."

By the 1930s, the majority of new waitresses were entering mixedgender locals. For these women, new strategies were required. The story of the women's committees they created – their brief organizational life and frustratingly piecemeal accomplishments contrast markedly with the longevity and achievements of the separate locals. The comparison demonstrates that separatism in and of itself could not always guarantee increased power and participation for women: the form in which separate organizing occurred was critical.

Of the culinary locals in New York City, at least four – Locals 1, 42, 302, and 6 – had large functioning women's committees at various times between the 1930s and the 1950s. Women were never the majority in any of these locals, but they comprised between 30 and 40 per cent of the membership in Locals 302 and 6. The failure of these committees is noteworthy in light of their numerical potential, persistence, and creativity.

Although the committees defined their first task as promoting female leadership, they made little headway. The executive board of Hotel and Club Workers' Local 6 generally had two women out of approximately fifteen to twenty members; the staff ratio of women to men was similar. Ironically, Local 6 prided itself on its progressive democratic character, but because one-third of the union throughout the 1940s and 1950s was female, clearly a major portion of their rank and file was not represented. The records of other New York City locals were worse. Cafeteria Workers' Local 302 did not have a female business agent representing its 3,000 women members until 1942. Fifteen years later, the picture was remarkably stable: only one of the fifty executive board members was female. The New York LJEB reflected the dearth of female leadership in its affiliate locals: Gertrude Lane, general organizer and later secretary-treasurer for Local 6, was frequently the sole woman in a delegate body of thirty to fifty members.

Women's committees also aimed to increase female participation in the life of the union. The barriers were numerous and ultimately impossible to surmount. Ida Brown, a Local 1 waitress, explained the source of the problem: "Many of us who can talk the legs off an iron pot when in our shops are smitten with stage fright at general membership meetings – and to tell the truth, we do not receive any particular encouragement from our brothers." A Local 302 cafeteria server admitted that "too many of us have qualms about going before a General Membership meeting and stating our opinions, but we wouldn't have any stage fright if we were part of a Council for women. Men just don't understand these things."

Women's committees initiated various programmes to foster wom en's participation. In conjunction with the New York Women's Trade Union League, Local 6 held leadership training classes for "women only" in organizing techniques and public speaking. Local 1 organized a parliamentary procedure class. Other committees organized social and sporting events to draw the "women members closer to the union." Bingo parties, swim and bicycling clubs, dancing events, and softball teams were commonplace. A women's dramatics class held through Local 302 helped create a musical, "Sunny Side Up," about the lives of cafeteria workers.

Women's columns in the union newspaper were begun. Even the women's committee of Local 6, which carefully pointed out that they "were not segregating" themselves "from the men... far from it... [because] men and women are dependent on cooperation with each other for the success of the trade unions," started a "women's corner" in the Hotel and Club Voice. "Yes, this is something new, a little corner all to ourselves" where we can get "by ourselves and let our hair down." The Voice of Local encouraged women to write letters for the "Woman's View" column and to attend their union meetings. Local 302's Cafeteria Call had a "Hello Sister" column for a number of years and later an "Our Sisters Talk It Over" column.

Early on, the columns emphasized the needs of women on the job, but as the committees lost steam, the columns shifted, appealing to women as housewives and mothers. Local 302's column changed tone in 1943, concomitant with a change in the Local's administration. After five years of broadsides directed toward workplace issues, a new columnist appeared who urged women to "join union activities to make this a better world for their children." In 1954, the "Woman's View" column in the Local 1 newspaper became the "Ladies' Corner" with articles on preserves, fashions, and household hints.

Significantly, women's home responsibilities were rarely mentioned as a potential source of conflict for women activists, nor were home responsibilities perceived as a duty from which women should be relieved. The chair of the women's committee in Local 6 reminded women that they had a duty to participate in their union even though they had household responsibilities and had to "go home, clean house and prepare meals." Remember the pioneer women, she exhorted. When the Indians attacked, they "didn't say 'excuse me, I have to bake a cake'... they came to the front and helped their men." Instead of attempting to rectify the problem of women's dual responsibilities in the workplace and in the home, women were expected to do both.

Determined to gain representation, women's committees pressured male-dominated locals for quotas regarding women and minorities. Local 6 passed a bylaw provision in the 1940s requiring that one black officer and one female officer be appointed "in the event that no Negro or no woman has been elected to serve either as a General Officer of the union or the Board of Vice Presidents." Local 1 women pushed through a resolution early in 1936 that at least two women would be elected to the Executive Board of the union. In the late 1940s, they amended the local bylaws to "provide that both the delegates to the WTUL must be women in addition to the mandatory two executive board members."

The most ambitious activities devised by women's committees involved organizing semi independent all-female councils that functioned almost as separate branches within the main local. The women of Local 302 started a Women's Council composed of representatives from each shop where women were employed. The Women's Council formulated bylaws and collective bargaining demands, and "other matters effecting [sic] women more than men. Similarly, under the auspices of the New York LJEB, Gertrude Lane set up a Women's Advisory Committee consisting of five women from each local with female membership. This all-woman group paralleled the male joint committee structurally but differed ideologically. As opposed to the collective bargaining thrust of the virtually all-male LJEB, the female group was committed primarily to legislative and organizing activity in regard to minimum wages and maximum hours.

Ironically, success could create problems for committees. Women's committees were in something of a double bind. The male leadership saw the principal function of women's committees as attracting women to the work of building the general union organization, yet the most effective way of involving women was by appealing to their special interests. Because the gender concerns of women were often at odds with the priorities of a male dominated union, the committees were stifled at precisely the point at which they developed a strong following among the women members of the local.

The demise of Local 302's committee is a case in point. From its inception in 1938, the committee defined broad and bold concerns. Besides the traditional entreaties for women's involvement in ongoing union activities, they wanted equal pay, a portion of the best jobs, and "important positions" in the union. They were tired of taking a "backseat" to the men. When the committee ran a letter-writing contest on "What do you want the Union to do for you as a woman member?" the winning essayist wanted a forty hour week with no reduction in pay – clearly a useful demand for women with family responsibilities – and the runner-up opted for the union "to create equal opportunity for women to earn equal money for equal work with men."

During the 1941 negotiations, the women's committee distributed "7-hour day for women" buttons and made other suggestions to the negotiating team such as having cots in the dressing room for emergencies... and having sanitary dressing rooms." The committee members elaborated further objectives, including a veiled reference to the problem of sexual harassment: "We felt that not enough girls in the union knew their rights and that sometimes they are laid off, or bothered, or something else like that."

During the early years of World War II, the committee toned down its feminist orientation in the actual activities they pursued, but their sassy rhetoric continued. One 1942 column grabbed attention with this opening: "What do you say to the wise guy who tells you that women belong at home in the kitchen? Or the bright boy who tells you women are taking men's jobs? Or the know-it-all who says girls are not as capable as men? Do you feel a slow burn creeping all over you while you want to tell him off – but good! Well, we have all the answers to those very short-sighted males who strut around this earth feeling that all things begin and end with them"

Nevertheless, although the committee elicited enthusiastic response from women members, the male-dominated executive board withdrew its support after a few years, effectively crippling the committee. Few lasting changes had occurred. The number of women in leadership remained small, and glaring inequalities in wages between women and men persisted.

On the other hand, those committees advancing only goals which complemented the interests of male coworkers found they lost the support of the very constituency they were trying to reach.

The committees within Locals 6 and 1, for example, steered clear of divisive issues" and in the end died from lack of female support. While agitating for more female staff for Local 6 and exhorting women to get more involved in the life of their union, the calls for women "to pitch in" and "shoulder the load" were directed at involving women in activities that did not challenge the ongoing traditional priorities of the union. In Local 1's Women's Column in the Voice of Local 1 – begun in 1948 for "the gentler sex... our waitresses, and the wives of our male members" – committee members urged participation on the part of women, but the column addressed the problems of discrimination based on race not sex: the grievants were all black men. Despite the urging of the local, few women members wrote for the women's column; there was "a deathly silence from our women," the editor admitted. A union administrator told women to visit the union office if they needed help writing, but to no avail.

In the end, without the autonomy, power, and institutional legitimacy enjoyed by the separate female locals, the impact of women's committees was episodic and ephemeral. Without a majority vote within the local or a separate institutional base of power, women could neither change the priorities of the male leadership, nor could they act independently. Moreover, the basic legitimacy of women's committees was always in question. The separate waitress locals had to overcome male (and female) skepticism toward their sex-segregated structure before they gained separate charters, but once their local was established, their basic right to exist was not challenged.

The committee form, however, was not an organizational structure recognized by the international union constitution.

Waitress locals also garnered credibility because they represented not just the women of the union but also the waitress craft; in contrast, women's committees justified their existence through establishing the special needs and interests of women. Waitress locals forged unity through combining craft and organizational loyalty with gender concerns; in the case of women's committees, organizational and craft loyalties often were at odds with gender.

Waitresses also experimented with various schemes for enhancing female power on the national level, alternating between arguments for equal treatment and special protection. Before the 1930s, for instance, female delegates to union conventions agitated against HERE's policy, instituted in 1909, "that one member of the Board shall be a woman to represent the women workers of our craft." In 1921, women delegates, all from separate-sex locals, submitted a resolution to abolish the special seat reserved for women.

During the floor fight that ensued, women objected to the quota as a "protective" measure that set a maximum for female representation rather than a minimum. Others saw it as demeaning and encouraging the view of women as the weaker sex in need of special treatment. "You must get away from the idea that women are less able than men," one delegate said. "We don't want to be patronized and that is what the present law produces." Male delegates opposed the motion and prevailed. Unable to do away with the quota or elect more women to the board, female delegates switched tactics.

In 1938; they embraced a recommendation that backed special protection for both women and dining car workers and increased the female quota from one to two. In these debates, waitresses now argued that women needed protection from the prejudices of their male colleagues and that, although the quota system at times seemed to limit the number of women board members, at least it ensured some female participation. Women delegates also expressed less optimism about their chances in open elections and appeared less sensitive to being categorized as a distinct constituency. In part, this shift may have been due to the increasing number of women entering mixed locals, the corresponding decline in female delegate proportions, and the general perception that the chances for increasing female representation by abolishing the quota system were slim. The resolution requiring two seats for women passed, and in the election following, waitresses secured three of the fifteen elected seats on the board.

Dissatisfied with the new policy, the general officers of HERE backed a resolution at the next convention eliminating one of the female vice-presidential slots. In contrast to previous conventions, male delegates now argued against paternalistic treatment of women, using the rhetoric of impartiality and equal treatment of the sexes. How can you support equal wages, GEB member and noted progressive Hugo Ernst asked the women delegates, yet desire differential treatment when it comes to elections? But Ernst showed signs of not being as fair-minded and consistent as he was exhorting the female delegates to be. "I believe you good sisters are clannish," he began, "when you insist that there should be more representation, proportionately speaking, than the number would warrant." In reality, of course, because women were at least one third of the membership, two board seats were hardly overrepresentation.

Despite pressure from male colleagues, not one of the 150 women delegates spoke in favour of the amendment. They stressed their numbers and their entitlement to proportionate representation. As delegate Anna Farkas succinctly put it: "We have probably one half females in this Hotel and Restaurant International Alliance, and I think we are entitled to female representatives." Taking a different tack, Gertrude Lane of New York City admitted that "women had very little chance to be elected on a district basis and that was one of the reasons it would be a fatal error for the organization to take away any of the women representation."

Besides, she added, in organizing she found that "one of the best arguments was the fact that our International recognized the importance of women in the industry." Despite "sharp debate from many different quarters," the quota requiring two female vice-presidents met defeat, and, as a result, HERE women lost one of the three women on the board. Nevertheless, waitresses retained two vice presidential seats on the GEB throughout the 1950s and 1960s even though they competed against men for those positions.

Thus, many waitresses supported sex-segregated policies on a local level, but they rejected the full implications of the "separate sphere ideology" at the national level: they argued against quotas for female representation on the highest body of the international until the late 1930s. Nevertheless, with the decline of female delegate strength, and increasingly frustrated with the lack of progress, waitresses shifted their tactics and argued for special seats reserved for female delegates. Although they never devised a system to ensure proportionate representation for women, waitress activists did manage to maintain and even increase their presence on the board – despite the declining female delegate pool.

To fully explain the achievements of women within HERE, one must look beyond the strategies devised by waitresses, even those as effective as separate locals. One must look to the nature and structure of the food service workplace itself and to the special family characteristics of waitresses. Waitresses created a work culture and community that promoted and sustained their collective activity. This activist consciousness was rooted primarily in the particularities of their work experience and family backgrounds.

The organization of the culinary workplace fostered women's leadership in subtle but powerful ways. The craft and sex segregation of work, for instance, solidified the occupational ties between waitresses while mitigating their identity with male workers in their craft. The strict categorizing of waiting jobs by sex meant that waitresses and waiters rarely worked together in the same house -women served at breakfast and lunch and in the lower-priced, informal restaurants; men worked dinner jobs in the fancier, more formal houses. This internal segregation of waiting work physically separated women and men food servers and created the basis for a collective identity among waitresses.

Yet unlike women in many other sex-segregated workplaces, waitresses continuously interacted with male cooks, bartenders, and busboys, as well as male customers. These exchanges were often fraught with conflict that derived in large part from the structure and demands of the workplace itself. Waitresses needed food and liquor immediately if their customers were to be satisfied; the cooks and bartenders, removed from the watchful and hungry eye of the patron, responded more to their own inclinations for a steady, unpressured work pace.

In order to fulfill their work duties, waitresses developed ways of manipulating these interactions and asserting their own ends. The daily adversarial maneuverings with men prepared waitresses for the conflicts that emerged in their own union. Indeed, the spats between waitresses and their male coworkers on the shopfloor affected their readiness to engage in conflict with these same union brothers in the union hall. How could they accept paternalism in the union when they so firmly rejected it in the workplace?

The kinds of skills acquired by waitresses in their daily interactions with customers were also directly transferable to union leadership. At work, waitresses learned to take charge verbally with customers, to deflect criticism and sarcasm by developing their own quick-witted retorts, and to be persuasive in their communication. Practice in "thinking on your feet" and in sharpening sparring skills came in handy during union debates, grievance meetings, and negotiation sessions. As William Why discovered in his classic study of the restaurant workplace, the women who survived as waitresses learned to control situations by initiating action rather than letting the customer define the interaction. This boldness became a habit with some waitresses and aided them in their union activities. They were not intimidated by men nor were they accustomed to following the male lead. Unlike the office environment, for example, waiting work discouraged traditional female behaviour.

Expert waitresses were keen judges of human character. They could assess an individual quickly, reading her or his nonverbal cues, and adjust their behaviour to the mood of the other person. This grasp of character allowed the waitress to interpret the best approach with the particular customer – the one which would not only enhance the tip but would also protect the waitress from potentially abusive behaviour. A customer perceived as a bully or a pest could be put in his place before he got a chance to launch into his routine. This ability to size up individual customers and predict their behaviour became a resource upon which waitresses could draw in their labour activities. The very qualities women needed in order to survive in the fast-talking, person-oriented, conflictual world of labour relations were fostered daily at the workplace.

Other aspects of the food service industry encouraged solidarity and group identity. Irregular hours and the custom of "split shifts" (which left workers stranded at the worksite between their stints of duty) fostered intergroup interaction and bonding. The employer practice of providing room and board also facilitated personal ties among workers. Those who "lived-in" formed the closest relationships, but even waitresses who resided off the employer premises could develop "passionate loyalties" based on the considerable amount of time they spent socializing and eating meals together. Some women in fact "chose" waitressing because of the opportunities for friendships and a substitute family it offered.

As one young recruit explained: "It's very unpleasant thinking about being a girl in a big city who must sit down alone and eat. The waitress however, doesn't do this. When her work is done she sits down with the other girls at a table and eats a good meal." The occupational community of rank-and-file waitresses which formed at so many workplaces underlay and nourished the waitress representatives who braved the masculine world of union conventions and high-level executive boards.

Waitressing may have also attracted a more unconventional type than other occupations, such as clerical or sales or even factory labour. Certainly, before Prohibition, waitressing was looked upon as a disreputable trade. Waitresses interacted with male strangers in public places and even served them liquor. The intimacy of food service, the tip exchange required, and the association – perhaps unconscious – between eating and sex, led many observers to link waitressing and prostitution.

Even later in the century, after more native-born women entered waitressing and attitudes toward sexual mixing loosened, waitressing still retained a somewhat unsavory cast. The "intemperate" personal qualities exhibited by waitresses on the job were also noticed by the public and frowned upon. The stereotype of the bold, free-talking, aggressive waitress was partially based in reality. For these women then, already working in a "unladylike" job, becoming a labour activist – clearly nontraditional behaviour for women – did not seem like much of a change of pace.

Lastly, the distinctive family backgrounds of waitresses may have predisposed them to workplace activism. Waitresses more than women in many other occupations tended to be either divorced, separated, or widowed, or if single, living apart from their family of origin. As recent scholarship has demonstrated, the particular household arrangements of women workers can be tied systematically with their propensity for collective action.

In his study of the union pioneers in the electrical industry, for instance, Ronald Schatz found that the distinguishing factor shared by the women leaders was their nontraditional family homelife: many were living alone, with sisters or peers, or divorced. These women rose to leadership, Schatz maintained, because they had either broken the patriarchal ties of their past family or challenged the authority structures in their current family. Waitress activists conform to Schatz's schema because they, like the women organizers in the electrical industry, also diverged from other women in their tendency to shun conventional married life.

Equally important, the nontraditional family status of waitresses meant that a disproportionate number were the primary support of themselves and their family and, at least until the 1950s, were attached to the workplace in a permanent fashion as full-time, long-tenure workers. The implications of these particular attributes for female mobilization are profound, as Louise Tilly and Carole Turbin have recently pointed out. Women who were primary wage earners were more likely to take the lead in labour struggles; they had a greater stake in improving their wages and enjoyed more independence from male authority.

Older women with more years in the labour force also appeared more committed to workplace struggles. They perceived their work as continuous and permanent, had developed more extensive workplace networks of support, and hence were more willing to invest in long term union building. Moreover, as I have noted elsewhere, older waitresses may have been more likely to take on union responsibilities because their energies were less absorbed in childrearing.

On the most obvious level, many of the factors which scholars have identified as linked to women's propensity for collective activity are also central to any understanding of women's ability to sustain such action. The particular family position of women and the characteristics of their "production unit" or workplace are critical in explaining women's ongoing union participation as well as their initial mobilization.

Yet of the instances of female mobilization detailed by Louise Tilly, only the cigar makers played a significant leadership role in their union and turned their activism into "an ongoing affair." Tilly attributes their unusual leadership flair in part to their "opportunities for solidarity and association not unlike male craftsmen" and their organization into predominantly female union groupings. The case of the waitresses suggests further generalizations about why activism among certain groups of women endured.

For here waitresses, like many other groups of women wage earners, the barriers to women's leadership – male hostility, the labour movement's masculine culture, the socialization of women for supportive roles, the often temporary attachment of women to the workplace, and the patriarchal institution of the family – could be mitigated in certain circumstances and ultimately overcome.

But the particular character of the craft and gender separatism that operated within the hotel and restaurant union proved key to preserving that participation. In other words, to understand the survival of collective action, we must analyze not only the family and work experiences of women but also the nature of the institutions within which they operated and the strategies they employed in negotiating their institutional arrangements.

It is not surprising that working-class women, like their middleclass sisters, found sustenance in the sex-segregated structures of their union organizations. What is startling, however, is that the craft form of unionism also proved nourishing. The few writers who have explored the relation between union organizational structure and women's subordinate status have emphasized the superiority of industrial unionism. And indeed, the "logic of industrial unionism" ensured that thousands of semiskilled and unskilled workers, including women, were organized. The history of waitress activism suggests, however, that although industrial union structures were more conducive to the entrance of women into unions, craft structures may have been superior in sustaining female participation and leadership.

Indeed, HERE waitresses benefited from a propitious mix of craft and industrial unionism. Food service workers – like many other AFL unionists in fact – never really adopted the exclusionary membership policies so often associated with craft unionism. HERE organized "semiskilled" workers, such as waitresses and dishwashers, as well as "skilled workers, such as cooks and bartenders. What made them craft unionists was their adherence to other organizational practices and philosophies: it was these aspects of craft unionism that promoted ongoing collective activity among women. The separation of workers by trade provided women with a space apart from male hostility and allowed the development of female perspectives and leadership skills.

The tradition of local control and decentralization – so characteristic of craft unionism – also allowed for female autonomy. Lastly, the craft union emphasis on pride in the trade and loyalty to others who belonged to the same occupation encouraged women's identity with work and with their sisters in the craft. The success of the waitress locals thus demonstrates how an organizational structure based on the logic of craft, rather than being incompatible with female mobilization, proved instrumental in its creation and maintenance.

Unions, then, are not static unchanging entities into which women must be integrated. Union responsiveness to women has varied widely over time and place. Even within the same international, let alone the same federation, labour organizations have exhibited a remarkable range of reactions. For those of us concerned with explaining that variation, the history of waitress activism redirects our attention beyond the stated ideological orientation of these institutions to the peculiarities of their organizational structures.

The surprising impact of craft unionism discloses an important caveat. Although the gender ideology of organizations may imply one outcome for women, their organizational structures, seemingly gender-neutral, may produce a totally different result. As Roslyn Feldberg has recently noted, those concerned about the future of women within the contemporary labour movement would do well to demand not merely a change in attitude but also the creation of structures that would allow women the space to define and implement their own priorities.

Chapter 7

Importance and Usage of Dress Codes

A survey was conducted to investigate the nature and use of employee dress codes of organizations that market professional services. The study sample consisted of personnel administrators employed in selected service organizations that are members of the American Society of Personnel Administrators; the total sample included 1000 administrators. The analysis of responses revealed that dress is important in marketing services and that compliance to a dress code is a criterion for employee performance evaluation. While most administrators agreed that dress is a significant factor in their companies' success, few organizations had formal written dress codes; dress codes are most often communicated orally.

Traditions in the professions, the expectations of customers, Chief Executive Officers of the organizations, and past experiences were the factors that dominate the development of dress codes. On the question of dress code requirements for male vs. female employees, the study revealed that more service organizations specify dress for males than for females. For traditional business attire, comparing the dress codes of the different service organizations revealed several significant relationships.

In recent years much emphasis has been placed on the importance of dress and appearance for professional success. Often organizations make an effort to manage dress and appearance so as to communicate to the client/customer in the most effective manner. Such controls have traditionally been manifested in policies called "dress codes." The responsibility for the administration of dress codes has conventionally been treated as a personal function.

"Proper" business dress has long been a part of the norms of professional services practitioners such as bankers, accountants, stock brokers and management consultants. However, it is interesting to note that in the marketing literature there is little attention devoted to dress as it relates to the marketing of professional services. This is particularly interesting when one considers the growth of professional service industries as a part of the U.S. economy and the broadscale increases in attention focused on services marketing by practitioners and academicians.

The marketing literature does, however, address the issue of personal appearance as it relates to the personal sales interview. It is well documented from a behavioural standpoint that dress has a significant impact upon perception and image formation as a part of the interpersonal communication process. Peak (1986) discovered that when personality traits are correlated with clothing styles, persons who wear conservative clothing are perceived as being more intelligent, mature, generous, sincere, trustful, understanding and dependable than those wearing more "daring" styles. According to Premeaux and Mondy (1987), dress establishes a level of respect and authority. This is often necessary to get the work done. In a study on occupation and grooming it was found that less positive characteristics are attributed to those who were groomed "poorly" than to those well groomed.

There is an essential difference between the professional salesperson and the professional service practitioner which underlies the justification of this study. Sales personnel are designated as the "front-line" customer contact persons for an organization which markets goods. Management, as well as salespersons themselves, are not only aware of the role of personal appearance and dress in interpersonal communication, but have employed the resources necessary to incorporate dress codes into promotion and marketing strategies. On the other hand, it is argued that professional service practitioners see themselves as "doers" rather than, sellers". Therefore, it is felt by some that these employees do not focus the necessary attention on those behavioural factors important in selling or marketing as would designated marketing personnel.

As Denny states:

One of the fundamental misconceptions many accountants have about marketing is that...someone else can bring in the new clients and then they can take over and do the work. Unfortunately they are wrong...It takes an accountant to sell accounting services.

The literature dealing with services marketing ends support to the premise that the dress behaviour of employees could be a salient attribute of the buyer when involved in the purchase process of a professional service. Two commonly cited characteristics of services, intangibility and inseparability, give credence to this postulate.

Because services are intangible in nature, perceptual and communication problems exist during the exchange process which make the true quality of the service difficult to evaluate and distinguish. Pricing and valuation problems result, leading the buyer to feel uncertainty. With complex technical services such as legal, financial or consulting research, the problem is magnified because of the lack of knowledge of the buyer. It can be argued that because the buyer cannot see (touch, smell or feel) the true quality of the service for evaluation that he might use surrogate criteria such as the behaviour of the practitioner, the physical appearance of the facility or other tangible cues. Dress behaviour, then, can become a tangible evaluative criteria for the buyer, regardless of the relationship dress has to the skills of the practitioner or quality of the service performed.

Another theoretical argument offered which distinguishes services from goods is that of inseparability. Often production and consumption of services cannot be separated temporally or spatially. Consequently, personal contact exists between the producer and consumer, allowing the buyer to have the perceptual exposure necessary to observe behavioural and physical characteristics of the seller.

The premise set forth as the rationale for this study is that through their behaviour, each practitioner in a service organization which has customer/client contact plays a role in marketing that organization's service. Since dress is an important aspect of that behaviour which plays a role in the communication process during this interaction, dress behaviour can be a salient factor in the exchange process. If this premise is accepted, and dress is perceived to be important in marketing of professional services, then the question of management or control of employee dress arises. One would assume that organizations would make an effort to manage appearance so as to communicate to the client/customer in the most effective manner.

The purposes of this study were to identify the nature and extent of usage of dress codes among selected service organizations and to determine the importance of dress in the marketing of professional services as reflected in the attitudes and opinions of personnel administrators and in the policies of their organizations. The study sample consisted of personnel administrators employed in selected service organizations that are members of the American Society of Personnel Administrators; the total sample included 1000 administrators.

The study involved a questionnaire designed to secure information about the perceived importance of dress codes among selected service organizations. Questions concerned the importance of employee appearance for service organizations, the factors used in developing dress codes, the requirements of dress codes, the effect of dress codes on employee performance evaluations, and the dress code requirements for male and female employees.

Questionnaires were returned by 304 personnel administrators, a 30.4 per cent return. Data was analyzed using frequency distributions, and cid-squares were computed to determine statistical significance. Listed below are the number of respondents from various types of service industries which were used in this study: Type of Service Organization Number in Sample Management/Marketing Consultants 51 Health Care and Human Services 47 Hotel/Restaurant/Entertainment 40 Financial (accountants/stock brokers/banking) 39 Employment Agencies (including temporary) 39 Other (not specified by respondent) 35 Engineering and/or Computer Services 30 Legal 13— Total 304

The personnel administrators responding to the questionnaire clearly indicated that appearance of professional employees was a significant factor when a potential client or customer evaluated their company's services. Most (81%) of the respondents indicated that personal appearance was a "very important" factor in this evaluation process.

Of the 304 responding personnel administrators, 73% indicated that a dress code, either formally or informally communicated, had been established for their service organizations. Among those respondents whose organizations employed any type of dress code, 67% noted that individual employee compliance to the code was a criterion for employee performance evaluation. Eighty-five per cent of the respondents indicated that compliance to a dress code was either absolutely necessary or very important when employers underwent performance evaluation.

As seen, the employment of an established dress code varied little by type of services, ranging from 66 per cent for management consultants to 83 per cent for employment placement services. But the differences in the formalization and use of compliance varied more dramatically. While only 19 per cent of management consulting firms had established written dress codes, 60 per cent of the hotel/restaurant/entertainment groups used written codes. The data revealed that differences in the use of written codes existed between types of services, and that these were statistically significant at the.05 level. Only 42 per cent of management consulting firms considered dress code compliance in evaluation of their employees, while 80 per cent of employment placement/ personnel services considered dress compliance as a factor in performance reviews.

The respondents were asked to rank the level of importance of eleven factors when developing a dress code. The scale ranged from "very important," "fairly important," "of little importance," to "no importance," with each given numerical weights of 1, 2, 3, and 4 in corresponding order. Mean scores and the percentages responding to each level of importance are reported. Customer expectations, tradition/ convention in the profession, and the opinion of the organization's C.E.O. were the three most important factors listed by the respondents in the development of dress codes.

Among those respondents whose organizations employed any type of dress code, chi-square analysis was performed to compare the classifications of the companies (local/ independent or multi-location/regional/national) to the formality of the dress codes. Though not statistically significant, the study revealed that more of the local/ independent service organizations used formal written dress codes, while more of the multi-located firms utilized dress codes which were informally communicated.

Over one-third (36%) of the respondents indicated that their dress codes had been established within the last 20 years. Many of the companies (43%) had made changes in their dress codes within the last 10 years. Though not statistically significant, it was found that the firms with revised dress codes were more relaxed in requiring a traditional business look.

The differences in the degree of requirement for wearing a "traditional business suit" by type of business organization (mean scores of weights assigned to responses were computed with a lower mean indicating that a business suit was required to a greater extent by these organizations). Of all types of services in the sample, financial services (accountants, stock brokers, banking) most required business suits, and engineering/computer least.

Those organizations classified as personnel services expected the wearing of suits with skirts more often than others, and again the engineering/computer services required the traditional suit with skirt to the least degree. Most of the respondents indicated that dress is important in marketing services and that compliance to a dress code is a criterion for employee performance evaluation. While most administrators agreed that dress is a significant factor in their companies' success, few organizations had formal written dress codes; dress codes are more often communicated orally.

The results of this study lend support to the premise that dress and appearance of employees could be a salient attribute of the buyer when involved in the purchase process of a professional service. Although the usage of dress codes differed among service organizations, many administrators agreed that dress and appearance are particularly important in making an initial impression and in progressing in a business career. More needs to be known about the actual impact of dress and appearance on the communication process with clients and customers in professional service organizations.

Quality into Small- and Medium-Sized Hotels

Total Quality Management (TQM) can be defined as a satisfaction of social shareholders via implementing effective planning, programmes, policies, and strategies, as well as using human and other assets efficiently and continually within an organization. This approach will continue to be one of the hot topics among practitioners, academics, and professionals in the new millennium.

This presents how a new TQM readiness model can be utilized for providing social shareholders' satisfaction (1) and continuous improvement in small- and medium-sized hotel organizations. Five-star hotel staffs appear to have better organizational strengths than four-star hotel staffs in North Cyprus. Four-star hotel employees indicate substantial differences in their perceptions concerning TQM readiness elements.

An extensive literature review has been conducted. Issues examined include the following: (1) Where to start? (2) Is it valuable to bring such a total system? (3) Should some parts be imported instead of the whole? and (4) Is there any cheap way to bring TQM to small- or medium-sized organizations? According to Oakland (1993), the first decision of where to begin can be daunting, referred to as the Total Quality Paralysis (TQP) problem in quality-management literature. This has been confirmed by other experts and academics who state that small- and medium-sized enterprises generally are less comfortable in bringing TQM into their organizations than large companies are due to limited managerial knowledge, skill, ability, incentives, resources, and time.

According to the literature, only a few studies have been developed on TQM readiness assessment criteria in small- and medium-sized firms. Scholars and others have a common understanding that the more clearly the TQM readiness factors are assessed, the healthier a transition can be achieved to the TQM process. The TQM literature states, "Organizations, which are ready for change in climate, have more opportunity to achieve a successful implementation in a shorter period of time".

A common point endorsed in the literature is that there must be a readiness survey before designing, developing, and implementing a TQM programme. This may help to determine TQM factors within an organization and to identify potential problems that may create resistance to TQM and will help to develop a database for future comparisons.

Walker and Salameth (1990) have stated that only a small percentage of hotels have heard "the siren call of TQM implementations" even in the U.S. It is interesting to note that after 10 years, the literature regarding hotels is still sparse. Although some viable hotels in limited geographical areas have reported that their TQM performance resulted in profit increased, employee satisfaction, and better usage of economic resources, only a few case studies have been published. As Bloomquist and Breiter indicate, "While those case studies are important in elaboration on the theme of quality management, there remain no reliable statistical data on (hotel) industry-wide performance credited to quality management."

Challenge for Hotel Organizations

Cyprus is the third-largest island in the Mediterranean. Cyprus has a great historical heritage, conserved environment beauties, and a good climate, and after the war in 1974, the island was divided into north and south parts. No study has been conducted on how TQM can be applied in small- and medium-sized hotel organizations in North Cyprus, which is a major deficiency since tourism is the leading sector. North Cyprus is certainly not the only country where tourism is the most important business sector. According to the World Tourism Organization (WTO) statistics, tourism in the world is expected to reach a volume of $US 4 trillion after 2000. This will mean that one out of nine people in the world will be employed in tourism industry in 2010.

The aim of this analysis is to provide a better understanding of how different groups of managers, chiefs, and employees perceive their readiness toward the TQM philosophy in North Cyprus four and five-star hotels. In June 1999, a preliminary investigation was carried out through one-on-one interviews with several assistant general managers, department managers, chiefs, and other lower-level employees from the four- and five-star hotels of North Cyprus. The aim was to design a more realistic TQM readiness model, as well as to prepare a better quantitative questionnaire for the targeted hotels.

The hypotheses of this study are as follows:

There is no difference between small-and medium-sized hospitality organizations' hierarchical levels (managers, chiefs and employees) concerning their TQM readiness.

There is a difference between small-and medium-sized hospitality organizations' hierarchical levels (managers, chiefs, and employees) concerning their TQM readiness.

A new model with its first selected eight factors of TQM culture (soft side) was identified. These factors are leadership, participation, teamwork, employee satisfaction, empowerment, influence, change, and training. It is important to mention that the assessment factors may not represent all the TQM readiness culture factors. In time, other related factors may be added to this group.

The Assumptions Underlying the Model

The assumptions underlying this model include the following:

1. The readiness model factors are iterative; in other words, every organization may use several different preassessment factors, and the rank of these factors also may be different.
2. TQM is not a completely new strategic system but rather is a process of developing the current system, opening its way to continuous improvement.
3. The readiness model will decrease the total cost, time, and energy of an organization in transforming it into a new TQM culture.

The model involves two important stages. The first stage is to understand and to monitor the present organizational system, especially when dealing with the factors of TQM philosophy and its soft components such as leadership, teamwork, participation, influence, empowerment, and employee satisfaction. The second stage is the process of examining the gap between upper, middle, and lower layers of personnel in order to prevent possible resistance from different layers at the time of transitioning to a new TQM culture, as well as preparing a database for future assessments. This database may serve as a benchmark where yearly data can be compared with the previous year, necessary precautions can be taken against weaknesses, and the organization can open its way to a continuous improvement process.

Of course, if the necessary proactive precautions can be taken successfully every year, the actual gap among the layers of staff will be narrowed in terms of employee resistance and inefficient use of time, money, and energy. As a result of successful TQM applications, the social shareholders will be more satisfied, and effects of internal challenges will be minimized for the organization.

The data in this study were obtained from four- and five-star hotels. In these hotels, the general manager, usually the owner or a relative who has a very close relationship to the investors, has overall responsibility for all activities. The department managers work under the control of the general managers and report directly to them. Department chiefs largely serve the role of supervisors, reporting to the department manager. The rationale for selecting four- and five-star hotels is because they attract the majority of tourists in North Cyprus.

A total of seven out of 10 hotels were included in the study. There are two hotels that are identified as five-star hotels; the remaining five are four-star hotels. All seven of these five- and four-star hotels were sampled, which provide an overall 100 per cent sampling ratio among five-star hotels and 87 per cent sampling ratio among four-star hotels. This stratified-sampling ratio is very high, and therefore the research is designed to be representative. Stratified sampling has been used in determining the number of employees of four- and five-star hotels. The stratified sampling technique "separates the population into relative homogenous groups".

The hotels employed approximately 550 permanent staff according to statistics gathered from the tourism ministry at the time of the research. The average return rate from the quantitative survey collected from the managers, chiefs, and employees was 73 per cent, 85 per cent, and 39 per cent respectively. Among the 500 questionnaires distributed, 267 were returned, 10 were not completely answered, and 13 were considered biased. Consequently, 23 responses were deleted from the analyses. The net return rate of 43.8 per cent (244) was quite adequate for the set of questions.

A perception survey, a self-administered questionnaire addressed to all managers, chiefs, and employees of the targeted hotels, was prepared in order to collect the necessary readiness data from a more comprehensive perspective. Respondents were asked to indicate their degree of agreement with each statement on a five-point Likert scale: 1=strongly agree, 2=agree, 3=somewhat agree / disagree, 4=disagree, and 5=strongly disagree. Furthermore, three questions were asked about the ranking of the hotel (four or five stars), type of ownership (public foundation, chain, or private family), and the job position (manager, chief, or employee).

Items for each subscale were subjected to a reliability assessment. The Cronbach coefficient alpha value for the total scale was .9602, and the subscales were 9092, .8425, .8812, .7177, .6993, .7164, .6976, and .7744 for leadership, team, influence, empowerment, participation, training, change, and satisfaction. Usually, a reliability coefficient above 0.50 is considered to be a sufficiently high reliability.

A factor analysis of the TQM readiness questions in the survey was performed. In order to identify the actual factors in the survey, all questions that did not load cleanly on one factor were dropped from further analysis, which left 61 questions. The frequency and one-way analysis of variance (ANOVA) were calculated as a second statistictical technique. According to Levin and Rubin (1998), ANOVA tests are used for determining the significance of the differences among more than two sample means.

The critical mean scores of the TQM readiness survey for the four- and five-star hotel mangers, chiefs, and staff. A one-way ANOVA analysis is used to explore whether there is a significant difference in the perceptions among upper-, middle-, and lower-level employees of the hotels. In terms of highest and lowest scores, it has been observed that there is little consistency in perceptions among the three staff levels (managers, chiefs, and employees).

Results for five-star hotels indicate that employees have significantly higher scores (negative) on seven items:

teamwork (I-33), leadership, and influence. For those seven items, employees had the highest mean scores. Considering all 61 questions, four-star hotel employees are less positive than five-star hotel employees. They have significantly higher scores on 32 items. For those 32 items, all staff has different scores on each item. Interestingly, the managers have higher mean scores than chiefs and employees on eight items, which are mainly dealt with through satisfaction, empowerment, participation, and leadership. The chiefs gave negative scores to change, empowerment, teamwork, and participation factors through six questions.

Four-star hotels had aggregate means (M) for the 61 items indicated by managers (M=1.94), chiefs (M=2.15), and employees (M=2.55). Both managers and chiefs expressed a moderate level of TQM readiness, while employees exhibited a low level of TQM readiness. However, in five-star hotels, the aggregate means for the same items were managers (M=2.13), chiefs (M=2.07) and staff (M=2.23), where all expressed a moderate level of TQM readiness. Therefore, the null hypothesis (Ho) was rejected, and the alternative hypothesis (Ha) was accepted.

North Cyprus is a suitable island for tourism because of its undeveloped industry, rich historical and cultural heritage, natural beauty, and relatively unspoiled environment. The various governments that have come to power all have stated that tourism is the primary sector in achieving economic development. The aim of this research was to find out how different groups of managers, chiefs, and employees of four- and five-star hotels in North Cyprus perceive their readiness toward the TQM philosophy With this study it is possible to point out to the owners arid managers the weak and strong aspects of the TQM soft side components they are practicing, and it also provides an opportunity to remove the resistance and conflicts that arise because of perception differences about this philosophy Some researchers point out that in many cases, TQM has been applied without any readiness research and has thus resulted in failure. As Weeks, Helms, and Ettkin mentioned, "The perceptions of managers, chiefs, and employees are crucial because individuals act as if their beliefs or perceptions are real."

Social shareholders are defined by the author as interested or chain parties who are in the same business arena and are a part of the same business life in a free market economic system such as customers, owners, employees, suppliers, government, municipality, and so forth. Two of the five-star hotels are in the same complex and therefore are considered as one hotel. Two hotels have been excluded from the research due to extraordinary reasons. One was under construction at the time of the survey, and the other one was degraded from 4 stars to 3 stars by the planning department of the Tourism Ministry of North Cyprus.

Competitive Advantage

This offers an in-depth treatment of conversion franchising, where new franchisees are added to a franchised system by recruiting existing independent entrepreneurs or competitors' franchisees. The first part of the paper examines conversion franchising as a source of competitive advantage. This discussion leads to the articulation off our propositions. The second part of the paper looks at the empirical results of our study of 72 North American franchisors.

Seventy-two per cent of these firms use conversion franchising in their domestic markets, and 26 per cent use conversions in international locales. The propositions relating to a franchisor's decision to use conversions based on increased levels of experience, economic resources, and to a lesser extent skills! knowledge, all were supported. These results lend support to the literature indicating that resources and skills serve as sources of competitive advantage. Implications for research and practice are discussed.

Franchising is emerging as a preferred method of doing business throughout the global economy. A recent study by the International Franchise Association estimated that, by early in the new millennium, nearly 50 per cent of every U.S.

consumer dollar would have been spent in franchised locations. Business franchising has spread rapidly to most continents during the past decade. Given the widespread use of franchising, how can firms leverage better this method of doing business? Some firms have gained increased advantage by adding mobility to their franchised operation by bringing their products/services to the customer where and when they demand them. But increasingly, firms are turning to conversion franchising as a way of enhancing growth and of gaining competitive advantage in multiple markets.

Conversion franchising occurs when a franchisor adds new franchisees to the system by recruiting existing independent businesses or competitors' franchisees. The purpose of this paper is to examine closely this emerging phenomenon by drawing on relevant literature and by reporting the results of an exploratory study of conversion franchising. Before discussing some of the competitive advantages that can accrue from employing conversion franchising, it first is instructive to review some of the advantages of traditional franchising.

Franchising's longevity and success also may be due to the fact that, organizationally, it represents a collaborative alliance. The alliance depends on the cooperation of two entrepreneurs (franchisor/franchisee) in order to be successful. Further, these partners depend on cooperation among a network of entrepreneurs to advance common methods and goals, like the sharing of information on innovations that potentially could benefit all franchise partners.

Franchising traditionally has offered many competitive advantages over independently formed and operated businesses. The franchisor has access to capital at lower risk; cost sharing with the franchisee; rapid market penetration at a relatively lower cost than establishing one's own distribution system; economies of scale; a motivated workforce of indigenous entrepreneurs; and reduced monitoring and control costs. The franchisee gets an opportunity to enter a business at less cost with a proven product or service and brand name. Additionally, the franchisee frequently receives management assistance in the areas of business location, facilities design, operating procedures, purchasing and marketing. These advantages have been born out by a superior survival rate for franchising over independent ventures. Next, we turn to a discussion of conversion franchising and its competitive advantages.

Conversion franchising occurs when a franchisor adds new franchisees to the system by recruiting independent businesses, chains, and/or franchisees from other franchised systems. Conversion franchising offers additional advantages to those discussed under traditional franchising. The use of conversion franchising appears to be expanding in recent years, as several industries (for example, fast food, lodging, real estate, and travel) have experienced changing environmental conditions that often have combined to favour this form of franchising.

The environmental conditions fostering conversions include economic, market, competitive, and technological changes. A contracting economy can mean tight credit policies, making it difficult to raise funds for new projects. During one such period, 3.7 per cent of the domestic hotels converted to a new brand affiliation.

A restricted real estate market has led many fast food franchisors to convert existing urban locations to their system rather than to devel op new sites. Saturated markets and increased competition coupled with the growing consumer demand for rejuvenated brand names have generated conversions in the real estate and hospitality industries. Independents have converted to ReMax and ERA, while Holiday Inn has converted some Ramada Inns and vice versa. Keeping abreast of changing technology has forced firms to seek conversions with systems on the cutting edge of technology, such as Century 21 and Coldwell Banker in Real Estate or Marriott's reservation system in the lodging industry.

Resource-based models of organization indicate that established know-how serves as a basis for competitive advantage.

Experienced franchisors have developed such managerial capabilities. Moreover, experienced firms often operate in more competitive arenas, in turn forcing them to try innovative strategies such as conversions. Experienced franchisors have learned to share their know-how with franchisees and have established a record of strong performance, in part because they have taken the time to build brand equity and economies of scale in purchasing, advertising, and distribution, all of which are attractive to independent businesses. Thus, we suggest the following proposition:

Proposition 1: The decision to use conversion franchising is associated positively with the experience of the franchisor.

Once a business has converted to a new franchise, is the conversion likely to lead to sustainable competitive advantage? Possible answers to this question are examined in the ensuing discussion.

Using the framework of competitive advantage from the field of strategic management is consistent with the view expressed by Castrogiovanni and Justis (1998) that researchers need to consider findings from outside the franchising field to assess their generalizability to franchisors. Competitive advantage is concerned with developing a value-creating strategy by uniquely combining bundles of valuable firm resources and skills to yield positional advantages (for example, differentiated or low-cost products/services) that result in positive outcomes (for example, market share, profitability). Firm resources include both tangible (for example, plant, location, capital) and intangible (for example, brands, copyrights, goodwill) assets. Firm skills include organizational, technical, and market knowledge, among others.

Aaker argues that a retail location superior to the competition's can act as a key asset, leading to competitive advantage. Barney (1991) suggests that a valuable location can act as an imperfectly imitable physical capital resource for the firm, while Day and Wensley see location as a tangible resource that can enable a firm to exercise its capabilities, leading to positional advantage. An existing location may be the only space available on a crowded playing field. This is particularly true in the restaurant, retail, and hotel industries, where location is a key element. Franchisors can acquire location resources in tight real estate markets by converting independents or chains that possess strategic locations.

A strong brand name may be regarded as a superior resource or as a key asset, leading to competitive advantage for today's firms. Consumers in every industry are increasingly brand conscious. At the core of the franchising concept is the bundling of a brand or a trade name with a good or service to sell to entrepreneurs in return for fees or royalties. The need to maintain brand equity motivates franchisors to grow their systems in order to develop promotion economies and, therefore, to spread promotion costs over more units.

Converting independents to a franchise system allows for rapid growth and increased name recognition. For example, in the hotel industry converting members of other chains (that is, rebranding) has been shown to lead to increased occupancy rates. Thus, conversions permit firms to reposition themselves under a new brand to enhance their competitive position.

Human resources are critical to the proper execution of any strategy Franchising taps into entrepreneurs who sign on as franchisees to manage individual business units. Sen provides an extended discussion of the franchisee as a source of managerial talent. While entrepreneurs may be motivated to do well, they often are inexperienced and require considerable training on the part of the franchisor. Using inexperienced franchisees poses a risk of adverse selection, that is, the franchisee misrepresents his/her abilities to the franchisor.

Conversion franchising enables the franchisor to bring in experienced franchisees who already have managed a similar business in the industry, either as an independent or as a franchisee for a competitor, thereby reducing the risk of adverse selection. Experienced managers are more likely to enhance a repositioned unit's performance than one with less industry experience. Furthermore, such an experienced franchisee requires less training support.

An existing customer base is a major resource that independents and members of other chains possess that can be internalized by the franchisor upon conversion. Since converts can resume business rapidly with existing customers, royalty streams also can begin flowing quickly to the franchisor. Of course, an additional benefit is that a competitor now has been co-opted into the system instead of working against it. Based on the discussion above, we suggest the following:

Proposition 2: The franchisor's decision to use conversion franchising is associated with the potential resource advantages provided by conversions.

It has just been argued that conversion franchising brings together key resources of the franchisor and franchisee that have a high potential for improving the competitive positioning of each alliance member. We now will examine important skills that can play a role in creating competitive advantage.

As a cooperative alliance, conversion franchising facilitates the sharing and enhancement of skills to improve the competitive position of both the convert and the franchisor in expanding markets. Skills or capabilities are those attributes that enable the firm to coordinate and to exploit its resources. At the core of the firm's capabilities are its knowledge base from which the skills originate. Thus, we now examine the role knowledge of markets, technology, and organization plays as key sources of competitive advantage provided by a firm's skills.

When a franchisor enters a new market, he or she does so with a limited knowledge of local market conditions and consumer preferences. Since cultures, consumer behaviour, and marketing methods are often different in various markets, franchised systems may need to be adapted to fit local requirements better. Feltenstein argues that firms need to think globally but to act locally and that much of the variability in sales, service, costs, and margins is determined by local market knowledge. Experience in growing the business provides enhanced knowledge for franchisors in areas such as market and site selection.

Acquiring experienced converts helps leverage the advantage of such experience. Moreover, converting independents or other chain members who have been operating in the local market for some time allows the franchisor to internalize these skills into the franchise system. Newly allied members also can aid the franchisor in maneuvering around local rules and regulations that otherwise could slow down or could block a venture.

Since conversions typically are of firms operating in the same type or in closely related businesses, converts bring their technical knowledge and expertise to the partnership. Two general types of technical knowledge are especially relevant in the case of conversions: industry and franchising knowledge. Knowledge relevant to the industry in terms of competitors, substitutes, methods of distribution, and general industry practices are critical to determining competitive advantage. A convert brings new perspective on industry knowledge to the franchisor, broadening the latter's knowledge base and vice versa.

Experience in a particular type of franchising is critical to a system's competitive advantage. The franchise concept is developed on what is believed to be a successful set of practices, and then knowledge bundles are replicated for franchisees. Independents who convert may obtain the immediate advantages of competing with a proven franchise concept. Converts who are previous franchisees presumably have switched because they perceive the new franchisor to have a superior franchise concept. Such franchise-experienced converts, however, also may provide additional knowledge from their prior franchising experience to enhance the concept of their new franchisor, thereby providing advantages for the entire system.

Converts' technical skills are enhanced by the franchisor through extensive training of new members through operating manuals and procedures, and through technical guidance and support. For example, PIP Printing, a leader in the quick-printing industry, offers its franchisees training workshops. The technical skills of the franchisee are enhanced further by the introduction of sophisticated computer systems. In real estate, 20 per cent of the firms in the U.S. are organized as a franchise. New franchisees in this industry gain access to nationwide databases of existing housing stock.

As mentioned previously, franchising enables a firm to harness the efforts of entrepreneurs while reducing the costs of monitoring a large multiunit organization. Thus, organizational skills revolve around monitoring to prevent franchisees who either may under invest in their units or may shirk on product quality because these actions affect the entire franchise system. The scale or size of the system contributes to improved organizational coordination. Increased size of the firm enhances monitoring capabilities of the franchisor by reducing the lower per unit costs of monitoring.

Conversions enable a franchisor to expand more quickly, thereby strengthening the organizational monitoring skills of the franchisor. Another way to control oppoı tunism is through the payment of fees to the franchisor; this provides financial incentive not to behave opportunistically because the franchisor risks forfeiting the fee if the franchisor suspends the relationship. Monitoring capability also can be enhanced by learning how best to control the franchisee's behaviour over time. Thus, the longer the franchisor has been offering franchises, the greater the likelihood of improved monitoring skills.

Independents can gain other improved organizational efficiencies, such as increased purchasing power, joint or pooled advertising, and other benefits of similar economies of scale, by joining a franchise system. Given the discussion above, we offer the following proposition:

Proposition 3: The franchisor's decision to use conversion franchising is associated with the potential skill advantages provided by conversions.

The literature on competitive advantages stresses those factors (for example, resources and skills) that facilitate the development of competitive advantage. However, traditional strategic management theory also notes that the acquisition of skills and resources may also be seen as threats or as challenges confronting the firm when undertaking a new strategy. Anecdotal evidence from franchise experience suggests that certain problems may be encountered when making conversions.

Some of the resource-related challenges posed by conversions include the added time it takes to implement a programme or to socialize or to retrain converts. Newly acquired entrepreneurs may be experienced but may be unwilling to work as part of a team or to readily adopt new business methods, thus diluting the advantages of a conversion. Market, technical, and organizational capabilities may be threatened because of the need to adopt new rules or methods to accommodate a new local market or to attract a convert to join. In short, the franchise concept and standard contract may be changed for opportunistic rather than strategic reasons in order to attract and retain new converts. The reality of the existence of such threats or barriers suggests the following:

Proposition 4: The franchisor's decision to use conversion franchising will he associated negatively with the perceived existence of threats posed by the conversion.

The purpose of this empirical section is (1) to provide a description of the current nature and extent of the use of conversion franchising among North American franchisors; and (2) to provide an initial examination of the propositions relating to the factors behind the decision to use conversion franchising by franchisors.

A random sample stratified by size and industry (1) of 250 North American (Canada and U.S.) franchisors were selected for the study from the Franchise Annual. (2) The top manager of each firm was sent a cover letter and a two-page questionnaire concerning their use of conversion franchising; one follow-up mailing was sent three weeks later. Seventy-eight firms responded. Six decided not to participate because of mergers, company policy, etc.; 72 firms returned useable questionnaires for a 29 per cent response rate. This compares favourably with other surveys of franchise companies that have reported similar return rates (26.3 per cent).

The profile of franchisors in our sample reveals a good distribution of firms across eight broad industry sectors. The firms are large, averaging 746 total units and having an average of 23 years experience in franchising. The majority of responding managers hold sufficiently high level positions in their organizations to be considered knowledgeable about their firm's franchise strategies. A comparison of respondent firms to a random sample of 40 non respondents in terms of industry (z = 0.24; p [less than or equal to] .91), size (t = 1.16; p [less than or equal to] .25), and age (t = 0.55; p [less than or equal to] .59) revealed no significant differences. This should reduce concerns of response bias in our sample.

The survey instrument consisted of 10 questions. After defining conversion franchising, the first question asked the respondents to indicate their agreement concerning 18 characteristics of conversion franchising. These characteristics represented the advantages and barriers of conversion franchising. Responses were made on a Likert-type scale ranging from 1 = not at all to 5 = highly descriptive of your experience. Other questions asked whether the firm used conversion franchising and explored the extent and reasons for doing so. The last three questions explored the use of conversions in international markets. Below we describe the variables used to explore the four propositions.

The decision to convert was assessed by the following survey question: Has your firm used conversion franchising now or in the past? A simple yes/no response was recorded. This is the categorical dependent variable for investigating the propositions. The remaining variables described below serve as the independent variables. Franchisor experience was expressed as the number of years the firm had been in business.

These were combined further into two factors using principle components analysis with varimax rotation; these factors explain 50 per cent of the variance in conversion advantages. One factor represents "market/location skills" and is comprised of 4 items (1, 7, 10, 16) and has an eigenvalue of 1.58 and a reliability of [varies] = .60. The second factor represents "economic resources" and is comprised of five items and has an eigen-value of 2.87 and a reliability of varies = .73. Two items (15, 18) did not load on any factor. A third item (1) was dropped from the market factor due to reliability problems. These latter three items were not included in any tests of the propositions.

Other sources of competitive advantages based on skills were drawn from the Franchise Annual. Technical advantages included seven dummy variables representing eight industry sectors. Franchising knowledge was assessed by the number of years the firm had been franchising. The organizational skills assessed were monitored through scale and financial bonding.

Scale was measured by the number of franchised units possessed and financial bonding was measured using the initial franchising fee charged by the franchisor. Competitive barriers/threats were assessed strictly with subjective measures drawn from the eighteen conversion franchising characteristics described earlier. Seven of the items represented potential barriers or threats.

These were reduced to two factors using principle components analysis. The factors explain 49 per cent of the variance in conversion barriers. One factor was labeled "changes" because of the adjustments to existing procedures required by conv ersions. This factor was comprised of three items and has an eigenvalue of 1.52 and a reliability of infinity = .50. The second barrier was labeled "effort" because of the extra effort required by the franchisor to make conversions and was comprised of four items and possesses and eigenvalue of 1.89 and a reliability of infinity = .60

The nature and extent of conversion franchising is described using descriptive statistics (for example, means or proportions). The exploration of the propositions was analyzed using discriminant analysis. The decision to convert represents a nominal dependent variable. The analysis derives a linear combination of independent variables (internal measures) that will discriminate best between the firms that use conversion franchising and the nonusers.

The analysis determines whether the competitive advantages and barriers posed by conversion franchising account for a significant variance in the decision to convert. In addition, this method of analysis determines both the predictive accuracy of the independent variables and their relative importance in explaining the decision to convert.

Seventy-two per cent of the firms surveyed use conversion franchising in their domestic markets. Almost half (49 per cent) began using conversions prior to 1987 (some as early as 1930); the remaining firms (51 per cent) have started using conversions since that time. Among the firms using conversions, an average of 26 per cent of their units are conversions (ranging from less than i to 98 per cent). In responding to an openended question as to why businesses converted to their franchise, our respondents identified eight major reasons.

The most frequently cited reasons were to acquire a brand name (26.6 per cent), which represents one of the major competitive resources conversions can provide businesses. Awareness, identity, and recognition on a national or global level were cited as the chief benefits of branding. Franchisor characteristics and operating results were tied for second as the most frequently cited (15 per cent each) reasons for conversion. Key franchisor characteristics included proprietary products and quality of operation and system. Operating performance benefits of conversions included better pricing, leading to increased sales and profitability.

Support services such as technology and research and development (R&D), as well as training, each were tied for third (12.5 per cent each) in importance for conversions. These represent technological and organizational skills frequently mentioned as advantages of joining a good franchise system. Cost savings (8.3 per cent) and other marketing benefits (6.6 per cent) represented the fo urth and fifth major reasons why franchisors believe that businesses convert to their system. These reasons appear to be congruent with the expected competitive advantages of conversion franchising discussed previously.

One of the difficulties in using conversions is that franchisors may have to make adjustments to their normal franchise plans in order to attract well-run businesses to convert. However, less than 25 per cent of the franchisors using conversions needed to make any changes to their normal conversion franchise plan. Most changes made to attract converts included reduced fees (23.6 per cent); added training (16.7 per cent); reduced royalties (11.1 per cent); covered remodeling costs (8.3 per cent); additional capital (5.6 per cent); longer contracts (5.6 per cent); and other (22 per cent). Thus, a variety of changes are made by a minority of franchisors in order to attract businesses to convert to their system.

The majority of franchisors who are currently using conversions to grow plan to continue using them in the future.

Thirty-one per cent plan to increase their use of conversions; 25 per cent plan to use them at the same rate as in the past. Only two per cent of the franchisors plan to decrease their use of conversions in their domestic markets. These intentions indicate that franchisors are satisfied that conversion franchising delivers distinct advantages over other forms of doing business.

The survey also briefly explored the franchisors' use of conversions in international markets. Twenty-six per cent of the respondents use conversion franchising in international markets. Half of these franchisors began using conversions internationally in 1990 or after, and currently an average 5.8 per cent of their overseas units are conversions. The country markets in which they have the largest number of conversions include Canada (37 per cent of respondents), Germany (21 per cent), France (16 per cent), and the U.K. (16 per cent). Importantly, of the franchisors using conversions internationally, 61 per cent intend to increase their future use of conversions internationally.

By way of summary, the descriptive data reveal that a substantial proportion of North American franchisors are using conversion franchising. Businesses were attracted to convert because of numerous competitive advantages associated with conversion franchises. The future of conversions appears to be quite promising, especially in international markets, as the domestic market becomes more saturated.

All four propositions advanced regarding the factors associated with a franchisor's decision to use conversion franchising were examined using discriminant analysis.

Since there were only two categories for the dependent variable, a single discriminant function was derived. The function, using competitive advantages and barriers to predict the decision to convert, is meaningful as indicated by the statistically significant Wilks' lambda of .45, p [less than or equal to] . The function accounts for 55 per cent of the variance in the decision to convert.

The validity of the function is ascertained by how well it predicts the classification of firms between those that use conversion franchises and those who do not. The derived function correctly classified 93 per cent of the firms. This is almost a 33 per cent improvement over chance alone. A statistically significant and valid function also may be interpreted. For interpretation, we use the discriminant loadings from the structure matrix. These loadings are simple correlations between each independent variable and the discriminant function. The loadings can be interpreted similar to factor loadin gs to assess the relative contribution of each independent variable.

The analysis of the discriminant loadings and their ability to discriminate between franchisors who convert and those who do not (F tests of group means) reveals five variables that significantly explain the decision to convert. According to Proposition 1, the decision to convert is associated with franchisor experience. Only experienced franchisors with an established reputation and system can use conversions meaningfully.

Proposition 1 is supported as "experience," has a relatively high, positive loading, and is also a significant discriminator between franchisors who use conversions and those who do not. Proposition 2, concerning the resource advantages associated with conversion franchising, is supported. "Economic resources" has a high positive loading, and its mean is also significantly different between the two groups of franchisors. Firms that use conversions perceive that they derive greater competitive resource advantages than firms who do not u se conversions.

Proposition 3 concerning the association of "skill/ knowledge" advantages of conversion partially is supported. Franchise skills (through experience), market skills, and industry knowledge all are associated with the decision to convert. Franchise and market skills have the two highest, positive loadings and are significant discriminators as indicated by tests of mean differences. The retail industry sector has a moderate but negative loading. The negative loading suggests that nonretail industry experience is more relevant in the decision to convert; other industry categories did not have high loadings, however.

The ability of this variable to discriminate between the two groups is marginal. Organizational monitoring skills achieved through scale and bondings had relatively weaker loadings and were not significantly different among the two groups of franchisors, contrary to our proposition.

Finally, competitive barriers did not add significant discriminating information to the decision to convert, contrary to Proposition 4. Neither effort nor changes had strong loadings, nor were their means significantly different between the two groups of franchisors. However, the negative sign of the loadings for effort was in the predicted direction.

Overall, our implicit model of franchisor experience and the competitive resources and skill advantages provided by conversion franchising appear to be significant predictors of the decision to use conversions. Although competitive barriers appear to exist, they do not appear to contribute significantly to the decision to convert, at least among this sample of franchisors.

Although conversion franchising appears to have been used for some time (since 1930 according to firms in our sample as reported previously), its use has accelerated recently. Over half of the firms have started using conversion franchising since 1987. While conversions appear to be more prevalent in domestic rather than international markets, a greater proportion of firms intend to increase their use of conversions in international (61 per cent) versus domestic (31 per cent) markets. The descriptive data also seem to support the franchising and strategy literature regarding why firms convert to a franchise system. Resources such as brand identity, franchisor support, and training were among the most frequently cited reasons.

Three of four propositions concerning the factors affecting the decision to use conversion franchising were supported in whole or in part. The most significant discriminant variables explained 69 per cent (38/55 per cent) of the variance accounted for by the discriminant function. Our results confirm that firm experience, economic resources, market skills, franchising knowledge, and selected industry experience all contribute significantly in explaining why franchisors use conversion franchising as part of their growth strategy. These results support the strategy and marketing literature, indicating that resources and skills serve as sources of competitive advantage.

The results also support the franchising literature regarding the various benefits of this form of business organization. Competitive barriers were related negatively to the decision to use conversions but did not have strong loadings, nor did the means of the barriers differ significantly between those firms that use conversions and those that do not. It seems reasonable to assume that franchisors tend to focus more on the advantages rather than on the threats when considering whether or not to use conversion franchising.

The results of this study should be examined in the light of its potential limitations. The sample size may be considered somewhat small, especially when analyzing the propositions due to missing data. The results are pertinent only to North American franchisors. However, North American franchisors are the most mature and therefore are the most likely to consider conversions. Our data reveal that business experience is a significant factor in the decision.

Our respondent companies had similar profiles to nonrespondents, minimizing response bias. Our measures of competitive advantages and barriers were drawn mostly from the field rather than the literature; this may reduce their explanatory power. However, both subjective and objective measures of competitive advantages were used to reduce same-source bias.

Slightly more than half of the variance in the decision to convert was accounted for by the variables examined in this study. Thus, these results provide a partial but not a complete picture of the factors affecting a firm's decision to use conversion franchising.

With the above limitations in mind, we offer some implications for practice and research. North American franchisors considering the use of conversions should possess significant experience in their business to develop both their business concept and a strong identity for their brand. Having done so, franchisors then have something to offer to businesses seeking to join their franchise system. When investigating potential businesses to convert, franchisors must evaluate carefully the resources needed to attract technically qualified businesses with a good track record in order to gain resource advantages.

Conversions may enhance the franchisor's market skills if the new franchisees are located in more distant markets and possess a prime business location. Conversions appear to be more attractive in nonretail sectors such as business and personal services and lodging. However, additional research is warranted to confirm these results.

North American businesses seeking to convert to a new or different franchise system are advised to seek a franchise with a proven concept and a strong brand identity in the markets in which they want to expand. Successful business converts should have a proven track record of financial performance. These potential converts should demonstrate that their management team is well experienced and qualified in their industry; however, they may lack some key resource or skill that the franchisor can provide.

This has demonstrated the relevance of employing theories of competitive advantage to guide systematic studies of conversion franchising. Future studies should develop more robust measures of competitive advantages and threats. Larger samples from other parts of the world also should be included to determine if the factors affecting the decision to use conversion franchising are the same in other national or regional markets. A particularly fruitful avenue for future research suggested by our data is the use of conversion franchising for international expansion.

While a minority (26 per cent) of the North American firms currently are using international conversions, the majority (61 per cent) of these firms intend to increase the use of conversions for international growth. Studies examining the factors affecting the international conversion decision also would be a valuable addition to the franchising knowledge base.

Chapter 8

Sociability and Models of Catering

MULTI-LAYERED MORALS

Picnicking is eating in the open, and thus being seen by others. In interpreting the behaviour of people eating in the open, it is crucial to consider frames of interpretation and connotation, grounds for moral and legal judgements. Places where alcohol was being served, especially, proved prone to moralizing and comments.

Results of new research on everyday and festive eating and drinking yield an interesting variation on the debate, launched by Peter Burke in the 1970s, about the growing divergence between elite and popular cultures. Differentiation is a key concept here, next to appropriation and demarcation. In this book Christoph Guggenbiihl makes use of emic interpretations of elite groups in Switzerland. He emphasizes that from the end of the eighteenth century a differentiation of catering businesses established itself. Guggenbiihl discusses the many functions of inns and shows how they were decanted into moral issues. The moralizing gaze was also present in middle-class observations of the (eating) habits of French labourers in the nineteenth century, as Anne Lhuissier demonstrates. Oliver Haid adds to this debate the case of Meran, where the introduction of a beer culture in a wine region did not pass unnoticed.

Beat Kumin discusses gastronomic culture in early modern inns. He questions the sharp cut-off before and after the 'modern' restaurant, with enhanced consumer choice, flexible dining times and menus with different dishes. Sources for early-modern Central Europe, in particular the Swiss republic of Bern and the principality of Bavaria, reveal variety, both in dining options and catering quality, a la carte selection options and table d'hote menus.

The major towns provided exquisite dining contexts. Kumin launches the thesis that what was crucial was not the invention of individualized service, but the creation of establishments exclusively dedicated to customer choice. Restaurants built on earlier practices but wrapped the eating experience in a special context, promoted an environment of leisurely and quality time consuming indulgence and bourgeois ostentation. In contrast to inns, they gradually moved away from the table d'hote system and the offer of accommodation facilities.

Maja Godina-Golija provides a case study of food available in catering establishments in the city and the countryside in Slovenia at the end of the nineteenth century and the first half of the twentieth century. The distribution of specific institutions of inns and then restaurants gives an insight into the kind of food potentially within reach. It is clear that a wideranging virtual menu of food and dining arrangements was available in Slovenia. Inhabitants and travellers in the region had access to many sorts of dishes, if they had the means.

BENEATH THE PAYING CUSTOMERS, THE CUSTOMS

There is a relation between eating out and having a home. Soup kitchens or charity meals in the open air, in city streets or squares, are not addressed here. People invited to a feast usually do not pay (but bring gifts and invite their hosts on another occasion). This is often embedded in what Pierre Bourdieu called an economy of symbolic goods.

Eszter Kisban emphasizes that in nineteenth- and early twentiethcentury Hungary wedding meals were the opposite of everyday meals, having their own rules and norms.

Alexander Fenton describes how, in mid-twentieth-century Scotland, employers had to provide meals free of charge to children granted exemption from school attendance for helping in the harvest. In a number of chapters of this book, 'cash' is suspended. Food can be carried to the field but it is not paid for there; it is distributed. Paying at the picnic is also not customary, although, as noted above, pooling was organized or people brought their own food. Nevertheless, the carrying has its price: a time investment at home, an effort to keep and store food on the way (and money is more economical, it takes up less space, volume and weight).

We may discover a number of occasions of eating and drinking out where the food or drinks are not paid for by the diners themselves. Marc Jacobs explores a tip of the iceberg of eating food for free (but, on a closer look, with social strings attached). Reciprocity and unwritten rules are important topics in the history of semi-public wining and dining. Eating in public is also a way to communicate with other groups or individuals. The concept of the tournee generale, when someone pays for all the clientele at an inn, is not usual in a restaurant. It is possible to invite a whole group to a restaurant, on the occasion of a wedding or a funeral, but at the time a number of the normal rules change (no menu, no open access for outsiders).

Rituals involving eating out, or in front of other households, remind us of alternative needs, codes and expectations and bring to mind a broad range of possibilities and repertoires. Symbolic violence often accompanied rites of passage or forms of collective action, resulting in free meals or in conspicuous food consumption.

Most chapters of the book show how menus gradually changed over time. Special occasions of eating in public functioned as a serving-hatch for innovations on the menu of everyday life. Kisban suggests that public occasions of hospitality, traditional feasts and the liminal zone of rites de passages in the country were important for the process of food innovation. Fenton emphasizes that eating out in peripheral areas is not frozen in time. He identifies a process of endogenous development: slowly, almost imperceptibly, but cumulatively, eating habits change.

Specific attempts at intervention, central direction, do not necessarily have a lasting effect on eating habits. However, eating landscapes do change. New objects are introduced (picnic baskets, hamburger packs ...). New settings are created. New dealers operate. New distribution lines are organized. New words are developed.

This is far from just a contribution to 'oral history': the history of eating out involves all senses, it is a total experience. Seeing the food, seeing the other eaters, the people serving, smelling the food, hearing the food and the other eaters, and the people serving, touching the food ... Eating out is also about reflecting on the food and the situation. The context evokes (or is the result of) all kinds of strings attached to the food: incentives of perception, being conscious of, or alert to, implication and obligations when eating the food (to pay, to shift to a ritual mode of etiquette, to be polite...).

This book reopens an old but never concluded debate of the 1980s: a discussion on popular and elite culture about the relations, actions, perceptions and interventions of elite groups seeking distinction and distance, on the one hand, and the vast majority of the population, on the other. Next to Roger Chartier, who discussed the concept of appropriation, E. P. Thompson temporarily closed the debate in his Customs in Common. He pointed to the definition that was propagated by Peter Burke, who approached culture as a system of shared meaning, attitudes and values, and the symbolic forms (performances, artefacts) in which they are embodied. Thompson added an agonistic view to this consensual view:

But a culture is also a pool of diverse resources, in which traffic passes between the literate and the oral, the superordinate and the subordinate, the village and the metropolis; it is an arena of elements full of conflict, which requires some compelling pressure - as, for example, nationalism or prevalent religious orthodoxy or class consciousness-to take form as 'system' [...]. The plebeian culture which clothed itself in the rhetoric of 'custom' [...] was not self-defining or independent of external influences. It had taken form defensively, in opposition to the constraints and controls of the patrician rulers.

Thompson emphasizes the relations of power, which are masked by the rituals of paternalism and deference. The history of the restaurant in the transition from early-modern to modern society and in the nineteenth and twentieth centuries is also the history of service. Rituals of deference and service are available in eating-out situations, when money is exchanged. E. P. Thompson formulated a programme of research that requires attention today in the study of popular culture, peripheral 1/or traditional communities. Needs and expectations should be major themes:

The industrial revolution and accompanying demographic revolution were the backgrounds to the greatest transformation in history, in revolutionizing 'needs' and in destroying the authority of customary expectations. This is what most marks the 'pre-industrial' or the 'traditional' from the modern world this transformation, this remodelling of 'need' and this raising of the threshold of material expectations (along with the devaluation of traditional cultural satisfactions) continues with irreversible pressure today, accelerated everywhere by universally available means of communication.

This is precisely a central problem in the book we present here, in particular in the contributions by Beat Kumin, Julia Csergo and Stephen Mennell.

Tradition and the dissolving or reoriented opposition between popular and elite culture, and the mediation between the two, is very present in the chapter by Virginie Amilien. Taking Norway in the last decade as her case, she investigates the confrontation between a traditional way of eating and thinking about food, on the one hand, and the very (post)modern style of eating in restaurants, on the other. She stresses the still prevalent traditional values of eating (in), observes the clamorous discourse on dining out in restaurants, and opposes both to the marginal success of eating out in restaurants. She emphasizes the fracture with traditional, indoor-eating Norway. In doing so, she accurately embodies the bridge as well as the tensions between Part I and Part II of this book.

One may directly connect today's elegant brasseries to the taverns of the seventeenth and eighteenth centuries, and to the restaurants and grand hotels of the nineteenth and the twentieth centuries. The main feature of the history of this particular type of eating out would then be the democratization of a once rather elitist practice. Eating out in semi-public places, therefore, would testify to a key element of the history of the West during the past three centuries.

Yet the difference between eating out in preindustrial, industrial and post-industrial times is not only a mere matter of scale, meaning that more people would be able to visit restaurants more regularly, and spend more money, crucial though this is. It is equally necessary to study the characteristics of eating places in that past and present, as well as how they were perceived, labelled, classified and represented. It then becomes clear that 'democratization' does not refer to question of access of the exquisite restaurant to all people, but that democratization of the restaurant involves the search for identification, status, distinction and pleasure for all. In the twenty-first century, there are 'restaurant' accommodations for every purse and budget.

Nowadays, Europeans are eating out on a larger scale than ever before, but definitely when they do so they purchase prepared food instead of bringing it with them. Norway may be an exception, but in most European countries since 1950, many individuals and households have started to increase their expenditure on 'eating out'. This growth has been accompanied by the multiplication of culinary columns and tips in the media.

Part II deals with this history of numerous innovations related to outdoors eating in Europe since the late eighteenth century and up to today. It focuses on the culinary capital, Paris, and on a number of neighbouring countries in Western Europe, in particular on France, on the United Kingdom, on Germany and the Netherlands. Adel den Hartog discusses technological innovations in an international perspective, while Stephen Mennell touches upon the public sphere of the modern era.

Cookery Writing and Culinary Zeniths

The perception, denotation, classification and representation of semi-public eating places may be explained by three intimately related phenomena, namely food, eaters and writers. 'Culinary zeniths', or places in certain periods that are generally viewed as successful with regard to food (in terms of gastronomy and sales), necessitate innovative supply, high demand and extensive discourse. An example of a successful culinary epoch would be the surrounding of the Parisian Jardin du Palais Royal in the 1800s, with great chefs, affluent eaters and culinary commentators.

Another example, suggesting that the gourmet connotation is not required, would be the global burger-culture in the 1990s, with the setting up of thousands of similar restaurants, a desirous public and extensive, albeit often hostile, writing (and action). The role of writing cultivating culinary zeniths has already been assessed, but it has primarily been limited to the culinary criticism of professionals like Grimod, Curnonsky or Gault and Millau.

'Culinary discourse' is understood here as the bundle of all written accounts dealing with food. The discourse actually contributed to the shaping of a new culture, for which it was a requirement. Such is a central point made by Karin Becker and Alan Warde in this book, and by Stephen Mennell, who attributes to gastronomic writing a cardinal place in the forming of 'public opinion'. All three authors stress the importance of writing with regard to the construction of gastronomy, gourmets and taste, and they explore further the information provided by culinary discourse.

Writers reported on food, prices, dishes and, perhaps above all, on places. Atmospheres were depicted, the clientele was discussed, the service and staff were valued, the decoration was commented on, and the general environment (music, conviviality...) was described. Particularly the new-style restaurant (a la carte, lavishly, expensive and elitist) enticed many to write.

Restaurants in All Forms, Dishes of All Tastes

Luxury food was, of course, not only prepared in fancy restaurants. Long before and after 1800, the rich and famous used professional cooks. Also, domestic caterers brought and served fine food at home. Against Kiimin's assertion, several authors suggest here and elsewhere that the emergence of the modern restaurant around 1800 marked an important qualitative leap in many respects.

First, restaurants were open luxurious places, in principle accessible to everyone (but totally different from the openness of a picnic!). Surely, the salle (or dining room) was a restricted area, only accessible to an elite. Their privacy was brought into the public: the ambiguity between private and public is nicely illustrated by the placing of individual ('own') tables in one room (opposed to the 'collective' table d'hote). Hence, our classification of 'semi-public' (or 'semi-private'). In this, Hans-Jiirgen Teuteberg stresses the emergence of the 'private' table, while Stephen Mennell addresses the issue of the 'bourgeois public sphere' of eating. Adel den Hartog, in turn, addresses a crucial condition of the restaurant's selective accessibility, namely technology. Among other things, he demonstrates the importance of subsequent types of lighting to create special effects, new gimmicks and prolonged opening hours.

Second, this 'private eating in public' entailed new rules and prescriptions. The eater could be recognized as a gourmet or a connoisseur by other eaters, the staff and - when talked and written about - the wider public, only if certain (invisible, subtle, discrete) rules had been met. Such rules did change over time (again, here was a crucial role for writers in judging and creating 'good' and 'bad' taste, places and manners). Social codes in restaurants were used to exclude and include, but they could also be acquired, interpreted and applied for transgression. In a way, the temperance movement (restriction and self-control) may be seen, mutatis mutandis, as an example of severe but clear rules and prescriptions.

Third, a restaurant offered a choice of dishes, thus leaving the decision of what to eat to the individual - a theme addressed by Teuteberg and Warde. The change of the menu card reflected this innovation: before the breakthrough of the restaurant (and still today at weddings or private parties) a menu was mostly a card that informed the eater what he or she would eat, but with the restaurant a menu became a card that informed the eater about the choice and the price. It was a key element that allowed the marking of boundaries, the stressing of preferences, the construction of good taste, and distinguished the connoisseur from the parvenu.

Fourth, restaurants were enterprises, confronted with market rules of price setting, production cost, sale figures, workforce turnover, productivity and competitiveness. Equally, wage demands, unions, strikes, apprenticeship, working conditions and schooling were part of a restaurant's daily life. Such matters have hardly been studied, except perhaps for businesses and businessmen if they had names like Escoffier, Bocuse and other stars. Alain Drouard explores the covert world of (French) cooks, stressing their search for status, recognition and professionalism.

Elements of coping with this, as well as with competition, were specialization, innovation and increasing of choice, a process that was bound to be incessantly renewed. This creation and retention of a niche in the bourgeois public sphere existed right from the start of the modern restaurant, and perhaps formed the most obvious - and surely the most commented upon - difference with regard to the traditional inn or tavern. Adel den Hartog shows how the use of technological devices contributed to such a creation.

Fifth, individual and collective pleasures were also of great importance, with fine food being one element among many to enjoy alongside conversation, flirting, joking, laughing, etcetera. Hans-Jiirgen Teuteberg and Virginie Amilien stress this element of pleasure. The combination of these five features resulted in a semi-public place that soon became the locus of nineteenth-century bourgeois culture in the entire world. The plot between chefs, eaters and writers consisted of a non-stop search for distinction, innovation, novelties, surprise and amazement with new tastes, new dishes, new drinks, new tastes, new experiences, new forms, new chefs, new everything... Amilien demonstrates that this plot is still very active nowadays.

Fast, Faster and Fastest Food

Accessibility, choice, expanding supply and pleasure are characteristics of fancy and tourist restaurants; it may be argued that the same goes for fast-food restaurants. The accessibility of such restaurants is general, though, in 1970s Europe, for various reasons (such as relatively high prices and a type of eating experience and an image that were culturally unfamiliar) there was some reluctance to enter a Burger King. Today, these places are wide open to a diverse clientele, with particular focus on youngsters.

The matter of choice and expanding supply seems more difficult to deal with. Whether a sandwich bar, a fish-and-chip shop or a burger restaurant, the supplied food is very similar in each type of restaurant all over the globe. Nevertheless, choice increases, adapting to custom and taste, with an enlarging supply of cheeseburgers, chicken burgers, nuggets or hulaburgers. Moreover, a local touch is added to the burger culture: in France during the summer of 2001, for example, 'a regional touch to your hamburger' was advertised, while sandwiches with daily changing regional sorts of cheese were sold. Such innovations are linked to the 'Happy Meal', which intends to make the food in this type of restaurant into a total experience of fun.

Sure, this is marketing talk. For many (young) children, however, eating out in a burger restaurant represents their very first 'restaurant experience', often during the celebration of a birthday party: a double rite of passage indeed. Quite clearly, eating in a fast-food restaurant may be a very enjoyable event. It remains to be seen whether 'shortorder cooking' arrangements provide as much pleasure to those preparing the meals.

This kind of eating out provoked the most sturdy reactions related to pureness, authenticity, identity, taste, gourmandise, and so on, brought together in the slow-food movement and erupting sometimes in assaults on burger restaurants. The intensity of this movement may be linked to globalization processes that conflict with national agriculture, the local restaurant industry and 'authentic' taste. Here, globalization andregionalization come together.

Yet fast-food businesses have long existed and can hardly be viewed as a pure US import. John Burnett shows that fish-and-chip shops, charcutiers, tea-shops?, coffee and sandwich bars and food stalls of various sorts were set up in cities and places with crowds long before the coming of the US-style hamburger restaurant. Two chapters address the history of the snack restaurant. Derek Oddy surveys the British fastfood industry since the 1880s, linking its development to work, shopping and leisure, and thus underlining once more the mixture between coercion and pleasure.

He surveys the development of various forms of eating out in the fast way, seeing a period of transition in the 1970s, and ends up trying to define the fast-food eater in the UK in the 1990s. Anneke van Otterloo and Adri Albert de la Bruheze discuss the Dutch variant of the snack restaurant, with special emphasis on 'eating out of the wall'. They detect a clear break around 1960, when the snacking started to reshape the traditional meal pattern. Van Otterloo and Albert de la Bruheze link these developments to broad social and economic changes, like the increase of purchasing power and leisure time, individualization and technological breakthroughs. They stress the implication of the food system, meaning that consumption of snacks cannot be studied without looking at production and distribution.

Diffusing Public Places of Discipline

It would be wrong to conceive the modern history of eating out solely from the angle of fancy and popular restaurants, taverns, snack bars or inns. If it is accepted that 'innovation' is an important feature of the modern eating-out industry, then innovative places were also to be found elsewhere. Evidently, the luxury Parisian Cafe Riche had a totally different aura than a school canteen of the neighbouring arrondissement, but such canteens were also places of innovation with enormous influence. This opens up the wide field of eating (out) in schools, factories, army and police barracks (and indeed aeroplanes).

It is a mistake to think of these public-eating places wholly in terms of coercion, control and the sphere of grimy barracks. In many such communities, eating was a cherished moment to which special meaning was attributed. It could be a source of joy when a particular dish was served, a special desert was put on the table, or an extra bottle of beer was allowed. However, discipline was more at stake. In this book Anne Lhuissier uses the investigation of the Le Play group into eating habits of workers in nineteenth-century France, which was conducted with a sheer moralizing end. The workers' lunch was frugal, prodigal or totally excessive (each time with a plausible reason). Control, however, was complete when workers (or students, policemen ...) were fed by the institution.

Feeding a larger group necessitated financial control, and administrators have long calculated the daily price per person. Efficiency was high on the agenda. One consequence was that technological devices were first introduced in larger kitchens, a point well made by Adel den Hartog. Second, feeding a larger group necessitated social control involving strict rules, hierarchy and organization. In many schools, for example, food was used as a means to punish or reward.

Third, 'mass feeding' permitted a contribution to the construction and spreading of ideology. In this book, Isabelle Techouyeres illustrates this by looking at the 'republican' debate on the educational aspect of school meals in the long twentieth century. In doing so, she also demonstrates the importance and interest France (be it teachers, parents, politicians, children...) has in taste and gastronomy.

This leads to the fourth point: according to the development and perception of nutritional science, administrators of larger kitchens considered the energetic values of food (often linking this to the cost), as well as hygienic rules. Ulrike Thorns considers here industrial canteens in Germany between 1850 and 1950, stressing the influence of nutritionists who promoted 'rational' feeding. In particular, she looks at the building of new canteens and kitchens, the technology of this type of food serving, and, again, social and ideological implications. Through the controlling of eaters in public eating and drinking places, many innovations were introduced. In this respect, the distance between the Parisian Cafe Riche and the army canteen of the adjacent district was not that big.

This introduction merely echoes the richness of all chapters of this book. It presents just one plat dujour of a kitchen that in facts serves many appetizing tapas with new approaches, questions and insights. Thus, the history of the cooks, the fast-food bars, the industrial canteens, the tourist restaurants, the writing on taste or the technology of eating out is highlighted. Other aspects, such as demographic pressure, the history of businesses, the influencing of eaters and eating, foreign restaurants or cooking techniques are present in this book and deserve equally to be discussed. We hope that the reader has found a nice carte dujour for many days here.

Up the Cost of a Meal

Of little-known origin, the term, unheard of in the sixteenth century, seems to have been used for the first time in the seventeenth century, more precisely by LaBruyere in Les Caracteres written between 1687 and 1688 and continued until 1694: If he has a picnic at home, he puts aside part of what was brought to him. This date is confirmed by Bloch and von Wartburg, who note the first appearance of the term in 1694 without giving a precise reference.

If we refer to the dictionaries of the period, the term appears neither in the Dictionnaire Universel by Furetiere (1690), although it is true that it precedes the first usage of the term by four years, nor in the Richelet (1719). The first time the word is mentioned is in the third edition of the Dictionnaire de l'Academie, which appeared in 1740. Therefore it was only officially introduced into the French language in the middle of the eighteenth century, when it is defined as an adverbial way of speaking that is only used in phrases such as a 'picnic supper', 'to have a picnic meal'. It is used to say, 'to have a meal where each person pays his or her share'.

That form fell out of use, pushed aside by its noun form, 'a picnic', which was used in the elliptical form of a meal in the picnic style, which later led to the simplified use of 'picnic'. How did this term come into being? Who invented it and what was the intention that could not be expressed in the existing vocabulary? None of these questions have any reliable answers. According to Bloch and von Wartburg, the expression comes from the wordpiquer (pick or to pinch/ swipe) but with the meaning of picorer (peck at or pinch food).(as in piquer les tables for someone who lives as a parasite) and from nique with the meaning moquerie ou chose sans valeur (mockery or something without value). According to them, the term, of French origin, was adopted throughout the rest of Europe, ending with 'picnic' in English in 1748 and picknick in German in 1753. That etymology is not universally accepted.

The Littre of 1869 and La Grande Encyclopedic of 1885 consider it of English origin, coming from 'to pick' (grasp) and 'nick' (an instant), and proposes the spelling pikenike, piquenique or picnic. One of the hypotheses proposed and later rejected by the Larousse universel of the nineteenth century (1866–79) shows the extent of the confusion: 'Pique-nique', says Larousse, 'aurait pu s'etre dit originairement d'un repas fait dans un village nomme "Pique-nique"' (Picnic could have come originally from a meal eaten in a village named 'Picnic'). He suggests another hypothesis, just as eccentric, according to which the term comes from a deformation of es beicktet nicht (sic), a phrase which a German traveller might have said after a satisfying meal eaten at a Parisian caterer's.

According to another hypothesis proposed by Larousse, it comes from the expression you offend me, I mock you this expression itself coming from the German nicken (to wink at someone in mockery) - an expression close in meaning to 'get back at someone'. The dominant idea here is both of revenge and a balancing out where 'each person will get his or her own'.

The term could then be used in all sorts of situations: one could love or hate 'in picnic', an expression used by Alphonse Karr, for example. Applied to a meal, the expression would therefore justify the definition 'repas ou chacun paye son ecot' (have a meal where each person pays his or her share), 'ou apporte son plat' (or brings their own dish), or a meal where no one owes anything to anyone else because participants all pay their share, paying in kind or with money. Payment could be of diverse nature: by paying money, by bringing one's own meal or by providing dishes for the group. In this way the term originated to express a practice that was not covered by any other term.

In 1870, Bescherelle's Dictionnaire National endorses that same meaning even if he suggests another etymology: the expression could come from the verb piquer (pick) and the term nique, an ancient small coin. Picnic would then express a meal where each person picks at a dish for their coin - for their money.

According to different publications, the definition of picnic as a meal where each person brings a contribution grows in three dimensions; spatial, hedonistic and convivial: 'a meal for two or several people, 'repas de plaisir ou chacun paye son ecot et qui se fait soil en payant sa quote-part d'une depense de plaisir, soil en apportant chacun son plat dans la maison ou on se reunit' (a pleasurable meal where people pay their part either by paying their share or by bringing a dish to the house where everyone meets), 'repas de societe [..., diner improvise' (a social meal [...] improvised dinner), 'repas, partie de plaisir' (a pleasurable meal or party).

Originally, then, 'to picnic' would be to eat together away from one's home, at someone else's home, but not necessarily outdoors. It would be to spend pleasurable time together and share expenses by contributing financially to the meal or by bringing something to eat. This definition is confirmed by the use of the term in literature. In his Essai sur la peinture (1766), Diderot, when addressing Boucher, mentions the convivial dimension of a picnic: 'Quand je suis en pique-nique avec mes amis et que la tete s'est un peu echauffee de vin blanc, je cite sans rougir une epigramme de Ferrand' (When I am 'picnicking' with my friends and I have been warmed by white wine, I quote without blushing an epigram by Ferrand). It is also used by Flaubert with the meaning of a meal in which everyone shares the expenses.

In Lucien Leuwen (1825–39), d'Antin and his gambling friends organize a picnic for which Mme d'Hocquincourt declares: 'Je vais m'occuper au nom du pique-nique d'avoir du vin et de le faire frapper' (In honour of the picnic, I will take care of the wine and make sure it is cooled). Used as a meal eaten 'together' 'away from home', but in various and private places, it is mentioned by Flaubert or George Sand, for example in Sand's L'Histoire de ma vie, published in 1855: 'Everard venait me chercher vers six heures pour diner dans un petit restaurant, avec nos habitues, en pique-nique' (Everard came to get me around six o'clock to dine in a little restaurant, with our regular companions, 'in picnic'). Again in Le Pieton de Paris (1932), L. P. Fargue mentions a Curiosity shop where 'des pique-niques s'improvisaient le dimanche' (picnics are improvised on Sundays).

Frederic Le Play's monographs about the working classes illustrate the colloquial and popular use of the term 'picnic' with this meaning. Among the twenty monographs about workmen in Paris (or in the near suburbs), it is used twice for meals where the expenses are shared. The first time is in an 1857 study of a shawl weaver from Gentilly where the term is used by poor families when they 'have a picnic meal' during a wedding 'payant' (where guests are charged):

Les invites sont alors avertis a 1'avance, et, au moment de se separer, apres les rejouissances, on fixe le chiffre de la cotisation qui doit etre fournie par chaque menage. [...] Cet usage a cela d'avantageux qu'il permet de conserver, dans les families les plus pauvres, 1'ancienne habitude des fetes celebrees au moment du mariage. (The guests are warned in advance and when it is time to go home at the end of the festivities, the cost is determined that must be provided by each family group. This custom has the advantage of allowing the poorest families to maintain the age-old custom of a celebration at the time of a wedding.) The second time it is mentioned is in a study carried out in 1891 concerning a Parisian cabinet maker who, during the summer, was accustomed to having 'picnics' at his friends' home in the suburb of Ivry: 'On se rend chez des amis et Ton paie son ecot sans fa?on, a litre de revanche' (We go to our friends' home and we bear the cost for our share without any fuss, to pay them back).

When they are referring to a meal eaten outdoors during a Sunday, the authors of monographs never use the term 'picnic', but expressions such as dejeuner (luncheon), diner sur I'herbe (luncheon on the grass), or dans la campagne (in the country), or even gouter ('snack'), which refers to a meal that the peasants eat in the fields. In this way, this form of a meal that can be improvised at anyone's home, at any time, and where everyone pays their share, this use of 'picnic', which can be defined as a way of sharing expenses of a meal, has lasted for a long time. Yet the term has become, in our imagination, a rural or rustic meal eaten outdoors, a dejeuner sur I'herbe (luncheon on the grass). It is worth noting that the last edition of Dictionnaire de I'Academie (1931–5) still gives the definition of 'repas ou chacun paye son ecot' (a meal where everyone pays their share), while only the contemporary supplements of famous dictionaries like the Larousse the Littre or the Robert mention a country meal. For the origin of this modern definition of 'meal with a group of people eaten in the countryside', Alain Rey reports in the Dictionnaire historique de la langue francaise (1992) that the word was borrowed from English probably before 1870, and that the English 'picnic' was itself a French loan word that had developed that meaning (1748, Chesterfield). We will now consider the reasons for this mutation and the steps leading up toil.

Necessity and an Exceptional Pleasure

First, it must be remembered that in spite of the importance and the prominence of the representations of which it is the object, starting from the last third of the nineteenth century, a meal eaten in the open air was a common practice during the pre-industrial era. There is frequent evidence of this practice ranging from an everyday necessity to an exceptional pleasure.

For field labourers, a meal eaten outdoors was a practice linked to their working conditions and to their meal break. According to the period, countries or regions, it goes by different names, but until the middle of the twentieth century nothing was written and no pictorial representation termed this meal eaten in a field a 'picnic'. These practices, born of necessity, were often seen in paintings or engravings of the seventeenth and eighteenth centuries, showing pastoral or romantic practices. Here, these images must be considered in the light of their depiction of a rural scene close to charitable Mother Nature. They would have the connotation of disgrace if they were situated in an urban setting where the act of 'eating outside', in the open air, was associated for a long time with a practice of the destitute and homeless.

However, both in town and in the countryside since the Renaissance, probably following Italian fashion, and later, when verdure and gardens were customary, dinners and light meals eaten out doors became part of the aristocratic way of life. Put aside hunting meals, which are a particular type of meal, and look at pictorial representations of outdoors meals in gardens of Eden where paradisiacal happiness reigns, such as in the works of Lancret or Vernet. Written evidence is abundant too. For example, we can read about the distinct taste of Catherine de Medici for improvised meals in the Tuileries Gardens. During the seventeenth century, elite Parisians liked to 'manger du jambon le matin aux Tuileries' (eat some ham in the morning in the Tuileries Gardens), where Anne of Austria herself 'joue la collation' (enjoys a light meal). Finally, what can be said about the revolutionary banquets organized in the streets, where everyone brought the food that was to be placed on the common table, and which led to the commemoration ceremony in France in the year 2000, with I'incroyablepique-nique (the unbelievable picnic) as a meal of fraternity?

Travelling was also a pretext for outdoor meals. During King Charles IX 's tour of France (1564–6), ambassadors tell of the taste of Catherine de Medici for meals in the countryside: as she travelled, she was followed by two beasts of burden carrying 'fruits et confitures' (fruit and jam) and a horse laden with 'la malette ou Ton meet la collation de ladite dame allant par pays' (the chest that contained the meal of the lady going through the country). Other sovereigns too appreciated these improvised meals during their travels: Saint-Simon reports that for his journeys, Louis XIV required that his carriage be supplied with meat, pastries and fruit and that he would often stop on his way to 'diner sans sortir de son carrosse' (dine without getting out of his carriage).

Other types of evidence testify to this taste of the aristocracy for rustic meals. For example, MarieAntoinette's travelling chest, a masterpiece of cabinet-making filled with choice porcelain, silverware and crystal glassware, gives us a foretaste of the picnic chests made by the most famous accoutrement makers in the era of the car. During the first third of the nineteenth century, the Prince of Faucigny-Lucinge reports the special fondness of the Duchess of Berry for the brilliant entertainment obtained from meals eaten unceremoniously in a carriage. It wasn't something that happened every day and was out of the ordinary. It was therefore a real pleasure.

For this, the butler would set up a table covered with a tablecloth made up of little boards folded one into the other, but once unfolded would be attached by little screws so that they would be stable. He would set the silver, the pitcher, the silver cups, pull the ivory spools from the armrests for the salt and pepper, and serve the meal of a perfect picnic: salami, prosciutto from Bologna, mortadella cold tongue, and chicken with the pieces which had been separated and then carefully put back and held in place with silk threads, fruit, and wine from Cyprus. These few references show that taking meals in the open air, only for pleasure, was a common activity among the elite, who were not obliged to do it for financial reasons.

Country Parties and Rustic Meals

During the nineteenth century several factors contributed to the practice of rustic meals: urbanization and industrialization, and at the same time the development of the hygienist trend, progress in the means of transportation, and new legislation on the duration of the working week. Some brief reminders. While the hygienist trend was gaining momentum in the name of public health, and leading to improvement in medicalization and sanitation in the country, representations of urban pathologies, previously based on demographic pressure, anarchical urbanization, deadly epidemics, pollution and physical and moral disorders (alcoholism and debauchery), were supplemented by a new imagery linked to the confusion caused by new technology and to an acceleration of the tempo of modern life. Surrounded by the pathologies of the modern world, including nervous fatigue, exhaustion and anemia, the hygienist trend favoured representations, extensively depicted since the seventeenth century, of nature as a healthy haven and a source of physical and moral rest.

At the same time the extension of the railway system and the rapid improvement of the speed of traveling, leading to a decrease in the price of railway tickets, prompted the growth of the social and geographical counter-urban phenomenon, the recreational day trip to the country called partie de campagne? A lot of evidence shows an increasing trend of Sunday invasions in the summer of the outskirts of a city like Paris to a distance that varied between 4 and 50 km. In 1878, Zola mentioned 500,000 Parisians, almost a quarter of the population of the city, who 'par certains dimanches de soleil [...] prennent d'assaut les voitures et les wagons pour se rendre a la campagne' (on certain sunny Sundays [...] storm the carriages and trains to get out to the countryside). Finally, the progressive and concomitant compression of work time brought about the 'profanation' of the values of Sunday free time.

This day was traditionally dedicated to religion, but from then on it was (also) used for rest, recreation and family sociability, especially during days spent outside of the cities in a natural setting that became a place of regenerating leisure. In spite of the increase in these recreational day trips and the generalization of rustic meals, the term 'picnic' to describe these countryside meals remains absent from our sources. For example, it never appears in the guidebooks of the outskirts of Paris printed in the eighteenth and nineteenth centuries.

It is worth noting that this meal on the grass itself was rarely given as a model. For each site mentioned, the guidebooks pointed out restaurants, caterers, guinguettes and cafes where food could be obtained. The Cuchet and Lagaranciere's Almanack des plaisirs of 1815, a classical guidebook which enumerates the pleasures and amusements offered by the towns surrounding the capital, only mentioned the possibility of a 'meal out of doors' for one of the twenty-nine sites proposed, and without reference to 'picnic': it is Saint-Germain en Laye and its forest that offers this possibility to the Parisian bourgeoisie

Some people loaded their car with excellent rouget pate, boned fowl and bottles of Chambertin, others brought a big basket with beef stew, salad with dressing, and are obliged to make do with the local wine. Everyone eats with a hearty appetite, enjoying the beauty of the site, the freshness of the air and that precious liberty so rarely found in the city.

Later Promenades aux environs de Paris pointed out only for Romainville, which attracted Parisians on holidays, that a great many groups dine in the woods, in the grass, and what cannot be brought along such as bread, wine, etc., is obtained from the game keeper or a caterer. It was not until the Guide Tinnenbrock of the outskirts of Paris that, when codifying the rules for an excursion in the chapter entitled 'Conseils donnes aux touristes pour une partie de campagne' (Advice given to tourists for a country party), the equipment and the menu of a 'country buffet' were specified without ever using the term 'picnic'.

However, a meal out of doors, as an amusing activity, seems for a time to have been an unavoidable activity for children in Promenades aux environs de Paris. In some of these works published between 1838 and 1850, engravings portrayed scenes on the lawns of Versailles, on the Island of Sevres or in the woods of Meudon. These scenes were called diner sur l'herbe, or diner de campagne (dinner in the countryside) - in Charonne, with a roast and a salad.

It is worth noting that the term 'picnic' was almost never mentioned in travel journals or chronicles. Here are a few examples chosen from a large sampling. When visiting in Paris in 1834, the naturalist Alfred MoquinTandon went to see the usual tourist sites in the capital and participated in the inevitable partie de campagne (party in the countryside) in SaintCloud, without mentioning a 'picnic'. Flaubert, although using the term in his novels, in his Garnets de voyages (1847) mentioned his supplies for the road several times and, after long and tiring hikes, his meals out of doors, which he calls casse-croute. A hand-written document like the Journal kept between 1854 and 1874 by Alexandre Bruyer, a Parisian employee who loved Sunday outings, never mentioned a 'picnic'. In the summer season, accompanied by his wife, he went on outings loaded with 'filets remplis de victuailles' (string bags full of food).

This custom did not come from a deliberate choice or from the desire for an entertaining meal, but was adopted because their modest financial situation only allowed them to eat occasionally in restaurants. So at the edge of a wood or forest, the couple would take a break 'sur le gazon, a 1'ombre' (on the grass, in the shade), and pull their meagre lunch our of their bag, to savour it 'avec la lenteur des gens qui ont envie de se reposer' (slowly like others at leisure) or 'garment' (joyfully) because they were 'heureux de se sentir libre' (happy to feel free).

However, a rapid examination of journals or correspondence of foreigners travelling in France shows that for the same period the term 'picnic' is used by Anglo-Saxon travellers to describe a rustic meal. Mrs Trollope, an English woman who stayed in Paris during the spring of 1835, tells of an excursion to Montmorency to visit the Hermitage, where a 'picnic' on the grass is followed by a walk on the paths of the foresters. Robert Louis Stevenson, who travelled on foot through the Cevennes in 1878, never used this term for the meals that he ate alone in the outdoors, which he was forced to do because of hunger and the absence of any inn.

However, in a short text, 'An Autumn Effect' (1875), he tells of an outing in a cart above High Wycombe and notes: 'The fields were busy with people ploughing and sowing; every here and there a jug of ale stood in the angle of the hedge [...]. There was a spirit of picnic.' It is a term that he associated with the pleasure of a social occasion. It was also the American Mark Twain who set sail on 8 June 1867 on the Quaker City for the famous first organized trip in the history of tourism. He gave the following subtitle to his travel journal 'A picnic in the Old World' because 'this book is a record of a pleasure trip [not] a record of a solemn scientific expedition'.

An outdoor Social Occasion or an Inexpensive Meal

Unlike its use in France, the term seems to have become a customary part of English as early as the beginning of the nineteenth century, used to designate a 'rustic meal' and not a way to share the expenses of a meal. In her Journal dated 1803, Dorothy Wordsworth uses the word to designate the custom of certain upper-class young people to eat on the grass on the banks of the Thames.

In his 1806 issue of L'Almanack des Gourmands, Grimod de la Reyniere subscribes to that definition of the term. Presenting the way to organize 'Parties de campagne erotiques et gourmandes' (erotic and gourmet countryside parties), he explains: 'Nous voulons trailer aujourd'hui de ces pique-niques a la campagne que Ton fait parfois entre amis pour tromper le temps, amuser son loisir' (Today we want to deal with picnics in the country that are sometimes organized among friends to pass the time, for entertainment in their leisure hours). The following model differs from the Anglo-Saxon:

On forme une societe d'hommes et de femmes bien apparies, mais qui ne doivent pas exceder douze personnes. On nomme un pourvoyeur qui doit etre choisi connaisseur, intelligent, probe, sachant bien acheter [...]; on lui remet les fonds pour lesquels chacun s' est cotise par egale portion, selon les depenses qu'on a voulu faire, et on le charge de tous les details nutritifs (A group of wellmatched men and women is formed, but not more than twelve people. A purveyor is nominated who must be chosen because he is a connoisseur, intelligent, honest, knowing how to buy. [...] He is given the funds to which everyone has contributed in equal shares, according to the purchases desired, and he is charged with all the culinary details.)

A gastronomic meal follows, carried in large baskets: fattened chicken fricassee served in bread, galantine of beef tongue, galantine of rabbit, cold roast turkey, ham from Mayence or Bayonne, boned pullet pate surrounded by some quail or larks, timbale of partridge, frangipane tart, Savoy cake, salad, seasonal fruit, petit fours, biscuits, macaroons, jams, without forgetting, for the men, Swiss or Roquefort cheese, all of which is served with table wine, wine from Juranfon, wine from Champagne, from Malaga, from Frontingnan, liqueurs and coffee. After having specified the order of the dishes, because Grimod's picnic is not an informal meal, he concludes:

> Nous ne parlerons point des joyeux propos, des couplets erotiques et des tendres discours qui auront assaisonne les mets de cette agape champetre. II suffit de dire que les femmes sont jeunes et jolies et que les hommes aimables et gourmands, le reste, on le devine (We will not talk about the happy remarks, the erotic verses and the tender speeches that will have spiced the dishes of this rural feast. We will only say that the women are young and beautiful and the men appreciate good food and are friendly, the rest we can guess.)

Is the above the reason why picnics in France have long been tainted with a certain immorality, considered as a practice of artists, students and grisettes, and bohemians of easy virtue? Is this why it was little used, at least under this terminology, in good company? The scandal caused by Manet's Dejeuner sur I'herbe could therefore be explained by the dramatic contrast between half-dressed women and well-dressed men because a gourmet sharing of food and women could be implied.

In prudish Victorian England, picnics have a prominent place in the bible for young women published in 1861 by Mrs Beaton, The Book of Household Management, which specifies in detail the art of organizing a picnic and a model menu similar to that of Grimod. This is in sharp contrast to the oracles of French manners, which are very reserved in respect to picnics.

In 1889, Baronne Staffe notes that Pique-niques and Cagnottes, a term that has today fallen into desuetude, are 'caisse commune a un groupe de personnes, alimentee par des cotisations ou des dons' (a common fund of a group of people which is financed by contributions or gifts), which goes back to the first definition of picnic:

> [...] il faut eviter les pique-niques. II regne en ces parties un laisser-aller qui mene vite aux inconvenances. Chacun est chez soi et les gens de nature un peu grossiere ne se sentent pas obliges a la retenue qui existe quand il n'y a qu'un seul amphitryon. Et puis, ces repas a frais communs donnent lieu a toutes sortes de remarques peu charitables, peu aimables, peu convenables: Mme une telle a apporte deux poulets et a amene six personnes. Mile X a donne un plat de fraises et elle a mange toutes les peches, etc. (Picnics must be avoided. Casualness prevails in these parties, which leads to impropriety. Each person feels at home, and people who are a little uncivilized do not feel obliged to keep up the reserve that is maintained when there is only one host. And then, these meals with shared expenses lead to all sorts of uncharitable, unfriendly and improper remarks: 'Mrs. Y brought two chickens and invited six people. Miss X brought a dish of strawberries and ate all the peaches', etc.)

A little further she adds: 'Les cagnottes ne me plaisent pas davantage. Au plus, pourrait-on admettre la cagnotte pour les pauvres' (Putting money in a common fund does not please me more. At the most, a money pool would be acceptable for the poor). To finish she concludes: 'Pique-niques et cagnottes ne sont pas en faveur dans le monde chic ni aupres des personnes dedicates' (Picnics and money pools are popular neither with stylish people nor with refined people). For Baronne Staffe, Garden parties, Lunch and Parties de campagne (country parties) are acceptable in good company with one exception, a recommendation for women:

> On part souvent en bande pour faire une excursion et dejeuner ou luncher sur 1'herbe. Les femmes prendront garde de ne donner lieu a aucune interpretation facheuse dans ces

parties ou regne un certain laisser-aller; elles doivent s'y monter tres reservees, ne pas s'isoler, enfin, pour tout dire, on ferait bien de s'abstenir de ces excursions qui ne sont possibles qu'entre hommes ou en famille (We often go out in a group, to go on an outing and to dine or have lunch on the grass. The women must be careful not to allow any misinterpretation in these parties, which are very casual; they must be very reserved and not go off alone, and finally, in a nutshell, it would better not to go on these outings, which are only possible among men or with a family.)

The Countess of Gence moderates this judgement of her Savoir vivre et usages mondains, dedicated to repas champetres (rural meals), she notes:

Les pique-niques sont generalement organises par la collectivite des jeunes gens ou des families qui en prennent 1'initiative. On a proteste centre la liberte un peu large de ces reunions tres gaies, sous pretexte que les convenances n'y etaient pas toujours parfaitement respectees. Entre gens bien eleves, tout est permis et les ecarts ne sauraient etre redoutes (Picnics are generally organized by a group of young people or families who take the initiative. There have been protests against the relative freedom of these gay gatherings, under the pretext that etiquette was not always respected. Among well-mannered people, everything is allowed and there should be no fear of lapses of conduct.)

The menu follows, which is almost invariable, with its cold meat, hot and cold pates and galantines, and the recommended financial organization refers directly to the first meaning of the term, still used in France: 'Quand on organise un pique-nique, les frais sont repartis sur chaque cavalier d'apres le nombre de dames presentes' (When a picnic is organized, the expenses are shared by each escort according to the number of women present).

Success of Outings and Recognition of the Picnic as a Country Meal

By the end of the nineteenth century the spectacular growth of various means of transportation and the henceforth-recognized success of tourism enabled 'picnic' to gain social recognition and become a standard term used to designate the practice of eating a meal in the outdoors. From now on, the term 'picnic' was to be associated with a meal eaten during a trip and just as often with one eaten during an outing or a country party. It was now considered a pleasurable meal and could even be a recreational objective.

In effect, the arrival, then the slow popularization, of the bicycle, which, a little later, was followed by the automobile, considerably reinforced the geographical displacement and transposition already induced by the railways, allowing a growing number of people to participate in various outings. At the end of the century, the new series of portable guidebooks that were printed reveal the substantial extension of the road network and the future of new transportation techniques. The Cyclo-guide Miran, the Guide Baroncelli or the Guide Michelin, written for cyclists 1/or motorists, indicate for the outskirts of Paris, for example, itineraries for day trips or longer, organized around natural or monumental, picturesque or imposing sites. At the same time, excursion company publications were becoming more numerous.

With the ease and increase in individual transportation, a pause for refreshment in the open air became for the 'sportsman' an indispensable part of the experience of a site. It added eating pleasure to the sensual and intellectual pleasures that came with the perception of a landscape from the point of view of its sounds, smells and sights. Integrated into the travelling experience, the word 'picnic' gradually took over as the generic term designating 'a packed lunch', formerly a necessity carried along during a trip but which has become a meal that is deliberately eaten in the outdoors, in order to savour the site visited, relish the pleasure of change that comes with travelling, nourish the physical activity enjoyed in nature, and reward the effort.

The automobile particularly favoured the birth of the nomadic picnic. On the eve of World War I, a motorist like Marius Carle who drove the roads of the Alps recommended that one should always have a supply of food in one's car in order to be able to stop to eat anywhere as soon as one found a pleasing location.

The most spectacular expression of this justification of the distinctive practice of 'picnics' is found in the increase in the number of new objects such as the punier Niniche, a chest equipped with plates, forks, tinware goblets, a coffee pot with a hot plate, and a rubber flask, the last accessory being recommended by the already mentioned Guide Tinnenbrock des Environs de Paris, which for the first time established the rules of an outing. They specified Tinvariable menu d'un dejeuner sur 1'herbe' (the usual menu of a luncheon on the grass): cold chicken and pates. This guide further provided a list of addresses where it was possible to obtain the first 'boites de conserves a chauffoir indispensables a toute partie de campagne' (heatable tinned goods indispensable for any country party).

These tinned goods, which were still used by campers during the first half of the twentieth century, contained full meals of meat and vegetables. The lower part of these tins had a small sealed container with a wick soaked in spirits of wine, which enabled the heating of the contents of the tin to boiling point. It must be remembered that tinned goods, which were not popular in France until after World War II, remained, for a long time, a luxury item: in other words, through advertisements for trips and outings in automobiles, they become a symbol of picnics for the well-to-do. For example, Amieux Frere put a 'Pic-nic' box on the market containing

> une assiette, deux serviettes japonaises, un tire bouchon renferme dans le manche de la fourchette, une fourchette, un cure dent, un verre a boire, une boite de sardines a cle, une boite de pate de foie gras truffe a cle, une bouteille de Medoc, une fiole de fine Champagne, une tablette de chocolat (a plate, two Japanese napkins, a corkscrew folded into the handle of a fork, a fork, a toothpick, a glass for drinking, a tin of sardines

with a key, a tin with a key of foie gras pate with truffles, a bottle of Medoc, a small bottle of Champagne liqueur and a chocolate bar).

During the 1920s, the number of luxury accessories continued to increase: chests, suitcases, kits, food boxes equipped with china, silver and crystal, and portable hot plates made by the most stylish accoutrement makers following the tradition of the royal chests that we have already mentioned. Around 1925, Hermes began selling a malette a picnic (picnic chest) - English spelling - containing all the necessary items: a platter for presenting dishes, thermos flasks, plates, goblets, closed cases, cups and folding tableware. In 1931 Hermes launched a new model that was a cloth case with a washable liner containing, for example, knives that could also be used as corkscrews and spoons as openers. In 1933 the chest was further improved as a folding table designed to be used for dining. Vuitton created other luxury items: folding tables and chairs, portable hot plates and even tents under which one could eat sheltered from the sun or unpleasant weather. All of these were proposed as picnic objects. To picnic now meant to eat in the open air but not necessarily on the grass. The practice was beginning to resemble 'camping', which was originally a sporty and elegant practice. This was how the term was used by Proust, for example, but with paid holidays, it later represented inexpensive and popular holidays.

Henceforth freed from the awkward notion of saving money or sharing the expenses of a meal, which was unacceptable to the customs, the savoirvivre and the conception of dining of the bourgeoisie, the Anglo-Saxon definition of 'picnic' was to prevail. Picnics came to be represented as a hedonistic pastime — a moment of shared pleasure centring on a meal eaten in a natural setting.

Chapter 9

Catering and Social Occasions

AT SOCIAL OCCASIONS

If you have become successful in making cakes or rolls or sandwiches or patties, or all of these things, people may already have begun to ask you to do other things, and have found that you can make many other dishes equally well. Somebody will soon want to know if you won't plan for and make all the sandwiches and cakes for the afternoon tea she is giving. If she is pleased, she or her friends will ask you to serve a more elaborate spread.

Before you know it you may be doing a catering business! It is far better to let your business develop naturally in this way than to open a catering establishment unless you have had considerable experience in cooking for large numbers of people or in the executive part of such a business. Before starting in to do a regular catering business on a large scale it would be well to secure a position in a well established catering firm to learn the many phases of this line of work.

Catering only would give an uncertain income at the best. It is usually carried on in connection with a cooked food shop, a lunch room, and hotel or community kitchen in order to make it a paying proposition all the year round. Like most businesses, catering is service. It also means much testing, tasting, time, thought and hard work, and no wasting.

Usually all dishes are prepared by the caterer and delivered to the place where they are to be served. As a rule no cooking is done on the premises, although facilities for reheating or keeping food hot may be found or provided. Special insulated coffee urns can be purchased of dealers in hotel supplies for $20 to $30, and containers for other hot foods will be made up to order on the principle of the thermos bottle. Frozen dishes are packed in molds and in tubs of ice and salt.

Experience will be your best guide as to the number of sandwiches, cookies and cakes, the amount of salad, ice cream and coffee to provide, but careful, intelligent planning in the beginning is also necessary.

Make up a definite amount of the desired food and note the amount necessary for one portion, and the number of portions in the amount you have prepared. Calculate from this data the recipe for one and then for the whole number to be served. During and after the serving of refreshments watch carefully and correct your estimates if necessary so you will have more accurate data another time.

BASIC PORTIONS

The following figures were taken from The Soda Fountain, a monthly magazine, and may serve as a guide in your computations. Lemonade, fruit punch, or other similar liquid beverage served in lemonade or punch cups10 quarts for each 60 people. Mineral glass portions10 quarts for each 56 people.

Ice cream - 6 standard portions to the quart. If bricks of ice cream are ordered, ready cut, they will make very satisfactory portions if each quart is divided into 8 servings. If a disher or ice cream scoop is used, know exactly how many scoops to a quart and a gallon you can get by using dishers of different sizes, and it will make a difference if these scoops are leveled off or just rounded out with all they will hold. Sometimes the profits go into careless measurements.

Frappe and Sherbet, hard frozen3 gallons for 50 people. Half frozen and beginning to melt2 gallons for 50 people.

Loaf Sugur: 1 pound to 24 people.

Berries: large sized ones10 quarts for 50 people. Medium sized ones8 quarts for 50 people. Smaller sized, sound, ripe berries 7 quarts for 50 people. Granulated or powdered sugar for berries 2 pounds for 50 people.

Fancy Wafers: 3 boxes -to 50 people.

Bonbons: 3 pounds to 50 people. OLIVES of medium size will run about 75 to the pint. Allowing 3 olives to a person, a pint will serve 25.

Boillon: hot12 quarts will serve 50 people, allowing about 7 ounces to a person. Jellied, 8H quarts will serve 50 people.

Whipped Cream: 1quart will make 50 rounding tablespoonfuls. One quart refers to the unwhipped cream, and the measurement by tablespoonfuls to the result after it is whipped.

Hot Chocolate: 25 to 30 cups to the gallon, depending on the cup measurement. This amount will take half a pound of chocolate.

Cakes: round loaf or layer, may be made to serve eight people if cut in triangles from the centre; or 16 people if cut in quarters and then sliced from.the centre outward toward the edge. In this case, the pieces are not exactly uniform in size, but the smaller pieces are thicker and the larger ones thinner, so each customer gets the same amount of cake in reality.

Croquettes: 6 pounds of meat will make croquettes for 50 people.

Oysters: Oysters on the half shell are apportioned at 4 to a customer. Solid oyster meats chopped call for 4 quarts for 50 people. Oyster stew allows 6 quarts to 50 people. If you wish a more generous allowance of oysters to a serving, allow 7 quarts.

Chicken: Turkey or Roast Meat. Remember that raw meats weigh from two to two and a half times their net weight when cooked. This is because so much of the moisture is evaporated when roasting. With meats which are boiled, or fried, or quickly cooked in any way, the raw meat will weigh about one and a half the cooked portions. Boiled meats will shrink almost as much as roast meats, much of the nutriment going to the gravy or broth. Twenty-five pounds of raw, dressed meat are allowed for the serving of 50 people, if the meat is hot. Cold meat goes farther because it can be sliced thinner, and 25 pounds can be made to serve from 60 to 70 people.

Salmon Salad. This calls for 6 pounds of salmon for 50 portions.

Chicken Salad: A 4-pound fowl combined with celery and the other trimmings should make 2 quarts of salad. 2 quarts of salad should serve 12 people or 1 quart to 6 people. 8 quarts will serve 50 people and 8 quarts of salad will call for 17 pounds of fowl. If larger portions are desired, and it is almost solid chicken meat, allow 20 pounds for 50 people.

Sandwiches: An ordinary sandwich loaf will make 24 sandwiches, or will cut into 48 thin slices of bread; or if you desire little thicker slices of bread and sandwiches with more substance, cut each loaf into 36 slices or 18 sandwiches. Each sandwich will be the full size of a slice of bread. Allow 2 sandwiches to a person. Or if the sandwiches are cut in two or in triangles, allow 4 to a person.

One pound of creamed butter should spread 3 loaves of bread. One quart of sandwich filling is the average allowance for one loaf of bread.

MENUS AND ESTIMATES

You should plan in advance several menus with standard dishes, suitable for afternoon teas, buffet spreads, wedding receptions, or other functions for which you may be asked to cater, and estimate the amounts required and the entire cost of serving fifty or a hundred or more people with these different menus. Then you will be prepared when you are called upon for an estimate of the expense for such service. With a change of menu there will probably be a change in the price, but something to work from for your patrons will be helpful both to you and to them.

When making up your estimate for any function do not forget to charge for transporting the food from your kitchen to the place where the entertainment is to be given, and do not neglect to charge for your own time including the time of consultation. The distance, the number of people to be served and the menu are important items that determine the price you must charge.

Your business may develop to such an extent that you will be asked to provide waitresses to set the table and to serve the refreshments, and you may also be requested to provide the tables, chairs, china, silver and linen, and even the decorations.

Equipment for Catering

You can probably get in touch with a caterer from whom you can hire such equipment as is necessary, on commission. In the same way you can make arrangements with one of the best florists in your vicinity, and make a commission on the flowers and other decorations that you have to provide.

If there are many people in your vicinity who entertain, it may be wise for you to purchase such equipment as is most frequently needed, as china, silver, linen, et cetera, that is not found in sufficient quantities in private homes. You can rent the equipment to your patrons, store it between engagements, and care for it instead of hiring from some one, and it will soon pay for itself, and be a distinct asset to your business.

Very careful figuring will be necessary to arrive at the proper charge to make for the equipment you lend. The original cost, loss by breakage, loss by theft, general wear and tear, cost of transporting, cost of washing, polishing, repairing, replacing, et cetera, must all be taken into consideration. Sometimes it is necessary to charge almost as much as the original cost of the china or glass each time it is rented.

Fifteen per cent of the total charge for serving a tea may be for the dishes used, while at an elaborate banquet as much as 75 per cent of the charge may be for the equipment alone. Prices charged for equipment vary with conditions. At one successful establishment the charges are as follows:

- One cent each for flat silver
- Fifty cents a dozen for cups, saucers, plates, et cetera
- One dollar and fifty cents a dozen for camp chairs.

A very large establishment may have to furnish awnings, carpeting, dancing crash, tables, etc., and also furnish footmen, musicians, dish washers and lumpers. There are special business houses in New York, Chicago, Cincinnati, and other large cities which will give you an estimate on the cost of such equipment as you find you need from time to time. Many of these firms advertise regularly in the Hotel and Caterers' Magazines.

Until your business has given you sufficient profit to warrant the purchase of an auto truck, you can hire a truck paying by the day or by the mile, for the transportation of food, equipment, etc. One large concern finds that waiters arrive in less dusty condition at their destination if they go by train or trolley instead of on the truck.

One waiter or waitress will probably be needed for each six to ten guests if an elaborate spread is provided. With simple refreshments and people coming and going during several hours, fewer waiters will be-needed. A dish washer will be necessary to scrape and rinse dishes before they are put back in their containers and returned to headquarters. Waiters and waitresses should be well trained and know exactly what they are to do while they are in your patron's home.

In this lesson we are giving lists of many dishes that may be used for different menus and for different occasions.

Afternoon Tea

It is not necessary to set a table for an informal afternoon tea, but a table should be ready to receive the refreshments in the room in which the guests are to be entertained. The table may be covered with a dainty tea cloth or centrepiece, spotless, unwrinkled, and as elaborate as one desires. A centrepiece of flowers may be in place on the table.

Coffee

With honey and whipped cream Add to these lists dishes that you yourself or your patrons like especially, and consult these lists constantly while planning new menus. As you note the cost of each dish and the amount required for a definite number of people, the figures may be placed in columns following the dishes. You will find it of the greatest help to have such lists to work from in planning meals for all sorts of occasions. A few notes are given to help in serving these refreshments.

- Boiled
- Filtered
- With cream and sugar
- With vanilla extract, sugar and whipped cream

Cocoa or Chocolate

- With cream
- With marshmallows
- With coffee flavor (Mexican chocolate)
- Iced chocolate

Soups

- Mock bisque soup
- Cream of chicken soup
- Beef Bouillon
- Chicken or clam bouillon with whipped cream

Punches

- Blackberry punch
- Cranberry bunch
- Cider arid white grape juice punch
- Gingerale lemonade
- Gingerale punch

- Grape juice and orange punch
- Grape juice lemonade with mint
- Ginger punch
- Loganberry punch
- Lemonade
- Orangeade
- Orangeade with gingerale
- Pineapple julep
- Pineapple lemonade"
- Tea lemonade
- Pineapple grape juice punch
- Tea punch
- Raspberry shrub punch

Frappes

- Cafe frappe with whipped cream
- Cider frappe
- Cranberry frappe
- Grape frappe
- Grape juice and mint frappe
- Orange frappe
- Raspberry frappe
- Strawberry frappe

How to Make Tea

Oolong, English breakfast, and Orange Pekoe tea are0 used for afternoon tea. It may be in the teapot when the tea tray is brought in. The water may be almost at the boiling point in a kettle heated by alcohol or electricity, and should be used as soon as it actually boils. It should stand on the leaves from 1 to 3 minutes only, depending on the kind of tea used. The tea should never be allowed to boil. Fresh leaves should never be added to those that have once been used for tea. Two level teaspoonfuls of tea and 1 pint of boiling water will make 3 tea cups of tea. Sugar and both lemon and cream are provided, and each guest makes her own selection. Other accompaniments are suggested above.

Where only 1 or 2 cups of tea are to be made at a time, a tea ball or perforated double teaspoon half full of tea may be used. Place in the cup, pour on boiling water, lift the ball up and down until the tea is the right strength as indicated by the colour, and remove tea ball immediately to another cup or a small dish. Two to 4 cups of tea may be made without refilling the ball.

Iced Tea

In hot weather iced tea may have a greater appeal than the hot beverage. The tea should be freshly made and poured while hot over pieces of ice in tall glasses. Sugar and lemon are used with it.

Coffee and cocoa are usually served from urns at which friends of the hostess preside. Filtered coffee may be made in the urn if it is provided with a strainer or if a linen bag is suspended in the urn. At a famous restaurant the rule is as follows:

One Gallon Filtered Coffee

Mix thoroughly 8 ounces medium fine ground coffee

- 1/2, of 1 egg white
- 1/2 cup cold water and
- 1/8 teaspoon salt; pour over
- 1 gallon of fresh water which is actually boiling

Draw off the liquid and pour over and over until of the right strength, then remove bag. If a percolator is used in which the water bubbles up and falls down through the coffee, it will probably take about 10 minutes to become of the right strength. Special insulated coffee urns should be provided in which coffee will keep hot for a number of hours if made in one place and served in another, or if it is served at intervals for several hours.

Boiled Coffee for Fifty

Put in coffee bag I pound ground coffee, place in container, add 6 to 8 quarts cold water and let stand several hours or over night. Bring to boiling point and boil 3 minutes. Remove bag and serve coffee as required. For After Dinner Coffee use 4 to 5 quarts of cold water.

Cocoa and Chocolate

Cocoa or chocolate may be served from the kitchen or from a chocolate pot at the table. Be sure the cocoa or chocolate boils with the water and sugar for at least 5 minutes before the milk is added, and that it is then kept hot over hot water or in a special container.

Mexican Chocolate

Scald

1 quart milk with 1 inch piece of stick cinnamon and 3 tablespoons ground coffee. Strain through cheesecloth, add 2 squares sweet chocolate melted over hot water and mixed with 1/2 cup boiling water. Cook three minutes over hot water, add 1/2 teaspoon vanilla and serve with Whipped cream.

Soups

Delicate cream soups are sometimes served at afternoon affairs, especially at bridge parties. A spoonful of whipped cream slightly salted or combined with sifted pimiento may be served on the soup.

Punch

Punch or frappe, which is a half frozen sherbet, is served with a ladle from a punch bowl, which should be on a small table that is covered with a luncheon cloth. Punch glasses should be on the table around the bowl. A block of ice should be in the punch bowl, also a garnish of thin slices of fruit or sometimes a bunch of mint leaves. Balls of lemon or strawberry ice may be used instead of ice in the punch bowl.

Whipped cream may be put on each glass of some varieties of punch as it is served. Gingerale or charged water should not be added to punch until just before it is served. Five o'clock tea sandwiches should be small and dainty. The bread should be thinly sliced, and the crusts removed. The serving plate may be garnished with cress or small lettuce leaves. White, graham, Boston brown or nut bread may be used. Be careful to spread the butter and filling to the edges and corners of the bread.

Sandwiches may be cut in circles, squares, rectangles, triangles, diamonds or strips. They should be wrapped in a dry cloth, then in a damp cloth as soon as made, and put in a closely covered metal receptacle or crock or wrapped in wax paper. Bread spread with creamed butter is always in good taste or the following fillings may be used.

Fillings for Sandwiches

- Chopped olives or pimolas
- Lettuce and mayonnaise dressing
- Chopped nuts and creamed butter
- Pimiento cheese
- Marmalade or strawberry jam
- Maraschino cherries and whipped cream
- Chopped preserved ginger, cream cheese and chopped nuts
- Cream cheese, lettuce and guava jelly
- Jam and cheese
- Sardine and celery
- Lobster and mayonnaise dressing
- American cheese and catsup
- Creamed butter and anchovy paste
- Radishes and mayonnaise dressing
- Horseradish butter
- Cream cheese and chopped olives
- Cream cheese, chopped celery and pimolas

- Cream cheese, chopped chicken and mayonnaise
- Melted sweet chocolate between buttered bread
- Strawberries sliced and mayonnaise
- Chopped ham and raspberry jam
- Ham and sweet pickles chopped and mayonnaise
- Raisins and almonds chopped and marmalade
- Raisins chopped and mayonnaise dressing
- Cucumber slices and mayonnaise

Ribbon Sandwiches

Layer sandwiches or ribbon sandwiches are made with three or more slices of bread 54 inch thick, put together with filling. They should be folded in damp cheesecloth, pressed under a weight until serving time, then cut in 1/4 inch slices, and arranged on a doily-covered plate. The bread may be all white, or alternate slices of white and dark bread may be used. Nut bread, graham bread, and Boston brown bread are all attractive. The middle slice of bread should be spread on both sides with butter or other filling, and the outside slices should be buttered on one side only. The effect is like a slice of layer cake.

Piquante Ribbon Sandwiches

- 6 tablespoons butter, work until creamy, add
- 4 tablespoons grated horseradish
- 1 teaspoon lemon juice
- 6 pimolas finely chopped
- Few grains salt

Spread a slice of white bread with this mixture, cover with a slice of graham bread, spread with the mixture and cover with a slice of white bread. Prepare other slices of bread in the same way. Wrap in damp cheesecloth, press under a board with a weight on top, and when ready to serve cut in thin slices.

Mosaic Sandwiches

Cut three slices each of white and graham bread one-half inch in thickness. Spread a slice of white bread with creamed butter and place a slice of graham on it; spread this with creamed butter and place on it a slice of white bread; repeat this process, beginning with a slice of graham. Put both piles in a cool place under a light weight. When butter has become firm, trim each pile evenly and cut each pile in three one-half inch slices. Spread these with butter and put together in such a way that a white block will alternate with a graham one. Place again in a cool place under a light weight, and when butter has become perfectly hard cut in thin slices for serving. Arrange on a plate covered with a doily.

Crackers

Small, toasted, unsweetened crackers may be served with soup or tea, or with a filling in place of sandwiches. These should be small and dainty for an afternoon tea. Cut cake with a soft frosting is difficult to handle, and had best be kept for some other occasion. Small cakes may be plain or frosted, and sometimes may be decorated.

Make up your own list of these cakes and add to it other small cakes that you have found popular. Use this list in planning your menus. A cross between a wafer and a cracker are the dainty

Swedish Tea Cakes

- Swedish Tea Cakes
- Beat slightly 1 egg,
- add 1/2 teaspoon salt and
- Flour enough to make a very stiff dough
- Knead, roll mixture very thin, cut out with small round fluted cutter, fry in hot oil and sprinkle with cinnamon and powdered sugar.

High Teas and Card Parties

At an elaborate tea you should not attempt to serve too many dishes, but whatever is served should be as attractive and appetizing as possible. The menu may consist of sandwiches or rolls, a hot dish, a salad, a jellied or frozen dessert, cakes, bonbons, salted nuts and tea or coffee. If the salad is a frozen one, the dessert should not be frozen; a charlotte ruses, or a jellied or fruit dessert, will be satisfactory.

At a card party the card tables are often covered with dainty cloths and the same kind of menu as suggested above is served at each table. The salads and desserts should all be served individually. Refreshments at card parties and club meetings may be easily served from the kitchen on individual trays containing the three or four dishes of the menu.

The Buffet Spread

At a formal reception, a wedding, a dance or other large party, a buffet spread may be served. At noon it may be called a wedding breakfast, at one or two o'clock a luncheon, in the afternoon a high tea, in the evening a spread or a reception. At any of these functions the guests may partake of the refreshments standing.

Buffet Service

When buffet service is used the food is placed upon an attractively laid table, usually all at the same time, although it may be brought to the table and served in courses. Plates, silver and napkins are arranged upon the table to make the service as quick and simple as possible.

The arrangement and service of a buffet luncheon and a buffet spread or supper are practically the same, except that the luncheon often presents heavier and more varied, courses, and in the evening lighted candles are used. The arrangement of the dishes depends largely upon the menu and the number of guests to be served. Rather than have the table appear crowded, it is better to have a maid replenish the dishes and supplies from the serving table or pantry.

The menu may consist of one or two hot dishes, one or two cold dishes, hot rolls and sandwiches, one or two frozen desserts, or one dessert frozen and the other an attractively garnished mold of jelly or cream; cakes, olives, bonbons, nuts, coffee or chocolate and punch. All food should be such as can be easily eaten with a fork or spoon.

The laying of the table should be as follows: After laying the luncheon cloth or the silence and dinner cloth, place the floral decoration in the centre, and the candlesticks, two or four, about the centrepiece (these may be omitted for a midday spread). Four dishes of bonbons, or two of bonbons and two of salted nuts or olives should be placed just outside the candlesticks for an evening spread.

Next, place two chafing dishes or platters at ends of the table in direct line. These should be filled just before the guests arrive. Each may contain a different mixture, or each may contain the same kind of mixture. The platters for the salad or salads are placed next, at opposite sides of the table. Around these platters and chafing dishes group the forks attractively and the plates in one or two piles. Place the serving silver in the most convenient position, fork at the left and spoon at the right of the salad platters and chafing dishes.

Rolls and sandwiches are arranged on doily-covered plates and placed not too far in from the edge of the table; rolls are served with the hot course, and sandwiches with the salad. Place small napkins piled diagonally, side and corner alternating, not too high, on two or four opposite corners of the table.

After the hot and salad courses have been served and removed, the ices, with serving silver, are brought in. Cakes arranged on doily-covered plates may be previously placed on the serving table, and passed or placed with ice cream on the dining table. Coffee alone, or coffee and chocolate, may be provided. Either one or both may be served from an urn placed at one end of the table, or the filled cups, either large or small, may be brought in on a tray from the pantry.

Punch is usually served from a punch bowl placed with the necessary glasses on a small table in another room. Friends of the hostess usually serve; sometimes the host and hostess assist, although a waitress may do the passing, removing all soiled dishes, bringing fresh ones and replenishing supplies. A buffet spread for a large reception, where people are coming and going during certain hours, varies from the spread served at a definite hour to a definite number in that all refreshments (hot, cold and frozen) and also the beverages are put upon the table at once.

WEDDING RECEPTIONS AND BREAKFASTS

The refreshments served at a wedding may be simple or elaborate. A Bride's Cake or a Wedding Cake or both may be used with a simple menu or omitted if more convenient. With an elaborate menu they may both be included. If only ice cream and cake are served the ice Cream may be brought from the pantry on individual plates by waiters, members of the family or friends, or it may be served in the dining room.

A folded napkin may be under each plate and a teaspoon, or an ice cream spoon may be on each plate as it is passed. The cakes arranged on doily-covered plates may then be passed. If served in the dining room the arrangement is the same as suggested under a Buffet Spread. The decorated Bride's Cake may be used as the centre piece.

Dishes that may Be Served at a Buffet Spread

Patties and Hot Dishes

Any delicate meat or fish, heated in a rich white or cream sauce, may be served in patty cases, timbale cases, ramekin dishes, from a chafing dish or as a croquette. Mushrooms, truffles, pimientos, green pepper or cheese may be added for flavor and garnish. Timbales are made of finely chopped chicken, sweetbreads, ham, veal, salmon, or delicate white fish combined with eggs, cream and crumbs, baked in timbale molds, turned out and served hot with a rich sauce. They may take the place of patties.

Suggestions for Hot Dishes

In the chafing dish or in patty cases

- Creamed chicken
- Russian oysters

- Creamed sweetbreads
- Creamed oysters
- Chicken a la King
- Crab meat a la King
- Creamed sardines and eggs
- Shrimps and peas in white sauce
- Chicken and mushrooms
- Lobster or other shellfish a la Newburg
- Cheese Rarebit
- Oyster Rarebit
- Tomato Rarebit

Croquettes

- Chicken Chestnut
- Lobster Chicken and mushroom
- Sweetbread Egg
- Oyster Oyster and Macaroni
- Salmon Salmon
- Cheese Veal

Scalloped Dishes

- Oysters Scallops
- Fish

Timbales

- Chicken
- Halibut
- Ham
- Lobster
- Sweetbread and Mushroom

Rolls and Sandwiches

'The rolls served at a buffet spread should be small, light, a delicate brown in colour, and buttered before they are served, or made so rich with butter that none is necessary. Cream fingers, Parker House rolls or luncheon rolls are usually served. Sandwiches may be the same as suggested for teas.

Salads

Salads may be made of vegetables, fruit, fish, meat, nuts or cheese, alone or in combination, mixed with salad dressing and served on lettuce or other green. Mayonnaise dressing, alone or combined with whipped cream, or a cooked dressing may be used. Every leaf of lettuce should be carefully washed and dried. The ingredients of which the salad is made should be cut in regular pieces of uniform size. The salad filling should be most carefully placed on the green used. Avoid any appearance of carelessness in the arrangement. Salads are very attractive if the ingredients are combined with 1 tablespoon gelatine soaked and dissolved in 3 tablespoons liquid for each cup of mayonnaise used. They may be molded in individual forms or in large decorated molds.

Frozen salads are popular. For a frozen salad as much cream should be whipped as you will use of mayonnaise dressing. Combine and mix with the fruit, vegetables, lobster, chicken, or whatever is used. Put into small brick molds or baking powder boxes, cover, pack in 1 part ice to 2 parts salt and leave about 2 hours or until frozen. Salad may then be sliced and served on lettuce leaves.

For a very elaborate affair whole small salmon, boned chicken or turkeys may be molded in aspic jelly. The molds are usually elaborately decorated and when turned out are garnished with cress or other green and mayonnaise dressing and make an attractive addition to a buffet table.

Aspics

Highly seasoned soup stock made from beef, veal, chicken or fish, is used for aspic jelly. Gelatine is dissolved in the stock; it is then cleared, cooled and used in a mold with boned chicken or turkey, salmon, eggs, lobster, chicken salad or other delicate ingredients. The mold may be a large one and garnished with hard cooked eggs, capers, olives, pickles, truffles, parsley, bits of cooked vegetables, et cetera. It should be well chilled before being turned out on a platter.

Dessert

The dessert served at a buffet spread is usually frozen, but jellies, charlotte russe, and Bavarian creams may be used. They should be attractively molded and decorated. They are frequently placed on the table on large platters and should be pleasing to look at as well as to taste.

Jellies

The jellies used are stiffened with gelatine. Powdered gelatine is especially satisfactory as it is quickly softened and dissolved. For flavor lemon juice, orange juice or almost any fresh or canned fruit juice may be used except fresh pineapple juice which has the property of digesting gelatine, thus preventing the hardening of the jelly.

Spanish Cream

Spanish cream is boiled custard stiffened with gelatine and made light and fluffy by the addition of beaten egg whites. The custard may be made of all milk and flavored as desired, or of part milk and part coffee.

Bavarian Cream

Bavarian creams are like Spanish creams with whipped cream folded in just as they are beginning to stiffen. Cooked fruit juices, as pineapple and apricot, may be used instead of milk.

Charlotte Russe

Charlotte russe is made of cream or fruit juice sweetened and flavored, stiffened with gelatine and combined with whipped cream. The mold is usually lined with lady fingers or thin slices of sponge cake.

Fancy Molded Desserts

Jellied desserts may be molded in layers. The mold should be placed in ice water and a thin layer of jelly put in the bottom. This may be decorated with fruit, nuts, etc. Then jelly should be carefully put over the decorations to hold them in place. When firm, more jelly may be added or beaten jelly, a whipped cream mixture or fruit may be used alternately with the jelly until the mold is full.

Artificial colours, as scarlet, rose, green, orange, etc., may be added to the mixture before it is stiffened. Fruits or nuts in small pieces may be folded into the mixture, may be arranged in the bottom of the mold, or may be used as a decoration on it or around it, when the mold is turned out.

Frozen Desserts

Recipes for many kinds of frozen desserts may be found in any good cook book. If two or three kinds of ice cream or ice cream and sherbet are to be packed in one mold they must each be frozen separately and then packed in alternate layers. This is called Neapolitan ice cream.

Sherbet

A sherbet is a mixture of fruit juice, water and sugar frozen like ice cream.

Frappes

A coarsely frozen water ice or sherbet. Equal parts ice and salt are used and mixture is stirred occasionally until frozen.

Ice Cream

Ice creams are mixtures of cream, sugar and flavoring, turned into the can of a freezer, surrounded with a mixture of 3 parts ice and i part rock salt, and frozen while being constantly stirred. Fruit ice creams are made by combining thin cream with sifted fruits and sweetening to taste. An ice cream stiffened with rennet or junket requires less cream than most other kinds of frozen desserts. Sometimes flour and eggs are both used to thicken the custard for ice cream. Ice cream made with many egg yolks is called French ice cream. Many commercial ice creams contain gelatine or other preparations to prevent their melting too rapidly.

When it is impossible to get cream for frozen desserts evaporated milk may be successfully substituted. When served with whipped cream and lady fingers a mold of ice cream becomes a charlotte glace.

Bisque Ice Cream

Ice cream to which chopped nuts or pounded macaroons are added is called bisque ice cream. Mousses are mixtures of whipped cream, sugar and flavoring. The mixture is put into a mold, covered with greased paper and with the tin cover, and packed in 2 parts ice to 1 part salt and left for 2 hours or longer.

Parfaits are made by pouring hot syrup over beaten yolks or whites of eggs and combining it with whipped cream and flavoring. They may be frozen without an ice cream freezer. Turn into a mold or empty baking powder boxes, cover with greased paper and with tight tin cover. Surround with 2 parts crushed ice and i part rock salt, and leave 2 hours or longer. The salt water that accumulates should be occasionally poured off to prevent the possibility of its getting into the mold.

Bombe

A bombe is made by lining a bombe, melon or other mold with frozen sherbet or ice cream, and filling the centre with frozen ice cream or unfrozen mousse or parfait of a contrasting colour. Many attractive combinations are possible. Pack for two hours or more before serving.

Variations

Any plain ice cream may be served with whipped cream or with a sauce. Many sauces are served warm and stiffen when poured over the cream. Nuts may be sprinkled on top of the sauce. Fresh or candied fruit may be used in a sauce, especially with vanilla ice cream.

Sundaes

Ice cream molded with a scoop, covered with a sauce and sprinkled with nuts. Ice cream freezers to be turned by hand come in sizes from i quart to 25 quarts. Where ice cream must be made daily and in large quantities, it is desirable to have a freezer that runs by electricity, and special methods for storing the frozen cream. Coils through which flows ammonia gas are frequently used instead of ice and salt in ice cream factories.

The Ice Cream Scoop

Ice cream scoops come in different sizes so that six, eight or twelve portions may be taken from one quart of cream. Some scoops are half spheres, and some are cone shaped. They insure uniformity in the size of the portions served. A large mixing spoon may also be used.

When serving, use two scoops or spoons and change them frequently, keeping one in hot water, while the other is being used to serve the cream, so that the ice cream will slide easily from the hot scoop or spoon into the serving dish.

Molded Ice Creams

Ice cream molds come in individual shapes. The best ones are made of lead and cost from one to three dollars each. Larger molds come in sizes holding from one pint to two quarts or more in many different shapes, such as brick, melon, heart shaped, et cetera.

Individual ices are of course served one to- a person. Large molds should be cut in slices for serving. Molds are filled to overflowing with the frozen mixture, covered and packed in 4 parts ice and I part rock salt until time for serving. The rim where the mold and the cover join may be bound with a strip of cheesecloth dipped in melted fat to prevent the entrance of salt water into the mold.

Frozen Mixture

A mold should be oiled and the oil wiped out with soft paper before a mixture is put in. Wet with cold water the platter on which the mold is to be served and do not dry it. If it does not fall directly in the centre, it can then be easily moved into place. If the mixture does not readily come out of the mold, dip it for an instant in, warm water or lay over it a cloth wrung out of hot water. A thin knife run around the edge will help to loosen it.

Frozen Dessert

The turned out mold may be decorated with:

Whipped cream forced through a pastry bag in which a rose tube has been inserted Candied or maraschino cherries Candied pineapple, plums and apricots cut in pieces Whole or chopped nuts, especially green pistachio nuts, toasted almonds and pecans Fresh or canned fruits especially strawberries and apricots Lady fingers Macaroons Kis'ses

FROZEN DESSERTS ATTRACTIVE FOR HIGH TEAS OR BUFFET SERVICE

- Vanilla ice cream plain or with chocolate or butterscotch sauce
- Chocolate ice cream with marshmallow sauce and nuts
- Strawberry ice cream
- Coffee ice cream
- Banana ice cream
- Vanilla ice cream with strawberries
- Strawberry ice with centre of vanilla or strawberry mousse
- Macaroon ice cream
- Lemon ice with centre of maraschino mousse
- Coffee caramel par fait
- Vanilla mousse with broken meringues frozen in it
- Pistachio ice cream with nuts or with peaches
- Neapolitan ice cream (three kinds of ice cream molded in brick mold)

- Cafe parfait Frozen pudding
- Strawberry mousse
- Caramel bisque
- Orange ice cream with crushed strawberries
- Strawberry ice cream between slices of angel cake, covered with chopped, sweetened strawberries

Butterscotch Sauce

In saucepan put

- 1 1/4 cups (1/2 pound) brown sugar
- 2/3 cup (1/2 pound) corn syrup and
- 4 tablespoons butter. Boil to 230 degrees F., and add
- 3/4 cup thin cream. Serve on ice cream and sprinkle with Chopped nuts. This sauce may be kept for some time. Stir well just before using.

Nut and Fruit Sauce

- Wash, stone and cut in pieces
- 1/2 pound dates; cut in pieces
- 1 cup maraschino cherries; mix and add
- 1/2 cup maraschino syrup
- 1 IO-ounce can of preserved figs cut in pieces and Syrup in which they are preserved. Chill thoroughly and just before serving add 2/3 cup almonds blanched, halved and browned in the oven.

If you have not the facilities for making or molding large quantities of ice cream, you can get in touch with a large city manufacturer who has the reputation of making the best ice cream of anyone about, and order from him as required. He will doubtless give you a commission, probably of I2 1/2 per cent, on all that you sell for him.

Cakes

Little cakes and cut cake may be served at the Buffet Spread. To the list of cakes that you have made up for afternoon teas, you may add:

- Pound cake
- Angel cake
- Devil's food cake
- Bride's cake
- Sponge cake
- White fruit cake

Accompaniments

- Olives Mints
- Stuffed olives
- Bonbons
- Salted nuts
- Tiny hard candies
- Candied ginger
- Chocolates

From previous lessons and experience you should have data as to the cost of sandwiches and little cakes. In estimating the cost of a menu, use cards. Have one card for each sandwich, each cake, for beverages, with their different accompaniments, and for nuts, olives, bonbons, et cetera. Then copy the totals from each card onto another card as follows, using cost and selling price of foods. It will be wise to make out a card, very carefully, for each menu that you propose to serve.

CATERING FOR A LARGE PARTY

Catering for a large party may not be beyond your possibilities. The following description of a successful dancing party will show a supper which was supervised by a young woman of little experience. It was largely prepared in her own home.

This is an extract from her letter:

"The dance hall was finished in ivory and old rose. We had festoons of paper vines and wistaria from each light globe and entirely around the room direct from the ceiling; in the space between each window were huge shower bouquets of real roses, four dozen to the bouquet, and at each drape at the windows and doors were like bouquets of roses; at opposite ends of the room were tall floor lamps and at opposite sides were tall candle stands of fifteen cathedral candles; tall stands with bird cages were in various corners. The punch table was in one corner and also decorated with roses.

"The supper room was decorated the same way; a huge bouquet of roses formed the centre piece, and festoons of roses and tulle decorated the tablecloth. Everything was served in silver dishes.

There were thirteen cakes, half white frosting, half pink; they were 8 inches wide by 12 inches long, one layer, nearly 2 inches thick; these were served in whole cakes, one of each colour, cut 21 squares to a cake, in a large silver tray, just the size needed. There were 1,000 sandwiches, 500 made of ham, ground in a meat grinder and mixed with sweet pickle and mayonnaise, the other 500 made of cream cheese, stuffed olives, pimiento, celery and mayonnaise. These were served on silver plates. Ten pounds of pecans and almonds mixed were salted after being cooked in olive oil. These were served in a large tall silver bowl. Coffee was served from a silver urn placed at one end of the table.

"Pink mints and long slender candy sticks, and individual ice creams in the shape of a full blown rose completed the refreshments for a party of 200."

MENUS FOR SPECIAL AND HOLIDAY PARTIES

Many women who have had experience in cooking and serving company meals in their own or in other people's kitchens, find profit in preparing meals for special occasions at the home of the person who is entertaining. If to a knowledge of cooking is added artistic ability that can be displayed in planning and arranging decorations, favours and menus in accordance with special occasions, a woman will find few unengaged days during the whole season. The best way to advertise such a business is probably to send out an announcement card something like the following to women who entertain frequently.

Almost no capital is needed in order to start such a business, but a very practical knowledge of all kinds of good cookery is essential. When no entertaining is being done, you can go once or twice a week to a few people and cook enough food to last several days.

Catering for Luncheon and Supper Parties

You will probably be called on the phone and asked if you are free on a certain date. On replying that you are free, a time will be set for you to go to the home of the hostess and discuss with her the menu she is to have.

You must be able tactfully to make suggestions, or graciously to follow her ideas as to the number and kind of courses, the style of decorations, and other details. For her selection you may have a list of dishes, and combinations for each course that will be served. After the menu is planned, a complete list of all the supplies required for the meal should be carefully made out. It will be well to go into the kitchen of the hostess

Do you want a tempting luncheon for company, a simple or elaborate dinner for guests? Let me prepare it for you while you are entertaining your friends. Let me come in for a day and "cook you up ahead" for several days. My rolls will keep tender, my roast will last for three or four meals. My pot of clear bouillon made up with different flavors will make a first course for a number of dinners. My pies, cakes, cookies and puddings will put something to eat on your pantry shelves and my luncheon dishes will be all ready for you to heat up and place on the table.

For several days after a day spent with you dainty dishes can appear like magic at meal time. Consultations in regard to menus and prices may be arranged for by mail or phone.

Most women find it necessary to take with them measuring cups and spoons, one or two sharp knives, special cutters and beaters and molds. The marketing may be done by the hostess or the person who prepares the meal.

The price charged depends upon the number of persons to be served and ranges from five dollars a meal up, according to the elaborateness of the meal and the number served. It is all clear profit as all supplies are charged to the hostess.

Table Decorations

The decorations for the table usually include a centrepiece which should be low enough or high enough not to obstruct the view across the table. This may be of flowers of appropriate colours, or tiny dressed figures suitable to the occasion. A Jack Horner Pie of crepe paper, containing favours, is frequently used as a centrepiece. If it is in the form of a huge turkey it is appropriate for Thanksgiving.

A1 lovely and enormous white crepe paper rose is appropriate for an engagement or a bridal luncheon. A stunning gray battleship of paper with tiny figures in uniform would grace the table at a luncheon for a navy man.

A chimney of crepe paper coloured to represent bricks, with a paper Santa Claus mounted on cardboard, and holding on his back brown paper bags from which protrude the family's presents, would be the delight of any Christmas party.

There are yellow tulip pies, and rose pies of all shades to celebrate the luncheon given to the returning college girl. All these centrepieces contain hidden favours which are attached to different coloured ribbons leading to the seat of each guest.

Other decorations may consist of appropriate place cards, individual favours, a small basket of fresh flowers, a small box of candy or a single but very beautiful flower at each place. It will be to your advantage to visit or otherwise keep in touch with favour shops in large cities. Study the suggestions found in magazines and originate or modify ideas. Keep a scrap book and note book.

Candle Sticks

Candles are not used for a luncheon but may be part of the supper decorations. Where sufficient candles are used they make the only light provided.

Points for the Caterer to Remember

- Take the greatest care of the hostess' possessions.
- Show consideration for other help in the house.
- Work in harmony with the help.
- Do not demand too much of the help.
- Be neat in appearance.
- Be agreeable in demeanor.

Waitresses

The woman who prepares the meal is not expected to serve, but she may be asked to engage the waiters or waitresses, having one maid for each six guests.

Luncheon Menus

A luncheon menu may consist of five or six courses.

1. A fruit course or shell fish or fish cocktail.
2. A bouillon or cream soup with croutons, crackers or rolls.
3. A fish or entree course if desired.
4. A main dish in individual services with two vegetables.
5. A salad with a cheese accompaniment or a sandwich.
6. Dessert, nuts, bonbons and coffee.

For special Holidays and other occasions, the colour scheme of centrepiece and favours, and the decorations of many of the dishes can be such as to suggest the special emblem for that day. With slight changes most menus suggested in this chapter can be adapted to every-day affairs or for a different holiday.

Supper Menus

A supper menu may be similar to that for a buffet luncheon or a spread. Ordinarily the guests will be seated at the table rather than be served while standing. Be sure the foods you select are obtainable at the time the meal is to be served. Do not repeat flavours or foods in a menu! For instance, do not serve tomato soup and tomato in the salad. Let each course be a contrast in colour to the one that precedes or follows it, unless you are carrying out a special colour scheme.

The Fruit Course

The fruit course may be of one fruit, a mixture of fruits, or one or several fruit juices. The fruit selected or its garnish may be of a colour that matches the colour scheme selected for the table decorations.

How to serve the Fruit Course

This course may be on the table when the guests enter the dining room. The fruit should be thoroughly chilled and attractively garnished.

The fruit may be served in

1. Single glasses similar to a champagne glass.
2. In a double cocktail glass, the inside glass being surrounded with crushed ice.
3. In the skin of the fruit, as grapefruit, orange or cantaloupe.

Sections of fruit or perfect whole berries, arranged on a small flat plate with a mound of powdered sugar in the centre.

Cocktails

A cocktail glass is served on a small plate covered with a doily with the spoon on the right-hand side of the plate. Fruit cocktails, made of fruit juices or fruit, are best sweetened with syrup made of equal parts of sugar and water cooked 3 minutes. A crabmeat, lobster, or a scallop cocktail may be served in place of fruit. The arrangement is the same, substituting an oyster fork for the spoon if the cocktail is served in a glass.

Fruit Cocktail Suggestions (Those with unequal proportions of fruits) Name & Method:

Apple Cocktail: Apple strips covered with apple or sweet cider packed in ice and salt until mixture is mushy. Served with maraschino cherries cut in strips and whipped cream.

Frozen Oranges Whole: Oranges packed in ice and salt until very cold. Served cut in halves with powdered sugar.

Grapefruit and Straw Berry Cocktail: Sections of grapefruit cut in thin slices, with slices of strawberries; garnish of sprigs of mint, and sauce of honey and lemon juice.

Roman Grapefruit: Grapefruit pulp seasoned with salt, Roman punch and sugar and chilled. Garnished with whipped cream flavored with sugar and Roman punch, and with maraschino cherries.

Straw Berry Cocktail I: Large strawberries cut in quarters. Served with a preserved marron cut in small pieces, sprinkled with syrup from bottle of marrons and served very cold.

Straw Berry Cocktail II: Unhulled strawberries and grapefruit sections arranged on plate and a sauce of maraschino cordial, powdered sugar and salt put in centre glass and garnish of sprig of mint.

Straw Berry Cocktail III: Combination of grapefruit juice, fresh strawberry juice, lemon juice, honey, sugar and White Rock. Serve very cold.

Winter Fruit Cocktail: Grapefruit pulp, orange pulp, and banana cut in small pieces, with Malaga grapes and walnuts. Serve very cold.

Cassaba Melon: Sections of melon served very cold.

Pineapple Cocktail: Portions of fresh pineapple, covered with syrup of sugar, water, orange juice and grapefruit juice and coloured pink.

Butterfly Cocktail: A slice of pineapple cut in two and rounded edges placed together. Decorated with bits of candied cherry, plum, angelica and pistachio nuts for wing spots and lines. Body made of whipped cream, and ornamented with paprika and cress.

Fruit Cup: Mixture of -white grapes, pineapple, oranges and strawberries in equal proportions. Season with sugar, salt, orange juice and pineapple syrup. Pack in ice and salt until barely frozen, and serve at once.

Cassaba Cocktail: Pulp of Cassaba melon mixed with an equal amount of Tokay grapes. Flavor with maraschino syrup and salt.

White Cherry Cocktail: Mixture of white cherries, pineapple and grapefruit. Served with dressing made of maraschino syrup, pineapple syrup, cherry syrup, lemon juice and salt.

Index

A

Accept 8, 15, 18, 21, 29, 34, 39, 58, 83, 85, 89, 167

Accommodation 59, 206

Account 17, 38, 42, 44, 53, 54, 55, 58, 62, 69, 102, 105, 106, 133, 197

Accountant 35, 175

Accounting 16, 25, 42, 89, 105, 131, 144, 175

Actions 122, 193, 208

Adjustments 197, 198

Administrative 86, 87

Advances 25, 52, 131

Advertising 6, 8, 15, 20, 38, 45, 46, 52, 53, 60, 78, 189, 194

Analysis 40, 42, 45, 62, 73, 78, 88, 89, 90, 93, 95, 96, 107, 109, 139, 141, 144, 145, 147, 173, 178, 181, 184, 196, 197, 199, 200

Announcement 261

Appeal 157, 243

Approach 42, 46, 47, 48, 52, 57, 64, 72, 78, 99, 102, 123, 125, 147, 168, 179

Assets 34, 52, 69, 70, 71, 72, 75, 76, 87, 88, 94, 97, 99, 179, 189

Association 76, 86, 169, 170, 200

Attracting 120, 130, 136, 161

Audience 24, 158

Automated 38

Availability 49, 116, 139

B

Background 9, 105, 122, 138

Banking 37, 38, 40, 45, 46, 51, 52, 53, 54, 55, 60, 100, 113, 117, 177, 178

Bars 22, 111, 215, 216, 217

Bartenders 151, 155, 167, 172

Beer 205, 216

Benefit 135, 139, 140, 187, 191

Blocking 28

Brand name 69, 70, 79, 94

C

Characteristics 66, 68, 76, 83, 132, 138, 166, 170, 174, 175, 176, 195, 197, 198, 210, 214
Check 16, 34, 37, 39, 60, 150
Communication 8, 11, 167, 174, 175, 176, 179, 209
Consumption 109, 110, 121, 131, 176, 207, 216
Credit card 22, 51
Customer 2, 4, 13, 14, 16, 34, 37, 39, 58, 59, 132, 167, 168, 173, 174, 176, 177, 187, 191, 206, 237
Customers 17, 28, 33, 37, 38, 39, 74, 82, 134, 136, 141, 167, 168, 173, 179, 186, 191

D

Dallas 102
Debit 39
Decision Making 17
Decision making 17, 108
Demographics 23, 123
Department managers 181, 183
Dissemination 88
Distribution 40, 44, 68, 139, 187, 189, 192, 195, 206, 208, 216
Diversification 76, 115

E

Earnings 37, 80, 89
Educational 133, 138, 217
Electronic 37, 38, 39
Elevator 3
Emergency 25
Employees 23, 29, 40, 41, 57, 58, 77, 78, 88, 111, 134, 137, 138, 139, 141, 142, 148, 173, 175, 176, 177, 178, 179, 181, 183, 184, 185, 186
Equipment 2, 5, 6, 7, 12, 29, 36, 58, 106, 112, 226, 239, 240
Event 1, 2, 3, 4, 5, 6, 7, 8, 10, 11, 13, 15, 19, 20, 21, 23, 26, 27, 30, 32, 33, 34, 36, 59, 100, 161, 215
Executive 18, 86, 87, 102, 156, 158, 159, 161, 162, 169, 235

F

Family 4, 25, 119, 125, 132, 138, 139, 143, 162, 166, 168, 169, 170, 171, 184, 221, 225, 231, 250
Feedback 11, 12, 16
Financial activities 48
Franchisee 71, 77, 79, 88, 187, 188, 190, 191, 193
Fundamental 47, 54, 130, 175

G

Generation 17, 119, 128
Globalization 85, 122, 130, 131, 215

H

Holiday Inn 188
Hospitality 16, 99, 102, 181, 188, 207

I

Implications 44, 51, 62, 67, 97, 166, 170, 203, 217
Importance 2, 19, 26, 40, 75, 78, 83, 85, 86, 87, 90, 91, 94, 102, 108, 126, 143, 156, 165, 173, 176, 178, 197, 198, 211, 212, 214, 217, 222
income 1, 21, 81, 92, 94, 96, 98, 103, 107, 114, 118, 130, 132, 133, 137, 138, 142, 147, 235
Independent 10, 78, 79, 84, 89, 90, 91, 95, 161, 178, 186, 187, 188, 189, 191, 196, 197, 200, 209
Innovation 23, 207, 213, 214, 216
Inquiries 32, 57, 64
Inseparability 175
Intangibility 175
International 67, 68, 69, 70, 71, 72, 73, 78, 79, 82, 84, 90, 93, 95, 96, 97, 107, 108, 109, 112, 113, 115, 116, 117, 120, 121, 122, 124, 125, 126, 127, 128, 129, 131, 151, 154, 163, 166, 172, 186, 196, 199, 201, 204, 211
Internet 32, 38, 39
Interpretation 92, 128, 200, 205, 230
Inventory 88, 144

J

Joint ventures 65, 70, 73, 89, 95
Journal 104, 154, 157, 227, 228

K

Knowledge 7, 35, 66, 70, 73, 74, 75, 76, 77, 81, 85, 88, 92, 93, 136, 156, 175, 180, 186, 189, 191, 192, 193, 196, 200, 202, 204, 260, 261

L

Language 134, 137, 145, 218
Location 1, 6, 22, 26, 31, 45, 66, 110, 132, 178, 188, 189, 190, 196, 203, 233
Lodging 104, 188, 203

M

Maintenance 101, 172
Management 8, 10, 14, 15, 16, 17, 21, 23, 24, 25, 26, 35, 65, 66, 67, 68, 69, 70, 71, 72, 77, 79, 80, 81, 82, 84, 86, 87, 88, 89, 91, 92, 93, 94, 95, 96, 97, 98, 99, 101, 102, 103, 104. 105, 117, 123, 124, 130, 174, 176, 177, 180, 181, 188, 189, 194, 203

Managerial 35, 66, 69, 86, 136, 139, 145, 146, 180, 189, 190
Market segments 2
Meetings 123, 126, 150, 159, 160, 167, 248
Motivation 14

N

Necessary 2, 7, 9, 10, 16, 24, 25, 43, 45, 50, 81, 101, 105, 106, 123, 150, 174, 175, 176, 177, 182, 183, 184, 210, 234, 236, 239, 240, 249, 252, 262
Neighbourhoods 136, 137
Nontraditional 104, 169, 170

O

Occupancy 57, 88, 106, 121, 122, 190
Organization 24, 74, 82, 83, 88, 95, 125, 129, 152, 153, 155, 161, 165, 166, 170, 174, 176, 178, 179, 180, 182, 183, 189, 191, 193, 202, 216, 231
Orientation 162, 172

P

Package 101
Personality 9, 29, 174
Personnel 1, 2, 6, 9, 10, 20, 35, 36, 71, 72, 75, 77, 173, 174, 175, 176, 177, 178, 179, 182
Physical 11, 49, 66, 69, 70, 71, 175, 176, 190, 224, 225, 232
Pleasure 109, 210, 214, 215, 222, 224, 227, 228, 232, 234
Policy 49, 154, 164, 165, 195
Procedure 54, 95, 157, 159
Professional 13, 19, 21, 22, 28, 34, 35, 46, 105, 146, 173, 174, 175, 176, 177, 179, 212
Property 4, 45, 68, 69, 70, 71, 72, 75, 77, 78, 80, 81, 83, 86, 89, 92, 93, 94, 95, 99, 101, 102, 103, 105, 115, 116, 120, 121, 253

Q

Quality 2, 12, 14, 16, 17, 20, 29, 32, 33, 34, 44, 58, 69, 70, 71, 82, 86, 92, 94, 118, 130, 175, 180, 181, 193, 198, 206

R

Recreation 111, 225
Religious 208
Reservation 69, 71, 72, 87, 94, 188
Revenue 7, 30, 73, 77, 111, 120
Room and board 168

S

Safety 35
Security 6, 22, 30, 38, 134

Services 2, 7, 9, 11, 12, 21, 22, 30, 32, 33, 35, 36, 39, 40, 41, 42, 44, 45, 46, 47, 49, 51, 52, 53, 54, 55, 56, 58, 60, 61, 62, 97, 101, 107, 109, 130, 131, 133, 173, 174, 175, 176, 177, 178, 179, 187, 189, 198, 203, 263

Sheraton 123

Software 25, 38

Solutions 23, 104

Super 34, 121, 208

T

Taxes 35, 102, 108, 120

TQM 179, 180, 181, 182, 183, 184, 185

Training 6, 14, 29, 72, 76, 77, 88, 91, 96, 128, 131, 159, 182, 184, 190, 191, 193, 198, 201

Transfer 37, 56, 74, 75, 81, 85, 92

U

Understanding 12, 13, 97, 103, 124, 170, 174, 180, 181

Universal 22, 50

V

Variability 192

Visit 109, 163, 210, 227, 262

W

Work experience 132, 139, 145, 166

Workload 8

Y

yield 42, 43, 44, 45, 47, 49, 50, 53, 94, 189, 205

Z

Zones 31